GREAT CAMPAIGNS

The Normandy Campaign

GREAT CAMPAIGN SERIES

The Antietam Campaign
The Atlanta Campaign
The Boston Campaign
The Chancellorsville Campaign
The First Air Campaign
The Fredericksburg Campaign
The Gettysburg Campaign
Jackson's Valley Campaign
The Little Bighorn Campaign
MacArthur's New Guinea Campaign
The Midway Campaign
The Peninsula Campaign
The Petersburg Campaign
The Philadelphia Campaign
Rommel's North Africa Campaign
The Second Bull Run Campaign
The Shiloh Campaign
The Spotsylvania Campaign
The Vicksburg Campaign
The Waterloo Campaign
The Wilderness Campaign

GREAT CAMPAIGNS

THE NORMANDY CAMPAIGN

From D-Day to the Liberation of Paris

Victor Brooks

Da Capo Press

Copyright © 2002 by Victor Brooks

Designed by K & P Publishing

Cataloging-in-Publication data for this book is available from the Library of Congress.

First Da Capo Press edition 2002

ISBN 0-306-81149-9

Published by Da Capo Press
A Member of the Perseus Books Group
http://www.dacapopress.com

Da Capo Press books are available at special discounts for bulk purchases in the U.S. by corporations, institutions, and other organizations. For more information, please contact the Special Markets Department at the Perseus Books Group, 11 Cambridge Center, Cambridge, MA 02142, or call (800) 255-1514 or (617) 252-5298, or e-mail j.mccrary@perseusbooks.com.

1 2 3 4 5 6 7 8 9—05 04 03 02

Contents

	Preface	7
I.	Genesis of an Invasion	13
II.	A Gathering of Titans	27
III.	A Blueprint for Victory	45
IV.	Countdown to Invasion	55
V.	Assault from the Air	67
VI.	Utah Beach: The Right Invasion at the Wrong Place	79
VII.	Omaha Beach: The Perilous Shore	91
VIII.	Gold Beach: The First Allied Link-Up	113
IX.	Juno Beach: Payback for Dieppe	125
X.	Sword Beach: First Lunge for Caen	133
XI.	The Road to Villers-Bocage	143
XII.	The Fall of Fortress Cherbourg	161
XIII.	Operation Epsom: The Battle for the Odon	181
XIV.	The Battle of the Hedgerows: The Struggle for St. Lô	193
XV.	Operation Goodwood: Climax at Caen	205
XVI.	Operation Cobra: Breakout at St. Lô	221
XVII.	Operation Luttich: Counterattack at Mortain	237
XVIII.	From the Corridor of Death to the City of Lights	247
	Epilogue: Alternatives and Evaluations	263
	Guide for the Interested Reader	279
	Index	282

Maps

D-Day, June 6, 1944:
  German Deployment and Allied Assault Forces   56
General Situation, June 10, 1944   150
General Situation, June 24, 1944   176
General Situation, June 30, 1944   186
General Situation, July 9, 1944   210
Operation Cobra Begins, Situation July 24–27, 1944   228
Falaise Pocket, August 7–20, 1944   248
March to the Seine, August 1944   260

Sidebars

Eisenhower before the Normandy Campaign, 1890-1943   23
Rivalries and Feuds in the Allied Forces   24
Table of Equivalent Ranks   25
Organization of the American Army   38
Organization of the British Army   39
Organization of the German Army   40
Allied Uniforms and Equipment   41
German Uniforms and Equipment   43
Omar Nelson Bradley   110
Infantry Weapons in the Normandy Campaign   111
Sir Bernard Law Montgomery   122
Genesis of the Waffen SS   158
Chivalry and Atrocities in the Normandy Campaign   179
Karl Gerd von Rundstedt   190
Rivalries and Feuds in the German Forces   191
Erwin J. Rommel   203
Armor in the Normandy Campaign   219
Gunther von Kluge   235
George S. Patton   246
Eisenhower after the Normandy Campaign, 1945-1969   278

Preface

The long summer days and brilliant June sunshine that brightened the French side of the English Channel would have been a welcome sight to holiday makers in ordinary times. However, June of 1940 was no ordinary time and the roads near the French seacoast were clogged with tanks, armored cars, and military trucks instead of tour buses and automobiles. Only a little more than three weeks earlier, Adolf Hitler had launched a terrifying lightning war which had knifed through the vitals of Holland, Belgium, and much of France and trapped most of the British Expeditionary Force (B.E.F.) against the blue-gray waters of the channel that separated the European mainland from the cliffs of Dover. A series of bold German armored thrusts supported by seemingly endless flights of Luftwaffe dive-bombers had sliced the French army in two and backed the British army against the sand dunes of the small port city of Dunkirk. Newly appointed British prime minister Winston Churchill and his military and naval advisors set in motion a plan called Operation Dynamo which was expected to possibly rescue a fifth of the quarter million Tommies who were now trapped in France. However, as Hitler dithered between finishing the British off with either panzer forces or Hermann Göring's vaunted Luftwaffe and kept shifting his focus to the capture of Paris, virtually every British vessel that was seaworthy enough to cross the Channel made its way to Dunkirk and plucked British and French soldiers from the beach. While RAF Hurricanes and Spitfires dueled with German Messerschmitts over the dunes, long lines of soldiers dodged artillery shells and dive-bombers to march up gangplanks or wade out to waiting rescue ships. An astonishing variety of mariners ranging from grizzled fishermen to sixteen-year-old Sea Scouts engaged in the rescue operation. A number of British noblemen and movie stars used their yachts to transport their countrymen back to England while Commander Herbert Lightoller, the senior surviving officer of the *Titantic* disaster, engaged in a rescue operation that dwarfed the scope of the events of that cold April night twenty-eight years earlier.

Early on the morning of June 4, 1940, advance units of the German army poked through the last defensive perimeter around Dunkirk and captured a brave French rear guard. However, 224,717 British troops along with over 60,000 French soldiers had been evacuated successfully and were now disembarking in Dover and the other Channel ports. On one level Britain had suffered a humiliating military defeat as the entire B.E.F. had been either evacuated or captured. Author J. B. Priestly called the Dunkirk experience "an excursion to hell" but insisted that the rescue of most of the army was in itself a miracle, as he noted, "Our great grandchildren when they learn how we began this War by snatching glory out of defeat and then swept on to victory may also learn how the little holiday steamers made their own excursions to hell and came back glorious." Lieutenant Christopher Seton-Watson of the 2nd Regiment, Royal Horse Artillery, was one of the thousands of British soldiers who realized the enormous good fortune of so many British troops yet appreciated the consequences of the German blitzkrieg. His letter of June 5, 1940, to his brother Hugh emphasized his enormous relief at avoiding capture or death in France and near shock at the tranquility of a still untouched Britain. However he then stated, "Just the other side of this blue, smiling Channel, there is hell raging and I think that it will come nearer home than Calais or Dunkirk."

The "miracle of Dunkirk" had rescued most of the British army to fight another day, but almost all of the weapons and equipment that supported a modern fighting force had been abandoned in France and Hitler's legions were sweeping to victory on the Continent. While German units fine tuned their tanks and other armored vehicles in preparation for a possible invasion of England, British Local Defense Volunteers practiced repelling enemy assault forces armed with shotguns, hunting rifles, and even broomsticks. Lieutenant Henry "Chips" Cannon was stunned at the meager defenses around London and as he walked through the British capital on an almost perfect Sunday in June noted, "I wonder as I gaze out upon the grey and green Horse

Guards Parade with the blue sky, the huge silver barrage balloons like blowing elephants, the barbed wire entanglements and soldiers about; is this really the end of England."

Several thousand miles away from a nearly besieged Britain, on the other side of the Atlantic Ocean, American military leaders and average citizens alike had followed the shocking events of the past few weeks and they began to discuss among themselves whether even the vast ocean was enough of a barrier to stop the Nazi juggernaut. The United States could deploy a reasonably formidable navy, but if the Germans ever penetrated that maritime shield there was little to prevent another blitzkrieg. On the same day that the last of nearly 230,000 British soldiers reached the safety of England, the *entire* United States army mustered only 190,000 men. One of the only American divisions anywhere near full strength was the 1st Cavalry Division at Fort Bliss, Texas, which listed on its rolls twelve thousand men and six thousand horses. A German army that penetrated American naval defenses would face only three half-strength infantry divisions armed mainly with surplus World War I rifles, machine guns, and mortars. The British Expeditionary Force may have been forced to abandon most of its modern weapons on the beaches of Dunkirk, but the American army did not even have much modern equipment to lose. Maneuvers and war games often featured stove chimneys designated as "mortars" and painted broomsticks doubling as "machine guns" while air units dropped "bombs" that were actually sacks of flour.

The U.S. Army Air Corps actually had real bombs in its arsenal but was hardly a match for the Luftwaffe in the summer of 1940. While The RAF could at least challenge the enemy with excellent Hurricane and Spitfire fighters, most American "pursuit" planes were outmoded P-35s and P-36s that featured slow speeds, no armor, no self-sealing fuel tanks, and were armed with a pitiful array of two 30-caliber machine guns. While the Air Corps was starting to add a few modern B-17 Flying Fortresses to its squadrons, the most readily available bomber was the obsolete B-18, a copy of a DC-2 airliner that had totally inadequate range, speed, bomb load, and defensive armament. America had the potential to become the "arsenal of democracy," but in June of 1940 that potential was largely unrealized.

However, while Americans began the long road of rearmament and British citizens prepared for bombing raids and a possible invasion, a few leaders on both sides of the Atlantic were already looking forward to the day when Anglo-American armies would breach Hitler's Fortress Europe and restore the light of freedom to what had now become a darkened continent. Almost four years to the day after the last British soldier was evacuated from the beaches of Dunkirk, a vast Allied armada would set sail to land a mammoth invasion force on the beaches of occupied France. Operation Dynamo would be a distant, but still emotional, memory as it was replaced with Operation Overlord, one of the most important events of the twentieth century. This book is the story of that decisive campaign of World War II which largely ensured that the century would end as an age of advancing democracy rather than as an age of tyrants. The author gratefully acknowledges the masterful work on this topic already provided by Stephen Ambrose, John Keegan, Carlo D'Este, Max Hastings, and other contemporary writers who have dealt with this vital moment in time. However, this book was written to add a number of hopefully innovative and original perspectives to this decisive campaign.

As an author whose ancestors fought under Wellington and Grant and whose grandparents were born in England, Ireland, Canada, and the United States, I am more than a little interested in presenting this campaign in the context of a Canadian, British, and American partnership. I am convinced that pride in the exploits of each victorious ally can be accomplished without detracting from the contributions of the other nations. I am also convinced that it is possible to acknowledge the often heroic fighting qualities of the German defenders while realizing that they were ruled by one of the most odious governments in the history of mankind. And that while many of these Wehrmacht forces fought bravely, they were not some form of legendary supermen and were, in actuality, defeated by Allied soldiers who were often braver, more tenacious, and more daring than their Axis adversaries. I make few attempts to hide my total disagreement with the popular scholarly opinion that the Germans were merely overwhelmed by superior Allied technology and manufacturing capacity. As will be seen in this narrative, the Wehrmacht was defeated due to the often appallingly substantial sacrifices of a "greatest generation" of Canadians, Britons, and Americans, who quite simply outfought, outled, and outsmarted the "master race" that Hitler deployed in Normandy.

Beyond these basic themes, this book will consider the Normandy campaign from several perspectives. First, as the author of several books on earlier wars including the American Revolution, the War of 1812, and the American Civil War, I am particularly mindful that this decisive campaign was fought much like earlier conflicts, especially the American Civil War. While that war was fought before any of the military leaders of World War II were born, the strategy and tactics of that defining moment in American history were still substantially influencing decisions made in the invasion of France eighty years later.

On the other hand, British and Canadian experiences in the Normandy battles were substantially influenced by their much more recent participation in World War I. The Great War with its huge numbers and appalling casualties continued to evoke haunting responses from the British leaders who were involved with planning and executing Overlord and would sometimes encourage a different Anglo-Canadian response to confrontation with the Germans than the activities of their American allies.

A second perspective found in this book will be a fairly specific and detailed evaluation of the leadership qualities of the military commanders who directed the Normandy campaign. Readers are certainly free to agree or disagree with my rating system, but I have attempted to provide the most balanced grades that I could develop. My use of the system in earlier books on the American Revolution and the American Civil War has elicited substantial responses from readers and I have no doubt that this volume will produce its own share of widely diverse opinions.

Finally, I have carefully considered a number of possible alternative outcomes to the Normandy campaign. The actual result of Overlord, the successful invasion of France, and the elimination of much, but certainly not all, of the German army defending Normandy, is only one of a number of potential outcomes to this decisive battle. A wide range of possible alternative outcomes, from an Allied victory of annihilation to a German obliteration of the invasion will be considered.

This volume could only be published through the assistance of numerous people, a few of whom can be acknowledged in this introduction. Robert Pigeon and Ken Gallagher, who provided the author with the opportunity to write his first World War II book and add the exciting world of Tiger tanks, Flying Fortresses, and Bren guns to a universe already populated with redcoats, minutemen, Union ironclads, and Confederate horse soldiers. I must also express my appreciation to three administrators at Villanova University, Dr. John Johannes, Vice President for Academic Affairs, Rev. Kail Ellis, O.S.A., Dean of the College of Arts and Sciences, and Dr. Henry Nichols, Chairperson of the Department of Education and Human Services. All three of these individuals have provided both encouragement and tangible support in the form of travel funds and reduced teaching loads that helped expedite the publication of this book. Within the Villanova

University family, a special thanks is in order for Dot Romano who provided the typing services crucial to this work and her husband, Silvio Romano, who was one of the brave citizen soldiers who landed on the Normandy beachhead to take part in the Great Crusade.

Within my own family, my sons Matthew, Gregory, and Stephen ensure that I keep at least one foot in the "real world" when I am writing. My brother Craig Brooks provided helpful expertise from his own career in the publishing industry. My sisters and fellow authors, Dr. Donna Brooks and Lynn Brooks, have provided invaluable leads on publicity and media relations. Finally, this book is particularly dedicated to my parents, both of whom died just before this project was undertaken. Major Victor Brooks Sr., USAAF, survived several plane crashes and terrible wounds in the service of the cause of liberty and Aurelia Kane Brooks of Rhoads General Hospital not only served her nation as well, but helped produce a wartime romance that had major implications for one as yet unborn author.

CHAPTER I

Genesis of an Invasion

All along the French beach facing the English Channel, the soldiers of the Wehrmacht relaxed from their duties and took time out to celebrate the approach of the new year, 1944. German troops had occupied this coastline for almost four years, but now it was becoming obvious to even the lowliest private that sometime during the coming spring or summer the Anglo-American allies were going to attempt to storm ashore somewhere along these picturesque beaches and attempt to drive deep into the heart of the Third Reich. The German soldiers patrolling the sandy expanses of the Normandy shore on this frigid New Year's Eve did not know it at the time, but a tiny British "invasion force" was already moving along the beach attempting to secure vital information. Major Logan Scott-Bowden, a 24-year-old Royal Engineer, and his assistant, Sergeant Bruce Ogden-Smith, were taking advantage of the festive atmosphere among the German sentries to conduct a reconnaissance of a stretch of shoreline that would soon become famous as Omaha Beach. The two commandos were furtively scooping up soil samples to provide information on whether or not the ground in this area was firm enough to support tanks and other heavy vehicles in the planned invasion, and despite the relaxed atmosphere among the enemy sentries, the two men feared imminent capture until they were finally hauled aboard a rescue craft with their vital samples.

While these two intrepid Allied soldiers had been scooping up containers of Normandy sand, three of the men who would be heavily involved in ordering tens of thousands of men to storm these same beaches a few months later were all greeting the new year of 1944 from a region where the Allies had already scored a significant victory over the Axis. The three men, two Britons and one American, were conferring in the luxurious Taylor Villa near the foot of the Atlas Mountains in Marrakech, Morocco, an area that was in the vortex of Allied-Axis fighting during the previous year. The host of this very informal, intimate parley was Prime Minister Winston Spencer Churchill, who had spent much of the past few weeks alternately conducting summit meetings with Franklin Delano Roosevelt and Joseph Stalin and recuperating from a serious bout with pneumonia that could easily have been fatal to the 65-year-old premier. Churchill had recovered enough to conduct limited government business but was still too weak to make the relatively long journey back to London. Protected by a crack force of Coldstream Guards and American military police, the prime minister sent frequent cables to Roosevelt, considered the direction of the war for the upcoming year, and met with the two generals whose talents would have a major influence on whether 1944 would be a year of military stalemate or decisive Allied success.

The American officer who was spending the last hours of the old year with Churchill was General Dwight David Eisenhower, a balding, gregarious fifty-four-year-old Kansan who was popularly known as "Ike" both inside and outside army circles. Almost exactly two years earlier Eisenhower had been plucked from the relative obscurity of being an acting brigadier general on the staff of an infantry division to become a senior planner for the post-Pearl Harbor war effort. The bewildered brigadier had received orders to fly to Washington and report to the chief of staff of the United States Army, General George Marshall. The stern-faced Marshall ordered Eisenhower to develop a detailed strategy for prosecuting the war against the Axis, rewarded him with a general's star, and soon dispatched him to Europe to significant command responsibilities in Allied offensives in North Africa and Italy. Eisenhower had expected to either remain in his post in the Mediterranean theater or be sent back to Washington when General Marshall, as was commonly assumed, came to England to take charge of Operation Overlord, the code name for the Allied invasion of France scheduled for the spring of 1944. However, exactly a week earlier on Christmas Eve, President Roosevelt had given an emotional radio address to the American people and confirmed the appointment of Dwight David Eisenhower as supreme commander of the Allied invasion of Northwest Europe. Now, as 1944 was about to begin, Ike found himself on the covers of magazines and commanding far more men than either George Washington or Ulysses S. Grant had. Eisenhower was scheduled to leave for Washington early on New Year's morning but he was spending the last hours of 1943 with two Britons who would emerge as key figures in the upcoming campaign.

Churchill's other houseguest was a fellow Englishman but a relative stranger to the prime minister up to this point in time. General Bernard Law Montgomery was the most famous and most controversial British commander of World War II. Montgomery, like Eisenhower, had begun the war well outside the inner circle of army leadership. He was a relatively obscure division commander when the British Expeditionary Force was dispatched to France in the wake of Hitler's invasion of Poland in September of 1939. However, when the German blitzkrieg of May 1940, sliced through the Allied defenses and threatened to annihilate the British army on the Continent, Montgomery emerged as an energetic, fearless leader who was instrumental in holding the enemy at bay long enough to engineer the "Miracle of Dunkirk." Montgomery rapidly rose to command of one of the key forces charged with defending England against a German invasion and by 1942 was placed in charge of the British Eighth Army at the decisive moment in the desert struggle against the German Afrika Korps. As Britain reeled from General Erwin Rommel's capture of over 30,000 British and Commonwealth troops at the bastion of Tobruk, Monty instilled a new confidence in his command and scored the most important British victory of the war to that point when he beat the Axis forces and their renowned "Desert Fox" at El Alamein in November of 1942.

Montgomery found himself idolized by British soldiers and the general public, loathed by more than a few British and American generals due to his supreme self-confidence, and seemed destined for a major role in the upcoming invasion of France. At about the same time that Roosevelt named Eisenhower supreme commander of Overlord, Churchill named Montgomery Allied ground forces commander and summoned his new commander to the Taylor Villa to discuss the upcoming campaign. While Churchill and Eisenhower bonded over clouds of smoke from the prime minister's ever-present cigars and the general's equally ever-present cigarettes and expressed their mutual appreciation for good liquor, the non-smoking, non-drinking Montgomery was somewhat odd man out in the confines of the villa's drawing room. However, when the action shifted to a picnic near a stream in the foothills of the mountains, Monty stunned the prime minister as he "leaped about the rocks like an antelope" reassuring

Churchill with his boundless energy and high spirits. Franklin Roosevelt would have quickly agreed with his British counterpart's insistence that Eisenhower and Montgomery had been assigned "a majestic, inevitable but terrible task" and as the two generals boarded separate planes for flights to Washington and London there was strong hope in both Allied capitals that 1944 would see the final unraveling of Hitler and his "thousand year" Reich.

The genesis of the Allied operation that would eventually become known as Overlord actually began just over two years earlier in the tumultuous days of December 1941. When the forces of the Japanese empire simultaneously attacked the territories of the United States and United Kingdom on December 7, both the American president and the British prime minister quickly agreed that "we are in the same boat," and vowed to work closely together to defeat the Axis. While the political and military leaders of Nazi Germany and Imperial Japan seldom fully shared confidences and largely conducted two separate wars, Franklin Roosevelt and Winston Churchill genuinely liked one another and fully appreciated that the combined resources and manpower of the British Empire and Commonwealth and the United States, along with a huge military contribution from the Soviet Union, would be needed to defeat an energetic, warlike, and utterly ruthless Axis. While a number of more recent works on the relationship of the Anglo-American allies during World War II have stressed American stereotyping of "supercilious Brits" and English exasperation with "loud boasting Yanks," this contention seems to be enormously exaggerated in the "real" world of 1941-45. Most British and American people of the time realized that they genuinely needed each other and differences over the temperature of serving beer or the proper side of the road on which to drive were miniscule compared to the massive threat to democracy and liberty imposed by Germany and Japan.

The commonality of the Anglo-American cause was illustrated very quickly when Churchill boarded a ship for America almost immediately after Pearl Harbor and found himself giving a White House Christmas broadcast to the American people at the side of Roosevelt. On the day after Christmas in an exhibition of solidarity that the Axis powers could only dream about, the prime minister delivered one of the most famous speeches of his career in the halls of the American congress. After impressing the members of the House and Senate with the services of his American mother's ancestors as officers in George Washington's Continental army, he thrilled the American lawmakers with his view of the lesson that the Anglo-

American alliance would teach the Axis tyrants. While admitting that "the forces ranged against us are enormous. They are bitter, they are ruthless, they will stop at nothing that violence or treachery will suggest," the British prime minister, echoed by an American president, stated that "we are linked in a righteous comradeship of arms, have joined all our life energies in a common resolve." Then, to the sound of rising cheers and applause, Churchill issued a warning to the common enemy. "What kind of people do they think we are? Is it possible they do not realize that we shall never cease to persevere against them, until they have been taught a lesson which they and the world will never forget?"

While no one listening to these fiery words in the last week of 1941 could imagine that much of the downfall of Hitler's Reich would be initiated on Normandy beaches with strange code names such as "Omaha," "Sword," or "Juno," the first tentative steps toward Overlord had now begun.

When the United States entered World War II in December of 1941 the global conflict was already more than two years old and the course of the hostilities was enormously fluid. Adolf Hitler had followed his lightning conquest of continental Europe with a savage air offensive against Britain which raged throughout the summer and autumn of 1940. When the Luftwaffe failed to produce the control of the skies necessary to attempt an invasion of Britain, the Führer quickly shifted his attention to his ultimate goal, the invasion and conquest of the Soviet Union. From June to December of 1941 an eastern version of the blitzkrieg annihilated entire Soviet armies and put German panzer units into the suburbs of Moscow. However, soon after Pearl Harbor and Hitler's declaration of war on the United States, the Soviets unleashed a surprise counteroffensive that saved the capital and inflicted tens of thousands of casualties on the stunned German army. At the same time, the Japanese forces followed their devastating attack on Pearl Harbor with an offensive against British-held Hong Kong and Singapore and American forces in Guam, Wake Island, and the Philippines. Thus Roosevelt and his military commanders confronted two competing priorities in the conduct of the war. First, they had to at least slow down Japanese operations in the Pacific enough to keep the enemy from capturing the two main springboards for an eventual counterattack, Hawaii and Australia. Yet at the same time Roosevelt, Marshall, and a number of other senior commanders agreed with Churchill and the British generals that Germany was by far the more dangerous enemy and should be confronted and defeated before serious thought was given to settling the score with the Japanese. American and British generals could agree enthusiastically on these general areas, but beyond this point significant differences began to emerge. George Marshall and most of his senior advisors were convinced that the Soviets were still very much in danger of collapsing after their devastating losses of the past few months and American strategists insisted that the only way to keep Russia in the war was to send a huge American expeditionary force to France as soon as possible and confront the Germans while they still had to contend with another enemy to their east. Marshall's plan was very much in the spirit of American planning in 1917 when the United States entered World War I. The United States had poured hundreds of thousands of men into France and, when the war reached a decisive state in the summer and fall of 1918, the Yanks had played a major role in defeating the Kaiser's forces. However, 1941–42 was not 1917–18. During World War I, British and French armies were able to keep the Germans out of about 75 percent of French territory including most of the major ports. Thus the divisions of the American expeditionary force could be ferried across the Atlantic on transport ships that were relatively safe from attacks by primitive German submarines, land in friendly harbors far from enemy guns, and then be placed in quiet sectors of the enormous trench line until they were fully ready for combat.

Unfortunately almost none of these advantages were in existence in this new world war. Far more sophisticated German submarines seriously challenged Allied passage of the Atlantic and the enemy controlled the ports and beaches of France. When American troops entered combat in Europe there would be no "quiet areas." They would have to go ashore shooting and then hope to hang on to the lodgment until enough follow-up forces could be landed. Beyond these risks, the invaders would have to contend with a Luftwaffe that was still a ferocious threat. Marshall's plan was very much in the bold, aggressive tradition of Ulysses S. Grant and John J. Pershing but it was also extremely risky as a short-term strategy.

Winston Churchill and his senior commander, General Alan Brooke, greatly respected and admired George Marshall and were delighted with his insistence that the war against Hitler should have priority over operations against Japan. However, these British leaders and their advisors were fighting World War II from a very different perspective than their American counterparts. First, every senior British leader was haunted by the spectre of the one million British deaths suffered in the trenches and fields of World War I. British forces had experienced over ten times as much frontline combat as the Americans in the Great War, and when it was over, half of His Majesty's soldiers were either dead or seriously wounded. Then, a little more than two decades later, a second frontal confrontation with the Germans nearly resulted in the annihilation of another British Expeditionary Force as the Tommies were barely extricated from the dunes of Dunkirk.

British planners were now convinced that it was high time to return to the traditional imperial strategy of using naval blockades, surprise raids, support of resistance forces, and other indirect operations to strike around the periphery of an enemy while waiting patiently for the opportunity to land a decisive blow once the adversary had been significantly weakened. While Marshall insisted on the need to engage the Germans in a decisive battle for Europe before the end of 1942, Churchill and Brooke were equally adamant about delaying such a campaign until the odds were much more clearly in the Allies's favor. As British and American military delegations flew back and forth between the two Allied capitals, a very tentative informal agreement was thrashed out. An operation code-named *Bolero* would be initiated during the last months of 1942 designed to transport divisions of American soldiers to England in time for a summer of 1943 invasion of France. Meanwhile a complementary plan code named *Round-Up* would be drawn up for contingency purposes. This operation would be initiated in the autumn of 1942 if it appeared that the Soviet Union was in imminent danger of collapse. At that point a small Allied expeditionary force of five or six divisions would be landed in the vicinity of Cherbourg, in order to ease the pressure on the Russians and provide a beachhead for the more general landings in 1943.

As the Allied commanders, now organized into the Combined Chiefs of Staff, bickered over the timing of an invasion of France, their German nemesis radically changed the nature of the debate. During the summer of 1942 Hitler launched two major Axis offensives, one in the Middle East with an eventual target of Alexandria and Cairo, and the other in the Soviet Union with designs on Stalingrad and the Crimean oilfields. The loss of over 30,000 British Commonwealth troops at Tobruk dampened already minimal British interest in the risky Round-Up venture even more substantially and since the United States as yet had few units in England to contribute to the enterprise, the Cherbourg invasion simply disappeared from the priority list. Marshall kept promoting a 1943 cross-Channel invasion but President Roosevelt was now under enormous public pressure to engage the Germans somewhere, anywhere, in 1942. At this point, Churchill offered his American counterpart an inviting alternative to an invasion of France. The British prime minister proposed an Allied invasion of French North Africa which offered major gains at minimal risk. The plan, code-named *Torch*, was to land a largely American expeditionary force in the western region of North Africa while General Montgomery's newly reinforced Eighth Army began a counteroffensive against the Germans from Egypt. The two forces could eventually converge on Axis armies in the area of Tunisia and hopefully eliminate an entire enemy army from the order of battle. Since Torch offered the Americans the opportunity to land somewhere away from the center of German military power, and because Marshall could not promise any serious ground operations in Europe for several months, Roosevelt issued an executive order for Operation Torch and the course of the war underwent a major alteration. Any major Allied-German battle in the fields of France would be postponed at least until 1944.

While battles between Allied and Axis forces surged across Tunisia, Sicily, and Italy during 1943 the prospect of an eventual cross-Channel operation loomed ever larger in Anglo-American planning. When Churchill, Roosevelt, and their senior commanders convened in Washington for the Trident Conference in May, a tentative date of May 1, 1944, was agreed upon while the subsequent Quadrant Conference in Quebec in August formalized a code name of *Overlord* for what was now agreed upon as the main Allied effort of 1944. Once the issue of confirming a cross-Channel invasion was finalized, the next significant task was to select a supreme commander for what was already emerging as the most ambitious amphibious operation in history.

It was becoming obvious to most people concerned with Overlord that the United States would most likely contribute the majority of troops to the invasion and thus the logical choice for a supreme commander would be an American general. The clear front-runner for the post was the most senior officer in the army of the United States, George C. Marshall. The chief of staff's singleminded determination had turned the American army into one of the most powerful military forces in history and Marshall himself was enormously respected by Churchill and most senior British generals. Roosevelt, who was under increasing pressure to name a commander by the end of 1943, was initially convinced that the appointment of Marshall was the most appropriate decision that he could make and the president seemed on the verge of sending the chief of staff to Europe to oversee Overlord while bringing Eisenhower back from command of the Mediterranean theater to fill Marshall's vacated position. Then, in the last few weeks of

1943, a subtle change of direction appeared in Roosevelt's reasoning. First, three other members of the American Joint Chiefs of Staff, Admirals King and Leahy and General Arnold of the Army Air Force, insisted that Marshall was the one man who could hold together that fractious body and begged the president to keep the chief of staff in his current position. Roosevelt responded by summoning Marshall for a personal interview to discuss candidates for command of Overlord. As the ebullient president bantered with the poker-faced general, small talk quickly petered out and Roosevelt finally informed the taciturn Marshall that the decision to either remain chief of staff or assume command of Overlord was entirely up to the general. While the president was apparently hoping that Marshall would selflessly refuse the high-profile European command, the general countered with an insistence that as commander in chief the decision was strictly Roosevelt's. The president realized that from the perspective of the military chain of command, the appointment of Marshall as supreme commander of the Allied Expeditionary Force would actually be a demotion from senior general of the army to a theater commander. Finally, insisting that "I could not sleep at night without you in Washington," Roosevelt informed Marshall that he would remain in his current role and Dwight Eisenhower, probably Marshall's highest profile protégé, would assume responsibility for Overlord.

On December 7, 1943, the second anniversary of Pearl Harbor, General Dwight David Eisenhower met President Roosevelt's plane as it landed in the North African city of Tunis. The president was on his way home from a series of conferences with Churchill and Stalin and had cabled the general that he wished to discuss important command decisions with him. Eisenhower was convinced that Roosevelt was going to affirm Marshall's appointment to Overlord and Eisenhower's transfer from field command to Washington. However, only minutes after the president settled into the back of the staff car he blurted, "Well, Ike, you are going to command Overlord!" The future commander of the most famous campaign of World War II stammered an emotional acceptance and suddenly realized that he now held an appointment that would to into the history books alongside Washington, Grant, and Pershing.

Winston Churchill would have much preferred the appointment of Marshall as supreme commander of Overlord but he genuinely liked Eisenhower and was also consoled by the prospect that most of the next tier of appointments would go to British officers. The most important subsidiary position would be that of ground forces commander, for this person would essentially direct the land campaign of Overlord. Eisenhower had dropped less than subtle hints that he would prefer that this appointment go to General Harold Alexander, a British officer with whom he had worked to mutual satisfaction in the Mediterranean theater. Churchill privately approved of this suggestion as he was an admirer of Alexander's abilities. However, Alan Brooke insisted that Alexander was not the best battlefield general in the British army and campaigned for his own protégé, Bernard Law Montgomery. The prime minister was enough of an astute politician to realize that the conqueror of the legendary Erwin Rommel at the battle of El Alamein was the most publicly revered general in Britain and, despite his prickly nature, was a highly intelligent commander. Also, while Ike and Monty were hardly close friends, they had developed a courteous, if somewhat formal, relationship in the Mediterranean and seemed quite capable of working together. Thus, as the tumultuous year of 1943 came to an end the invasion of France finally had a tentative target date and its two senior commanders. Now these commanders would face the enormous challenge of penetrating Hitler's Atlantic Wall and ending a four-year Nazi occupation of the heartland of Europe.

Eisenhower before the Normandy Campaign, 1890–1943

The general who would emerge as the supreme commander of the largest Allied operation of World War II was born in Denison, Texas, but grew up in Abilene, Kansas. His parents and ancestors had strong links with German pacifist sects but Dwight's father was hardly a pacifist in his treatment of his sons—he was a demanding parent who made liberal use of corporal punishment. Even when Dwight entered West Point in 1911 the tight regimen of the military academy probably seemed far less harsh than the future general's home discipline. During his career at West Point, Ike was known as an outstanding football player and a rather mediocre student and when he graduated, his extremely positive personality seemed more of an asset than his intelligence.

Unlike future commanders such as Patton and MacArthur, Eisenhower's experiences in World War I were strictly American-based training duties, yet his ability to excel in staff work won him promotion to major and an assignment to Command and General Staff School where he finished first in his class in 1926. Two years later Ike was posted to the Army War College and then spent much of the next decade linked to Douglas MacArthur, serving under that general while he was army chief of staff from 1933-35 and also when he took over command of Philippine Commonwealth forces during the period 1935-39. However, despite excellent reviews from MacArthur, when Eisenhower returned to the United States for further assignments his career seemed to have plateaued as a middle-aged colonel.

Eisenhower's star began to rise only days after Pearl Harbor when General George Marshall summoned him to Washington and ordered him to draw up a list of possible responses to the Japanese juggernaut that was beginning to sweep through the Pacific. Eisenhower proposed the rerouting of some resources to provide aid for the now besieged American forces in the Philippines and suggested a daring use of blockade runners to break through the Japanese naval cordon. But despite his personal attachment to the islands, he admitted that there was little substantial aid that could be provided and insisted that ultimately the war would be won or lost on the battlefields of Europe.

Marshall was deeply impressed with Eisenhower's reasoning and rewarded him with promotion to brigadier general with the warning that he would probably spend the rest of the war as a Washington-based staff officer with little hope for future promotion. However, when Marshall decided to use Eisenhower's talents to make an on-site evaluation of British military capabilities, a chain of events developed which found Ike skyrocketing up to command of the European Theater of Operations in a remarkably brief time. When the Allies invaded North Africa in November of 1942, Eisenhower was senior American general and held this same position in the Tunisian and Sicilian campaigns. When the invasion of France began to crystalize in the autumn of 1943, the conventional wisdom was that George Marshall would go to England to command Overlord while Eisenhower would return to Washington as army chief of staff. However, President Roosevelt gradually came to the conclusion that Marshall was far more valuable where he was, and in December of 1943 the chief executive personally informed Eisenhower of his assignment to the highest-profile command of the war.

Rivalries and Feuds in the Allied Forces

While there was never an Allied equivalent of the "Night of the Long Knives" or similar violent confrontations within the ranks that were part of the German regime's character, the Normandy campaign was directed by a group of leaders who did not suffer from too much humility. The constant interaction of men with huge egos and little room for tolerating one another's mistakes created ongoing feuds that simply shifted back and forth across a number of sometimes predictable and sometimes surprising fault lines.

The emergence of Dwight Eisenhower as supreme commander of Overlord immediately initiated feuds and rivalries based on varying opinions of Ike's fitness for the job and attempts to gain admittance to his inner circle. While Eisenhower enjoyed an excellent relationship with Winston Churchill and a number of senior British generals, admirals, and marshals, he never fully gained the approval of the most powerful man in the British army, General Alan Brooke. Brooke was convinced that Ike was an intellectual lightweight and embodied a number of negative "American" characteristics such as impatience, failure to read extensively in military history, and frequent development of shallow relationships with large numbers of people. In turn, many of Brooke's prejudices were adopted by the general's main protégé, Bernard Montgomery. On the other hand, if some British leaders found Eisenhower too "American," a number of U.S. leaders saw Ike as too "British." Some American generals were convinced that Eisenhower's haste in sending home officers who made anti-British comments, his affectation of British words such as "tin" for "can" and "petrol" for

"gasoline," and his commissioning of his personal driver, British-subject Kay Summersby, even though it was technically illegal, demonstrated that Ike had "gone native" in England and become an "adopted Briton."

However, even those leaders who found Eisenhower objectionable still realized that he exercised enormous power and they went to great lengths to secure admission to the SHAEF inner court. Their attempts resulted in shameless flattery of one of the most unpleasant members of the American officer corps, Ike's chief of staff General Walter Bedell-Smith. Bedell-Smith's less than sunny disposition and penchant for court intrigue produced a rare unanimity of opinion among a number of British and American officers who simply loathed the man, but his position as a gatekeeper to the inner circle also produced abject pandering by the same men who hated him.

Beyond the ongoing rivalries to gain Eisenhower's attention and secure his goodwill a wide variety of other rivalries and feuds erupted at regular intervals throughout the Normandy campaign. One point of contention within the American army was the running feud between those officers who had been transferred from positions in the Pacific war and believed that they had secured vital experience in amphibious warfare against the Japanese, and the commanders who had spent the whole war in the European theater of operations and dismissed the Pacific battles as "sideshows" and "bush-league" campaigns compared to the "real" war against Germany. An ongoing feud in the British ranks involved those officers who had become too "Americanized" through their service in SHAEF and those leaders who had refused to become "seduced" by Ike's influence. One British officer who especially incurred the wrath of his colleagues was Lieutenant General Frederick Morgan, an officer who worked closely with Eisenhower in drawing up Overlord and became so friendly with Ike that he was largely ostracized by his peers during and after the war.

While most of the senior German generals failed to survive the war or its immediate aftermath, the Allied leaders, with the notable exceptions of Leigh-Mallory and Patton, lived long enough to continue their rivalries through the medium of postwar memoirs. As each high-ranking leader justified his key decisions in print it was almost inevitable that he would blame someone else for whatever aspects of the campaign were less than fully successful. The result was a series of printed feuding in books that resembled the post-Civil War memoir battles—now with the enhancement of modern radio and television. The controversies have yet to be fully resolved now five decades after the end of the war.

Table of Equivalent Ranks

BRITISH/U.S. ARMY	GERMAN ARMY	WAFFEN SS
Field Marshal (U.K.) General of the Army (U.S.)	General Feldmarschall	Reichsführer SS
No Equivalent	General Oberst	SS OberstgruppenFührer
General	General der Infanterie	SS Obergruppenführer
Lieutenant General	Generalleutnant	SS GruppenFührer
Major-General Brigadier (U.K.)	Generalmajor	SS Brigade Führer
Brigadier General (U.S.)	Oberst	SS Oberführer
Colonel	Oberst	SS Standarten Führer
Lieutenant Colonel	Oberst Leutnant	SS ObersturmbannFührer
Major	Major	SS SturnbannFührer
Captain	Hauptmann	SS Hauptsturmführer
1st Lieutenant	Oberlfutnant	SS Obersturmführer
2nd Lieutenant	Leutnant	SS Untersturmführer
Sergeant-Major	Hauftfeldwebel	SS Sturmscharführer
Master Sergeant	Oberfeldwebel	Hauptscharführer
Staff Sargeant	Unterfeldwebel	Scharführer
Sergeant	Unteroffizier	SS Unterscharführer
Corporal	Obergefreiter	SS Rottenführer
Private–First Class	Oberschutze	SS Oberschutze
Private	Schutze	SS Schutze

CHAPTER II

A Gathering of Titans

A dense winter fog covered most of the British Isles as General Dwight David Eisenhower returned from the United States to assume his new post as supreme commander of the Allied Expeditionary Force. When Eisenhower landed in Prestwick, Scotland, on the morning of January 15, 1944, he was pleasantly surprised to discover a private train had been acquired to whisk him southward to London. As the train clattered through the mist-shrouded villages and cities of Scotland and England, Ike adjusted to his new surroundings in a special rail carriage code-named "The Bayonet." The plush coach included a sofa, desk, conference table, and telephone and symbolized his new status as one of the most important leaders of the western alliance. He had spent the first two weeks of the new year alternately engaged in emotional reunions with his wife, brother, and elderly mother, and discussing upcoming operations with General Marshall, Secretary of War Henry Stimson, and a bedridden, exhausted Franklin Delano Roosevelt. Now he was back on the eastern side of the Atlantic Ocean and charged with preparing the most awesome amphibious operation in the history of warfare.

Eisenhower now had a clear-cut mission and an energetic, if prickly, ground forces commander in Bernard Law Montgomery, but it was vital to fill out the other members of the Anglo-American team that would be responsible for implementing Overlord. Monty himself had used the past two weeks to establish himself in new headquarters at St. Paul's School, Hammersmith, and must have taken special delight

Dwight D. Eisenhower (left) and Bernard L. Montgomery (right) were chosen to lead the critical Operation Overlord. Here they observe troops practicing amphibious landing operations in England in March 1944.

in being able to select the headmaster's private study for his personal office. The British general admitted that in his own days as a student at the illustrious school he had never been invited inside this exclusive sanctuary and yet now he could turn the room into a nerve center for the decisive campaign in the largest war in history.

While Eisenhower and Montgomery would never enjoy a close working relationship, the two senior generals were very much in agreement that the initial drafts of the Overlord plan needed a substantial overhaul and that the achievement of air and naval superiority was absolutely vital to any prospect of success in the invasion. As other senior commanders entered the Overlord "family" these points would become substantial issues for debate. Five senior officers, three Britons and two Americans, were in the process of joining an inner circle that would include more than its share of contention and controversy.

The position of deputy supreme commander went to Air Chief Marshal Sir Arthur Tedder, a fifty-four-year-old Scot who was a careful, methodical planner and a skilled administrator. He had developed an excellent relationship with Eisenhower during the earlier Mediterranean operations. Tedder had been almost sacked by Churchill early in the Desert Campaign but he had survived to provide excellent air cover for Montgomery's El Alamein campaign. Although Tedder avoided publicity, Eisenhower thought enough of him to call the Marshal "one of the few great military leaders of our time."

The officer in charge of Neptune, the maritime element of Overlord, was Admiral Bertram Ramsay. Sir Bertram had gained a prominent place in British history as the officer responsible for the "Miracle of Dunkirk," the successful evacuation of the B.E.F. from France, and was now charged with overall command of the largest armada deployed in the history of naval operations. Ramsay, like Tedder, outspokenly supported Eisenhower's concept of a truly allied war effort and the cooperation between American, British, Canadian, and other Allied naval forces during Neptune would be quite high.

Another hero of Britain's "Finest Hour," the dark days of 1940, was the commander of air operations for Overlord, Air Chief Marshal Sir Trafford Leigh-Mallory. Leigh-Mallory had played a significant role in the Battle of Britain as commander of fighters in one of the two vital southern operation regions opposing the German blitz. However, the air marshal was viewed as a scheming incompetent by a number of both American and British officers and was branded as gloomy, hesitant, and incapable of being a team player. Eisenhower and Leigh-Mallory had no particular animosity toward one another and Eisenhower seemed to have faith that the RAF marshal would make proper use of the formidable air power at his disposal for Overlord.

The most senior American field commander besides Eisenhower was the person responsible for United States ground forces in Overlord, Lieutenant General Omar Bradley. The fifty-one-year-old Missourian had emerged from the same modest roots as Eisenhower and had risen from division commander to leadership of the entire American First Army in little more than a year. While few of his contemporaries viewed him as a brilliant or charismatic commander, he was steady, reliable, and unassuming, and according to Eisenhower, could "read" a battle better than any American general. Bradley also had a dour, sometimes petty side that would complicate the command structure of Overlord.

The final member of Overlord's inner circle was Lieutenant General Walter Bedell-Smith. The 49-year-old officer was often Eisenhower's alter ego in his role of chief of staff of Supreme Headquarters, Allied Expeditionary Force (SHAEF). Bedell-Smith was brusque, laconic, and moody and had few close friends among either British or American officers. Generals who dealt with this often harsh and demanding officer called him "cold blooded," "stiff faced," and "tricky." However, Bedell-Smith was an excellent administrator who often performed the duties for which Eisenhower's personality did not prepare him. He enjoyed the absolute confidence of both Eisenhower and Marshall and would emerge as a key figure in the genesis of Overlord strategy.

Eisenhower and his senior commanders had been given a straight-forward but Herculean task by the Combined Chiefs of Staff. The Allied Command had ordered the men of SHAEF to "enter the continent of Europe, and in conjunction with the other Allied Nations, undertake operations aimed at the heart of Germany and the destruction of her Armed Forces." Now the leaders of Overlord would have to devise a strategy that would enable the Allied Expeditionary Force to crack Hitler's Atlantic Wall and defeat one of the most formidable armies in modern military history.

The German Wehrmacht that barred the way to the liberation of Europe was a bloodied but still unbroken force at the beginning of 1944. The previous year had seen a series of decisive defeats for German forces at Tunisia, Stalingrad, and Kursk with nearly a million Axis soldiers removed from the chessboard of the war in those three battles alone. During 1943 the British, Canadian, and American navies had significantly turned the tide of the battle of the Atlantic against the Kriegsmarine's U-boats, Soviet forces had pushed the German army out of much of the territory captured in the early stages of Operation Barbarossa, and the American Army Air Force and Royal Air Force's bomber commands had begun to penetrate into the heartland of the German Reich.

However, while Germany had absorbed some stunning blows in that disastrous year, the same resiliency that would haunt the Allies until almost the end of the war was becoming a hallmark of the Nazi military machine. German generals had conducted a masterful withdrawal from the crumbling front in Sicily, turned the expected rapid Allied advance through Italy into an agonizing crawl, and inflicted terrible losses on the still largely unescorted Allied bombers that penetrated German airspace.

The person who personified National Socialism, Führer Adolf Hitler, seemed to alternate between lucid plans and delusional rapture as the decisive year of the war approached. He saw the alliance of the fading British Empire, the aggressive American republic, and the fanatically anti-capitalist Soviet Union as a political absurdity and was convinced that the relationship would shatter if even one member received a smashing defeat. He also viewed the approaching American presidential election as a referendum on the war in the United States and was convinced that if Roosevelt lost the contest an executive more amenable to a negotiated peace might gain the White House. Therefore, the German dictator formulated a bold strategic plan for the coming year. He was convinced that the decisive theater of the war was in western Europe and that was where the tide could be turned. The Führer's plan was to merely hold the Soviet army at bay on the eastern front while significant reinforcements would be deployed in the west. Hitler fully expected an Allied landing in the spring or summer and was determined to utterly crush the invasion in its earliest stage. Then, with a second Anglo-American invasion delayed for a year, or perhaps forever, much of the western army would be shifted eastward to launch a new German offensive against the Soviets. If the Allies were still not willing to settle for a negotiated peace, a new arsenal of Wehrmacht weapons including guided missiles, jet planes, and upgraded submarines would be employed to defeat the British, Americans, and Russians in detail.

The key to the annihilation of the expected Allied invasion was a force of sixty German divisions, divided into four armies from the south of France to the coastline of Belgium and Holland. If the entire power of this formidable military force was properly utilized, an Allied invasion could probably be annihilated, but the men most responsible for implementing a successful strategy could not agree on the best use of their armies. General Gerd von Rundstedt was the senior German commander in the west. The 69-year-old Prussian had been chief of staff of XV Corps in World War I, commanded Army Group South in the campaign of 1940, and held the same position in the invasion of Russia the next year. After resigning his command at the end of 1941 in a feud with Hitler, he was recalled to duty as commander in chief in the west in 1942. Von Rundstedt was honest, flexible, and cranky and more loyal to the concept of Prussian military honor than the Führer whom he referred to sarcastically as "that Bohemian corporal." He insisted that it would be impossible to keep the Allies from landing on invasion beaches as their overwhelming naval forces could not be fully countered by German coastal batteries. Therefore, von Rundstedt proposed a plan in which the most formidable weapon in the Wehrmacht, the armored divisions of Panzer Group West, would be fully utilized. The elderly German commander wanted to entice the Allied ground forces well inland, out of support range of their naval forces, and then launch a vicious armored counterattack at a point most geographically favorable to the Germans. Von Rundstedt insisted that his trump cards were the sixteen hundred tanks assigned to defend the Western Front and they could only be used effectively if concentrated into large formations. Thus wherever the Allies chose to land, the decisive battle would probably be fought somewhere in the interior of France.

Von Rundstedt's chief rival for the ear of the Führer in the defense of the Western Front was his immediate subordinate, Field Marshal Erwin Rommel. While von Rundstedt symbolized the old-guard Prussian nobility, the fifty-three-year-old Rommel was the son of a schoolmaster who had only risen to prominence with the emergence of Hitler. Rommel had played an important role in the invasion of France commanding the 7th Panzer Division, then gained fame on both sides of the Channel for his role in the North Africa campaign where he earned the nickname "Desert Fox." After scoring a decisive victory over the British garrison at Tobruk, he lost an even more important battle to Montgomery at El Alamein and was eventually reassigned by Hitler to prevent his capture as the Allies closed in on the Axis forces in Tunisia in the spring of 1943. On New Year's morning of 1944, only days after Eisenhower and Montgomery had received their Overlord assignments, Rommel was made commander of German forces in Belgium, Holland, and Northern France as general in command of Army Group B. The Desert Fox now commanded the two largest armies in the west, the Seventh and Fifteenth Armies and he quickly became embroiled in a running controversy with von Rundstedt over the best way to meet the looming Anglo-American invasion.

Rommel had seen the power of his Afrika Korps unravel in the desert war as the Allied air forces gradually wrested the skies from the Luftwaffe, and by early 1944 it appeared that the Anglo-American air superiority over Western Europe might be even greater than had occurred in North Africa. Therefore, despite the significant mutual respect and admiration between Rommel and his superior, the Desert Fox insisted that von Rundstedt's plan for a decisive confrontation inland was unworkable; Allied air power would annihilate the panzer divisions on their way to their showdown with the enemy. Rommel insisted that the enemy had to be defeated on the beaches, while they were still most vulnerable to counterattack and before they could concentrate their superior numbers of troops and tanks. The commander of Army Group B requested that Hitler allow him to station powerful armored battle groups near any possible invasion beaches and then unleash these lethal weapons before the Allies had the power to

The Germans built a series of defensive concrete bunkers and forts, known as the Atlantic Wall, along the coastline. These heavily armed fortifications placed along the landing site beaches were often the first source of firepower the Allies faced on landing.

deflect them. According to Rommel, the first twenty-four hours of the campaign would be decisive, a period he would famously refer to as "the longest day."

Hitler respected the talents of both von Rundstedt and Rommel and believed they were among his best generals. Surprisingly, for a person with little empathy for others, the Führer did not want to injure the pride of either field marshal and he imposed a rather cumbersome compromise. Rommel could deploy some of the panzer divisions relatively close to the French coast but they would remain under von Rundstedt's operational command until the Führer directed otherwise. Also, to placate the senior general, about half of the armored forces would be held well inland to allow von Rundstedt to launch his massive counterattack if conditions permitted. Thus as the leaders of Overlord debated the proper strategy to defeat the enemy, the German defenders were also emotionally debating how to stop the invasion. As this gigantic chess match gathered momentum leaders on both sides of the English Channel reviewed the assets available to themselves and their adversaries and considered how to maximize their advantages and negate those of the enemy.

The British faced some of the best German units in their landing sector, but they were heavily armed for the offensive, as in this photograph depicting British soldiers firing mortar rounds.

The U.S. Army's most common artillery piece for the invading divisions in the Normandy campaign was the 105mm howitzer, shown here.

While there is a popular modern impression among many Europeans and Americans that the Anglo-American allies wielded enough power to simply overwhelm the German defenders during Overlord, the reality is one of a far more balanced checksheet of advantages and disadvantages on each side of the battle line. In overall numbers of combat soldiers available, the forty or so Allied divisions available for Overlord only marginally outnumbered the Germans assigned to the sixty Wehrmacht divisions guarding France and the Low Countries. The Allies could deploy far more support troops than their adversaries, but the number of frontline riflemen, gunners, and tankers was not overwhelmingly larger than the Germans could field. While the Russians would enjoy a superiority of combat soldiers of almost four to one against the Germans during the final year of the war, the Anglo-Americans would fight most of the Normandy campaign with an advantage of about three to two over an enemy that almost always had the advantage of fighting on the defensive and utilizing excellent terrain. Red Army generals may have found comfort in the realization that they could suffer enormous casualties and still overwhelm the Germans with sheer numbers; Anglo-American commanders would not enjoy that "luxury" during Overlord.

The weapons that the opposing armies would employ during Overlord reflected particular strengths and weaknesses of the contending nations' armaments industries. The British Enfield and German Mauser rifles were both bolt-action weapons of approximately similar range and firing rate. However, the American infantrymen would enter battle equipped with the Garand M-1 semiautomatic rifle that was arguably the best personal weapon of World War II as it featured reliability, range, and rapid fire. The Germans compensated for their relatively slow-firing rifles by lavishly deploying submachine guns, machine guns, and other automatic weapons throughout their infantry companies. German units were heavily equipped with "burp guns" and machine pistols and their superb MG42 machine gun could fire twelve hundred rounds a minute compared to five hundred rounds for most comparable British and American weapons. Both sides made frequent use of hand grenades and the German "potato masher" featured a stick for better throwing accuracy while the American "pineapple" was less accurate but held twice as much explosive charge. Thus the Anglo-American allies entered the last year of World War II with only rough parity against the Germans in basic weapons.

The contest between gunners would present a similar range of particular Allied and Axis advantages. The German 88mm dual-purpose gun was probably the most valuable artillery piece of the war as it provided deadly firepower against Allied airplanes, tanks, and ground troops. However, the superb British 17-pounder was much easier to transport and an effective weapon against German panzer units. American 105mm howitzers and huge 155mm howitzers became the nemesis of German counterblocks and provided excellent support for large-scale offensives.

The most-feared weapon on both sides of the Overlord battlefields were the tanks and here again a fascinating parity of advantages and liabilities quickly emerged. The Allies began operations in France with about twenty-two hundred available tanks compared to just sixteen hundred of these weapons assigned to German forces. The Germans would defend the Western Front with a bewildering variety of tanks which included now obsolete French and Czech vehicles captured early in the war and the two most feared tanks in the Axis arsenal, the Panther and the Tiger. The enormous, powerfully armored, and powerfully armed Tiger was particularly viewed as the scourge of the battlefield by Allied infantrymen watching these ponderous behemoths lumber toward them, but the Germans could deploy only about one hundred of these weapons and their breakdown rate was appallingly high. The Germans would much more often enter battle equipped with the standard Panzer IV which was a solid but not quite as daunting weapon.

One of the main German defenses used in France were their tank forces. Above is the much-dreaded Tiger tank, their most powerful and largest armored vehicle.

In the months leading up to the invasion, huge stockpiles of weapons were assembled in England. The M-4 Sherman tank, shown here, was used by many American and British units because it was easy to mass produce, extremely reliable, fast and maneuverable but it was also poorly armored and undergunned.

The Allies would employ their own diverse range of tanks including Stuarts, Churchills, and Cromwells, but the armored battles of Overlord would largely be lost or won with the controversial M4 Sherman medium tank that was supplied to the majority of British and American armored units. The Sherman was easy to mass produce, extremely reliable, fast, and maneuverable but also poorly armored, undergunned, and very likely to blow up when hit. In a one-on-one confrontation the Sherman could marginally hold its own against a Panzer IV and would be heavily outgunned by a Panther or Tiger. However, there were plenty of replacement Shermans available if the Allies could get far enough inland to unleash their armor.

Thus as Eisenhower and his commanders surveyed the men, weapons, and equipment available to their own forces and those of the enemy, the man responsible for Overlord quickly realized that while this invasion was no suicide mission, neither was it a likely pushover. Attackers and defenders seemed to be evenly balanced and it was now imperative for the titans of Overlord to develop a strategy that would decisively tilt the balance of battle in their favor.

Organization of the American Army

On the day that Great Britain and France announced a state of war with Germany, the United States Army numbered 190,000 men enrolled in five understrength infantry divisions and one full-strength cavalry division. Yet two years later, as the United States enjoyed its last few hours of peace before Pearl Harbor, American Ground Forces commander General Lesley McNair confidently predicted that the rapidly expanding army would jump from its current strength of thirty-six divisions to two hundred divisions between one and two years after the outbreak of an increasingly inevitable war. Five weeks later General George C. Marshall raised the estimate of combat divisions needed to fight a two-front war to 334. However, when the Allied high command began planning Operation Overlord, the actual strength of the American army had plateaued at eighty-nine divisions and this figure would actually drop to eighty-eight by the end of the war. This force seems rather modest for a sprawling nation of 130 million people, especially when compared to the four hundred divisions fielded by the Soviet Army, three hundred divisions deployed by the Germans, and one hundred divisions raised by Imperial Japan. Yet, there was a very rational background to this relatively small number of combat divisions.

The United States was obliged to engage not only in a gigantic military effort all over the globe, but also a huge manufacturing effort that would supply all of the American forces and many of the British and Soviet allies. Thus roughly half of all eighteen to thirty-five-year-old males who could be utilized for military service were exempted to work in the war industries while the navy, army, air forces, and marine corps were expanded beyond prewar projections. When all of these obligations had been met there remained just under 2.5 million men available for the Army Ground Forces from which combat divisions would be organized. This pool of men could support roughly ninety divisions which included eighty-eight authorized divisions and two provisional divisions a grand total that was reduced to eighty-nine when the 2nd Cavalry Division was inactivated in the spring of 1944.

An American infantry division was a "triangular" unit in which three squads formed a platoon, three platoons deployed as a company, three companies were organized into a battalion, three battalions deployed as a regiment, and three regiments were organized as a division. The total strength of 14,000 men would be organized around 6,518 riflemen, 243 automatic rifles, 157 .30-caliber machine guns, 236 .50-caliber machine guns, 90 60mm mortars, 54 81mm mortars, 557 bazookas, 57 of the 57mm antitank guns, 54 105mm howitzers, and 12 155mm howitzers. This force was the most motorized infantry division in the world as its authorized vehicles could be augmented by six quartermaster truck companies to provide motorized transport for the entire force.

An American armored division also revolved around a spectacular level of overall mobility. The sixteen American armored divisions included some exceptions from a "normal" strength, but the typical unit included 10,937 men, 186 medium, and 77 light tanks. However, these tanks were augmented by 650 armored half-tracks and nearly 2,700 other assorted vehicles from jeeps to self-propelled guns. This lavish provision of vehicles gave American armored divisions a high degree of cross-country mobility that would produce significant consequences once the Americans became unleashed from the hedgerow country in the later stages of the Normandy campaign and meshed perfectly with the American tactical emphasis on speed, mobility, and a massive focusing of firepower at a point where the enemy was least able to counter it.

Organization of the British Army

The British Army had entered World War II designed as a constabulary force to police a huge empire utilizing relatively small units to defend British interests and keep the peace. The main reference point for British soldiers was not the division but the regiment which encouraged a special sense of loyalty in every man who served in these organizations. However, the British regiment was actually more an administrative unit than a combat force as the main fighting group within this unit was actually a battalion that could be linked up with two other battalions from other regiments to form a brigade. Three infantry brigades and an artillery brigade would then be amalgamated to form an infantry division of 18,400 men. This arrangement produced some minor confusion between American and British allies. The United States Army which had substantially used a brigade structure in the Civil War and World War I, virtually abandoned that formation during World War II while heavily focusing on regiments that in turn were nothing more than parent organizations of battalions in the British Army of 1939–45.

The organizational table for British armored units was also fairly varied. A normal armored division deployed 286 tanks, mostly Shermans and Cromwells, with an infantry brigade of three motorized battalions and an armored brigade of three armored battalions, which were also called regiments, plus another infantry battalion assigned to ride in half-tracks. This complete unit could put fifteen thousand men into the field, but because each individual battalion or regiment was so autonomous, cooperation between infantry and armored units could be quite spotty. Also, the British army fielded a number of independent tank brigades that often were equipped with relatively slow, heavy, Churchill tanks deployed to support the infantry along with the special tanks of the 79th Armoured Division whose "funnies" were dispersed throughout the army.

The reliance on a regimental system produced a high degree of cohesion, sense of belonging, and geographical commonality in the British army which was often envied by American officers. However, the regimental system did include at least one serious drawback. Once combat battalions began taking heavy casualties in Normandy, it became difficult, sometimes impossible, to send replacements from men who came from one section of the United Kingdom to a division representing a different area. The British War Office seriously overestimated the percentage of casualties that would come from artillery or armored units and underestimated the losses of infantry units. Soon there would be only one available trained infantry replacement for every three infantry casualties further hampered by the inflexibility of the regimental replacement system. At the time of the Normandy campaign the entire British army of just over 2.8 million men contained only 550,000 infantrymen supported by a very limited pool of replacements. This resulted in a short-age of over thirty thousand British infantrymen in Normandy and forced the breaking up of the 50th and 59th Divisions to provide replacements.

Organization of the German Army

By the summer of 1944 the strain of a long war was beginning to force alterations in both the organization and tactics of the German forces. German infantry divisions that had invaded Poland and France with 17,200 men enrolled in three regiments of three battalions apiece were fighting the Anglo-American army in Normandy with only 12,800 men organized into either three regiments of two battalions or two regiments of three battalions. Additionally, a whole new category of infantry divisions had been created. The "static" divisions that comprised much of Rommel's beach defense force on D-Day, had almost no readily available transport vehicles and were populated with large numbers of older or previously wounded German troops blended with "*Ost Truppen*," foreign "volunteers" captured on the Eastern Front and given the opportunity to fight in the west rather than face the bleak survival prospects in German P.O.W. camps.

A fairly conventional German infantry division engaged in the Normandy campaign tended to be formed around three infantry regiments fielding two infantry battalions, an antitank company, and a cannon company while the divisional and organization would also include a reconnaissance unit, an engineer unit, a signals force, a medical company, military police troop, veterinary company, and several artillery batteries.

The high command had also been paring down the strength of the panzer divisions and by the summer of 1944 a German armored division was reduced to 14,727 men organized into a single two-battalion tank regiment, a pair of two-battalion panzergrenadier regiments, several batteries of mobile anti-aircraft guns and antitank guns, an armored reconnaissance unit, and an armored signal unit. The tank regiment was usually divided into a battalion of Panzer IVs and a battalion of Panthers while each panzergrenadier regiment included one battalion equipped with armored half-tracks for mobility. While a conventional panzer division still boasted a considerable amount of firepower, its actual tank strength was only half as powerful as in the early days of the war as the authorized number of tanks had been whittled from 328 to 165 with often inefficient maintenance operations slashing that number even lower. A typical panzer division fighting in Normandy was usually fortunate to deploy 100 tanks in any given battle. Also, the most-feared German tanks, the Mark VI Tigers, were kept out of the divisional organization and assigned to special Heavy Tank Battalions which were kept under army control and only utilized in specific missions after which they would be returned to headquarters.

While the numbers in Wehrmacht divisions were beginning to contract, Hermann Göring and Heinrich Himmler generally ensured that their semi-private armies at least started the Normandy campaign at something closer to their original strength. Luftwaffe parachute divisions and Waffen SS divisions were likely to contain a full nine combat battalions and be equipped with the best available weapons. For example, the Hitler Youth of the 12th SS Panzer Division began the Normandy campaign with 21,386 men in a unit that probably boasted the firepower of three or four static divisions.

The organizational nature of German fighting units was not the only thing that had changed during the past five years. The German army began the war as a primarily offensive weapon based on a deadly combination of infantry, tanks, and air power slashing through static enemy armies and then annihilating them before they fully realized what had hit them. Now the German army was caught in a gradual retreat on every fighting front and generals who could fight successful defensive battles were becoming increasingly valuable. The idea of blitzkrieg was based on the availability of generally superior tanks and air superiority or even supremacy over the battlefield. Now, conditions were dramatically altered. The Germans still deployed excellent tanks, but the Allies were producing four tanks to every panzer and even the Panthers and Tigers couldn't stave off those odds indefinitely. The Stuka that was the terror of the skies in 1939 Poland and 1940 France was now unmasked as a dreadfully slow and vulnerable plane that was almost useless unless protected by swarms of German fighters, a luxury that was now increasingly a rarity. However, the Germans proved to be excellent at improvising techniques for holding their ground or at least preventing annihilation in retreat.

One of the focal points of German defensive tactics was the Kampfgruppe which was simply an ad hoc force of mixed arms smaller than a division but with no fixed structure or size. Kampfgruppe commanders soon became adept at cobbling together an effective fighting force from an assortment of grounded Luftwaffe personnel, engineers, slightly wounded infantrymen, and perhaps a tank or two all melded together into a very temporary, but often effective, combat fire brigade. The German high command wanted to use these very flexible Kampfgruppe to be utililized winning as many firefights as possible which in turn was expected to provide a tactical advantage and encourage the Allies to see the invasion of western Europe as either unwinnable or so bloody as to be not worth the effort.

Allied Uniforms and Equipment

The Allied soldiers who were fighting their way across Normandy in the summer of 1944 displayed a fascinating mix of similarity and diversity in their uniforms and equipment. The clothing worn by British and American soldiers during this campaign marked the continuation of a trend towards comfort and utility that had been accelerating since the days of the Great War. British troops who had fought the Americans at Bunker Hill, Saratoga, or Yorktown had been encumbered with perhaps the most uncomfortable, least utilitarian uniforms of any army in history as hats that were purposely too small perched on ridiculous powdered wigs; overly tight breeches and collars cut off circulation; and scratchy, hot, red coats proved a godsend for enemy marksmen. Now, the scarlet coats were no longer seen in battle; comfortable berets replaced the tri-cornered hats; and lightweight cotton uniforms were available for dealing with excessive heat. However, while the British soldier of 1944 exhibited a dramatically different appearance than he did under Burgoyne or Wellington, he still looked more like his Great War predecessor than did his American counterpart.

The most important visible similarity between British soldiers of 1918 and 1944 was that most units were still equipped with helmets that were very similar to those worn in the Great War. Also, the basic color of the tunic and trousers were almost the same shade of brown as the units that fought at the Somme or Ypres. On the other hand, at closer inspection, there were increasing variations that were appearing by the time of the Normandy campaign. By June of 1944 a number of British units were being equipped with the newly developed Mark III helmet that featured more sloping sides and a look that was somewhat distinctive from its familiar predecessor. Also, the brown shoes and the almost knee-high leggings of 1918 had been replaced by low black shoes and ankle-high gaiters. Much of the heavy equipment in forward units was now attached to a leather, vest-like jerkin that could carry large amounts of ammunition, rations, and spare clothing.

If the transformation of the Tommy was somewhat subtle and gradual, the GI who stormed the Normandy beaches looked almost nothing like his Great War predecessor. The British-style hel-

met that most doughboys of 1918 utilized survived into World War II, but just barely. A radically different headpiece, the M-1 steel helmet, was authorized in November 1941 and used by most combat units by late summer of 1942. This helmet gave excellent protection in combat, could serve as a portable basin and was made more comfortable with a lightweight compound fiber liner that could be worn alone for parade use. The helmet's poor protection from cold weather was improved by an M-1941 wool knit cap worn underneath.

The rest of the combat uniform for an American soldier in the summer of 1944 was a garrison or "overseas" cap, a cotton or wool olive-drab shirt and trousers, an M-1941 field jacket, brown leather shoes, low canvas gaiters, and a variety of web field equipment. This uniform was designed for comfort and ease rather than for strict military looking appearance so that many American troops appeared less "soldierly" than their British or German counterparts. On the other hand, American dress uniforms, especially for enlisted men, were considered far smarter in appearance than the outfit available to the average Tommy. American units stationed in Britain utilized a salary that was three times as high as their British counterparts and a uniform that appeared to equal or exceed even British officers for what was sometimes seen as an unfair advantage in the more friendly battle for the attention of eligible women in the British Isles and France.

German Uniforms and Equipment

Many popular American films and television programs have contrasted the apparent snappy appearance of German soldiers with the "sad sack" depiction of GIs. However, while officers and members of elite units were still being issued relatively smart uniforms at the time of the Normandy campaign, the average German enlisted man probably envied his Allied counterpart's appearance. A typical German soldier fighting in the summer of 1944 wore a uniform that included a service cap, M-1943 field tunic, belted trousers incorporating a reinforced seat and tapered legs for anklets, short lace-up boots, and an M-1942 "coal scuttle" helmet. The officers who led these men were still enjoying access to uniforms that dramatically distinguished them from their enlisted subordinates.

Less than two months after the invasion of Poland, officers in the German army who held a rank below general were ordered to wear enlisted men's field uniforms in order not to be targets in battle, but most officers essentially ignored the order for the rest of the war. Officers had access to specially designed peaked caps, special tunics, a distinctive brown leather belt, officer's breeches, black leather riding boots, gray suede gloves, and a pistol and holster all made of superior materials that enlisted men would almost never see. A combination of the fact that the German army commissioned only a third the proportionate number of officers as the Allied armies and the traditional social gulf between officers and men in the German military tradition instilled a broad-based desire for officers to dress very differently than their enlisted men.

The enlisted men who had access to uniforms that were superior in material and appearance tended to belong to elite services such as the Luftwaffe or SS. Hermann Göring's contention that the men of his command were essentially "knights of the air" induced him to order a design of uniforms that would be far more visually impressive than ordinary ground soldiers. Thus even those Luftwaffe personnel assigned to antiaircraft units, paratroopers, or the growing number of "field divisions" maintained wardrobes that included numerous items in some offshoot of a blue color not unlike the RAF or the United States Air Force after its separation from the army.

Heinrich Himmler also wanted to maintain a distinctive appearance for his SS troops and he utilized earlier German military regalia to uniform his elite troops. The distinctive SS collar runes, commonly called the "double lightning flash," harked back to the days of the Vikings and the highly coveted forester's dagger went back to the mists of Gothic lore. The Death's Head cap insignia were used by Hussars as late as World War I and the black dress uniforms were also at least partially used as a link to early German forces as it was a predominent color of elite cavalry regiments under the kaisers and also by units involved in the war of liberation against Napoleon from 1813-15.

CHAPTER III

A Blueprint for Victory

As the senior Allied commanders absorbed the monumental task facing them in the coming invasion, they began exploring possible means of stacking the odds more favorably towards Anglo-American success in Overlord. Three potentially pivotal decisions soon became apparent. The commanders would need to choose an invasion site where the landings would not be either annihilated or checkmated; they would need to persuade the Germans to deploy as many divisions as possible somewhere other than the landing site that was chosen; and finally, they would need to make it as difficult as possible for the enemy to reinforce the landing areas once the invasion had occurred. If all three of these conditions were met the odds of a successful campaign would rise substantially; if one or more of these decisions or operations were seriously flawed, the momentum of the war would most likely shift to Hitler.

The first crucial decision was to select a landing beach for Overlord and six potential sites quickly emerged. The list included the North Sea coastline of Holland and Belgium, the Pas de Calais beaches directly opposite the British port of Dover, the mouth of the Seine River near the port of Le Havre, the Calvados Coast and Cotentin Peninsula of Normandy, the Brittany Peninsula, and finally, the Bay of Biscay coastline down to the region of Bordeaux. Each site was carefully considered, and in a fairly short time, the list of contestants was pared to two. The Dutch and Belgian coast offered the advantage of relatively close access to the heartland of Germany but the beaches featured soft sand dunes that would play havoc with Allied vehicles, there were few exits from the beaches, and the region was at the extreme limit of Allied fighter cover. The mouth of the Seine offered somewhat better air logistics and featured the tempting prospect of the capture of the huge port of Le Havre, but an Allied invasion army would be forced into the extremely dangerous situation of advancing inland along opposite sides of a major river which would be an invitation to disaster in the event of a well-planned German counterattack. Brittany featured the availability of a number of first-class ports such as Brest, Lorient, and St. Nazaire, but these cities were sure to be heavily garrisoned and the region was two hundred miles from most Allied fighter bases. The Bay of Biscay was even less appealing as it was totally out of range of most Allied fighters and required a sea voyage of such distance that many of the vital smaller invasion craft would have to be left behind.

When these four contenders had been eliminated, Pas de Calais and Normandy remained. Calais was probably the logical choice for a landing since the beaches were only twenty miles from the Dover dockyards and the region offered a straight path to both Paris and the borders of the Reich. However, Calais presented one overwhelming disadvantage to the Allied planners. The site was *so* logical as an invasion point that the Germans would probably concentrate their best troops, best tanks, and best artillery along this segment of the coast. On the other hand Normandy had just enough disadvantages to possibly convince the enemy to look elsewhere for a landing. The fifty miles of coastline that stretched roughly from Ouistreham on the Bay of the Seine to the Cotentin beaches beyond the crossroads town of St. Mère Église was about two hundred miles from Paris and about four hundred miles from the German border. The beaches in this region had an acceptable, but hardly abundant, number of exits to interior roads and were a tolerable but not ideal distance from Allied airfields. While it was obvious that this region would hardly be undefended, there seemed to be a reasonable chance that the Germans would deploy much of their army somewhere else, especially if they could be subtly convinced by the Allies that the "real" invasion was going to develop at another place at another time. This was a fantasy that British and American commanders were more than happy to instill in their German counterparts.

The deception operation designed to keep as many Germans as possible peering across the water everywhere but Normandy was one of the most successful disinformation campaigns in military history and dramatically improved the odds in favor of Allied victory. Code-named *Fortitude*, this operation was designed to keep large numbers of German troops deployed near beaches the Allies had no intention of attacking while convincing the enemy high command that the Normandy landings were either a ruse or a clever feint.

One facet of the operation, Fortitude North, was designed to draw German attention to the stark coastline of Scandinavia as a place for imminent Allied invasion activities. Hitler and a number of his military commanders suspected that the Anglo-Americans had developed plans to invade Germany through Norway and Denmark and a powerful force of seventeen divisions had been deployed to counter that threat. Allied commanders were delighted to see a substantial part of the German army defending a region they had no intention of invading and they now allowed enemy intelligence services to "discover" the presence of the British Fourth Army in Scotland poised for a lunge across the North Sea toward Scandinavia. Actually the Fourth Army could not have attacked a Scottish sheep farm as it consisted of nothing more than a handful of radio operators and communications specialists. While these personnel kept up a steady stream of orders for phantom "corps" and "divisions," using codes they knew the Germans had broken, Luftwaffe reconnaissance planes were allowed to penetrate Scottish air space to photograph dummy landing craft and prop tanks preparing relentlessly for the great invasion. This deception worked so well that most of this powerful garrison was still defending Scandinavia on the day that Germany surrendered.

Once Allied intelligence had detached the Scandinavian garrison from the coming invasion the next step was to convince the Germans that the complimentary offensive against the European mainland was scheduled to strike Calais rather than Normandy. Fortitude South was an even more elaborate hoax centered around a real general and a fictitious American army group. The bogus American force was the First United States Army Group or FUSAG for short. The army consisted of dozens of army divisions that had received numerical designations but had never been added to the army table of organization. Their commander, however, was the very real and very controversial General George C. Patton.

Patton had been the first American general to enjoy significant success against the Germans during the North Africa campaign and then commanded the American element of the invasion force that captured Sicily from the Axis. However, just at the peak of his success he had been involved in two incidents of slapping hospitalized soldiers who the enraged general insisted were cowards because they had not suffered battle wounds. Patton's superior, Eisenhower, had briefly considered relieving the controversial general of his command and sending him home but had realized Patton's genuine combat abilities and decided to use him as an army commander sometime after the initial Normandy landings. During the summer of 1944 Patton would burst on the scene as the commander of the hard-driving Third Army. However, during the winter and spring of that year the outspoken general was assigned the unrewarding but vital job of decoy for the enemy.

Allied intelligence officials knew that the Germans considered Patton the most dangerous American commander and they reasoned that if the enemy could be convinced that the opinionated general was about to lead an army group from Dover to Calais, the charade would seem extremely realistic. In turn Patton, who was desperate to get back into Eisenhower's good graces, played his role superbly. He diligently inspected real units that were then sent back to their camps to prepare for the Normandy operation. He gave speeches in the towns and cities of Kent dropping broad hints that these were the jump-off points for the invasion of Calais.

Patton was soon receiving high-level assistance in maintaining his charade. Local papers ran articles detailing the damage that American tanks were causing on area roads and phony letters to the editor from outraged Kent landowners detailed the property damage being caused by First Army Group maneuvers. A huge pier was built at Dover to convince the Germans that the Allies were about to lay an oil pipeline across the Channel to Calais and soon dummy pipes made of canvas and wood were being photographed by Luftwaffe reconnaissance planes. The "construction" site was visited by Eisenhower, Montgomery, and even King George to add an authentic touch to the drama. Finally, British and American movie personnel were brought in to deploy fake tanks and landing craft in locations that would most likely convince the enemy of their authenticity.

Once an invasion site had been selected and a plan to decoy much of the enemy army from the Normandy beaches had been implemented, another major challenge had to be confronted. The Allied high command would have to develop a strategy that would simultaneously prevent large-scale German reinforcements from reaching the invasion area while permitting the Anglo-Americans to pour additional men, vehicles, and supplies into Normandy unhampered by their adversaries. Both of these activities would involve the integral participation of the two major Allied air arms, the Royal Air Force and the American Army Air Force. The proper use of these two formidable aerial weapons would quickly ignite one of the most emotional debates of the entire Overlord operation.

When Dwight Eisenhower was appointed supreme commander of Overlord he soon came to realize two fundamental realities concerning the air component of the Normandy invasion. First, given the relative parity in ground combat forces between Allied attackers and Axis defenders, an invasion of Fortress Europe was very unlikely to succeed unless the Anglo-Americans established at least air superiority over the Luftwaffe during the operation, or preferably, total control of the air. Given the inherent advantages the German defenders would enjoy on the ground during the invasion, it was absolutely vital that the RAF and AAF keep the Luftwaffe away from the landing beaches. Second, Ike also realized that the two major Allied air arms had now developed into essentially autonomous forces that were largely fighting their own war against the Germans almost independent of any current or future ground campaigns. Eisenhower would have *access* to the most powerful aerial armada ever deployed but his *command* over that power was to become a contentious issue.

While Eisenhower, Montgomery, and the other leaders of the Allied Expeditionary Force were hammering out the early drafts of the Overlord operation, the bomber commands of the RAF and AAF were entering a critical phase of Operation Pointblank, the Combined Bombing Offensive of the Reich. The British and American "bomber barons" led by Marshal Arthur Harris of British Bomber Command and General Carl Spaatz of the newly formed U.S. Strategic Air Forces in Europe (Eighth and Fifteenth U.S. Air Forces) were convinced that Overlord was either a waste of time or at best a mopping-up operation as they asserted that a constant bombing offensive, night and day, over key targets in Germany would bring the enemy to its knees without the need to actually launch a risky ground invasion.

By early 1944 the air offensive was gradually penetrating ever further into the heartland of the Reich and even Berlin was being subjected to aerial punishment. However, the "bomber barons" had already committed an enormous blunder. They had insisted that heavy bombers equipped with a formidable array of defensive weapons could accomplish bombing missions deep into Germany with acceptable losses among the attacking squadrons. However, the Luftwaffe had countered these attacks with improved night fighters, deadly rocket firing "destroyers," and speedy cannon firing interceptors, and casualties among Allied air crews grew to alarming proportions. Not only was German morale not cracking and German industry not collapsing, but British and American bomber personnel were suffering casualties that were heavier than the infantrymen who had fought in the bloody trench warfare of World War I. As perplexed and harried bomber commanders groped for a solution to this expanding crisis, Eisenhower suddenly loomed on the scene with a demand that the powerful assets of the Allied air forces should now be channeled toward the initiation of the Overlord campaign.

The test of wills between bomber barons committed to exclusive use of their forces for strategic bombing and a supreme commander determined to add these forces to his invasion arsenal created reverberations that went as far as Downing Street and the White House. While senior American and British air officials complained that Overlord was distracting them from a war-winning offensive of their own, Eisenhower, Montgomery, and the other members of SHAEF insisted to Churchill, Roosevelt, and others that the whole premise of an invasion of France was based on extensive air force cooperation. Finally, Eisenhower played his trump card. He informed the prime minister and president that if he was not provided with authority over one of the key weapons of the invasion, the air force, he would simply resign from his position and "go home." Ike was playing the ultimate bluff of his career and he largely succeeded. The strategic air forces were placed under his "direction" for several months in a compromise that substantially favored Eisenhower over his air force adversaries. Now, armed with this enhanced authority, Eisenhower exhorted his deputies to explore the most promising avenues for utilizing the Allied air forces to strengthen the odds in favor of success in Normandy.

Eisenhower's deputy commander, Air Chief Marshal Arthur Tedder, introduced the general to a somewhat rumpled scholar, Dr. Solly Zuckerman. The Oxford University professor had worked closely with Tedder in both planning and evaluating Allied air operations in the Mediterranean theater and had conducted extensive research on how the selection of targets for aerial bombardment affected a ground campaign. Zuckerman was convinced that the best way to prevent the enemy from substantially reinforcing their garrison in Normandy was to destroy the signal centers, locomotive repair facilities, and marshaling yards for rolling stock of the French railroad network. He insisted that successful air attacks on a relatively short list of rail centers had virtually paralyzed the Italian railroad system during the Sicilian and southern Italian campaigns and the process could definitely be repeated in France. By February of 1944 Zuckerman had compiled a list of seventy-eight key targets in France and Belgium which included loco-motive depots, rail junctions, switching systems, and roundhouses, and he asserted that 45,000 tons of Allied bombs should be sufficient to largely eliminate this system.

Zuckerman's concept was quickly dubbed the "Transportation Plan" and the idea was strongly supported by both Eisenhower and Tedder who both insisted that the operation would finally make effi-cient use of strategic bomber forces that seemed to be accomplishing very little in their own private war against the Reich. As a member of SHAEF noted, "The railway areas cover from 50 to 500 acres and are ideal targets either for precision bombing by day or, in a large number of cases, bombing at night, thus effectively using American day bombers and British night aircraft."

The plan may have seemed ideal to Eisenhower and his staff, but

The B-17 bomber was know as the Flying Fortress. B-17s such as the one shown here were used for bombing raids in Germany during the Normandy landings.

the "bomber barons" were astounded at this diversion of their power-ful bomber fleets from their war-winning offensive against German industrial centers. Solly Zuckerman was vain, self-assured, and sar-castic and gave the impression that any other opinion than his own was concocted by a far inferior intellect. The tweed-coated academic quickly locked horns with Harris, Spaatz, and their team of experts, most of whom were as prickly and egotistical as he was. Harris quick-ly challenged Zuckerman's plan by asserting that if the strategic bomber forces carried out the "Transportation Plan," the operation would inflict a minimum of 60,000 casualties on French civilians. This argument resonated strongly with Churchill and most members of his cabinet as they realized that French casualties of this magnitude would hardly endear the Gallic peoples to Britain in a postwar world.

While the bomber command of the RAF opposed Zuckerman's plan on the basis of civilian casualties, Carl Spaatz and the American bombardment chiefs challenged the Oxford don with an alternative proposal of their own. Spaatz supported a group of Americans bomb damage experts who insisted that Zuckerman had chosen the wrong target. They insisted that the best way to immobilize enemy counter-attacks during Overlord was to devastate the German petroleum industry. Spaatz and his advisors asserted that a mere twenty-seven fuel plants in the Reich and allied countries produced 70 percent of Germany's refining capacity; if these relatively few facilities were annihilated, the Wehrmacht would virtually grind to a halt as tanks, planes, and trucks would be largely immobilized. Moreover, this "Oil Plan" offered the added bonus that the Luftwaffe would fight to the death to protect these targets and Spaatz insisted that newly available American long-range escort fighters could engage the enemy over these threatened areas and destroy many of the planes that might oth-erwise challenge the Overlord landings.

Spaatz and his advisors had produced a legitimate alternative to Zuckerman's program and the issue came to a head on March 25, 1944. On that blustery early spring Saturday, Eisenhower convened a high-level conference at historic Norfolk House on St. James Square in London. Among the invited participants were British Air Minister Portal, Tedder, Leigh-Mallory, Harris, Spaatz, and an assortment of staff officers and civilian experts from the Ministry of Economic Warfare, the Joint Intelligence Committee, and a number of related agencies. Tedder and Spaatz emerged as the spokesmen for the two competing opera-tions and each presented cogent reasons for Eisenhower to select their plan. While Eisenhower had already been leaning in the direction of the

Transportation Plan, the general shifted even further toward Tedder when a representative for the Ministry of Economic Warfare produced conclusive statistics that even if all twenty-seven enemy petroleum plants were destroyed, German stockpiles of fuel would keep the Wehrmacht reasonably mobile for another four or five months.

Eisenhower listened carefully to all arguments and then produced a masterful compromise. The Transportation Plan would be fully implemented as soon as possible. However, Eisenhower admitted that Spaatz had discovered a potential long-term Achilles heel of the Wehrmacht and as soon as most of the rail targets had been destroyed the strategic bombers would be shifted back to attacking the fuel industry while fighter-bombers and medium-bombers finished up the transportation offensive. Finally, those same aircraft would then begin a massive interdiction campaign just before the invasion to destroy bridges, tunnels, key highway junctions, and any other target that would affect the mobility of enemy reinforcements.

Thus during April and May of 1944 air combat swirled over much of northern France as British and American planes pulverized rail yards, locomotive repair shops, and marshalling yards. By May 25, seventy-three rail centers had been attacked with 49,000 tons of bombs. Forty-two roundhouses were either destroyed or badly damaged, four thousand French locomotives were smoldering hulks, and tens of thousands of passenger and freight cars were useless. Then key bridges, tunnels, and highways from Calais to Cherbourg were pounded into rubble as the Allies kept the attacks widespread to blind the Germans to their actual landing site. The bombs, machine guns, and rockets also took a large toll of French civilians, but only about one-sixth the number that Churchill feared.

Equally important to the success of Overlord, the arrival of increasing numbers of the formidable P-51 Mustang long-range fighter enabled Allied strategic bombers to penetrate ever further into the enemy's heartland. By early June, most of the Luftwaffe's best fighter squadrons had been pulled back from France to Germany to battle the Allies over the skies of the Reich. Only a handful of German fighters and bombers would be available to challenge the largest air armada every deployed in warfare. The Allies now had a viable landing site while the enemy reconnaissance was largely blinded, many of their troops were improperly deployed, their mobility was compromised, and their air cover seriously weakened. The stage for invasion was now clearly set and while success was hardly assured, the odds were clearly swinging in the Allies's favor.

CHAPTER IV

Countdown to Invasion

On an unseasonably cold Good Friday morning a group of the most powerful military leaders in the western world squeezed through the narrow pupil entrance of St. Paul's School in Hammersmith, London, and filed into the tiered seats of a large lecture hall. While young British students might have acclimated themselves to the hard wooden benches and heating system that made the room only marginally warmer than the street outside, the current occupants of this amphitheater were middle-aged or older men accustomed to the perquisites of high rank. Winston Churchill, clutching an enormous cigar, and Dwight Eisenhower, fumbling for one of his ever-present packs of cigarettes, glanced at the no smoking signs posted all around them, and then took their seats in the front row. Meanwhile, deputy commanders, AAF and RAF generals and marshals, American, Canadian, and British naval officers and ground forces army, corps, and division commanders filed into the rising tiers and tried to make themselves as comfortable as possible in this cramped, cheerless classroom. The focal point for everyone present was a gigantic scale model of the Normandy beaches that was laid out on a floor space as wide as a city street and featured an amazing level of detail of even minor aspects of the future battlefield.

At precisely 10 A.M. General Bernard Law Montgomery entered the classroom attired in new battle dress and as confident as a teacher about to deliver his most popular lecture. American military policemen were posted outside the doorway to bar any latecomers. Then,

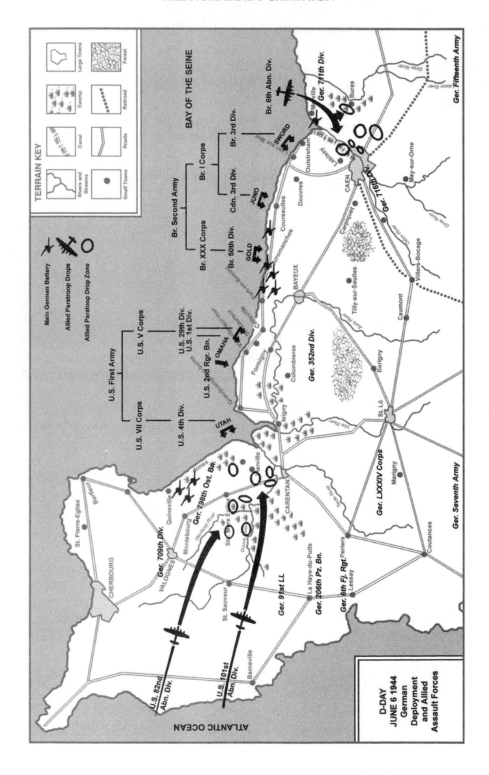

D-DAY
JUNE 6 1944
German
Deployment
and Allied
Assault Forces

moments later there was a ferocious commotion outside and finally, General George Patton pushed his way through the doors and engaged in a glaring contest with Monty as he took a seat. The exasperated ground forces commander recovered his composure and proceeded to open the first full-fledged briefing on Overlord.

The feisty British general, armed only with a long pointer, hopped over miniature buildings like a modern Gulliver in Lilliput and, in an enormously confident tone, discussed every major element of the Allied landings in a two-hour presentation without using a single note. The model of the landing area depicted a roughly fifty-mile beachfront from the Orne River on the left flank to the beaches opposite the crossroads town of St. Mère Église on the Cotentin Peninsula on the right flank. Monty exuded optimism as he insisted "this is an allied operation being carried out by British and American forces with the forces of our allies cooperating. It is a great allied team and none of us could do any good without the other."

The purpose of this massive operation was "to assault simultaneously immediately north of the Carentan estuary and between the Carentan estuary and the River Orne with the object of securing as a base for further operations a lodgment area which will include airfield sites and the port of Cherbourg." Montgomery had already squared off against Rommel in North Africa and he felt that he understood the Desert Fox's tactics. "After he is certain where the main landings are being made, he will then concentrate his mobile divisions quickly and strike a hard blow while his static divisions will endeavor to hold on to important ground and act as pivots to the counter attack." Allied intelligence had already informed Eisenhower and Montgomery that Hitler seemed reluctant to give Rommel operational control of the panzer divisions and Monty felt that this oversight would give the invasion army a window of four or five days to secure the beach head and prepare for the inevitable counterattack. Montgomery insisted that by this point the Allies would have as many as fifteen divisions ashore and should be able to withstand an enemy thrust.

The six infantry divisions to be deployed in the initial phase of Overlord would land at beaches code-named Sword, Juno, Gold, Omaha, and Utah. The British 3rd Division would land on Sword Beach just east of the Orne River and drive toward the important rail and road center of Caen just over eight miles inland, while a force of French naval commandos seized the small resort town of Ouistreham where the Orne ran into the sea. The 3rd Canadian Division would land at Juno Beach, strike out for the Caen-Bayeux road and then head for the western outskirts of Caen to add muscle to the British advance on that university town. The 50th British Division would land at Gold Beach push through the small beachfront town of Arromanches and then attempt to seize Bayeux, about five miles inland.

While the British and Canadians secured the eastern flank and drove for Caen, an American combat team including Rangers and regiments from the 1st and 29th Divisions would storm ashore at Omaha Beach and gain a foothold for a drive on the Carentan estuary. The extreme right flank of the invasion would be Utah Beach which was assigned to the U.S. 4th Division. Utah was the gateway to the port of Cherbourg, one of the first vital targets in Overlord.

The senior Allied commanders were fairly confident that the invasion force could secure a foothold on the beaches, but they were very concerned that the Germans might be able to organize a quick, powerful counterthrust from the high ground east of the Orne River or from the causeways that led from the Utah beaches to the interior of the Cotentin Peninsula. Therefore, Eisenhower, Montgomery, and Bradley all enthusiastically supported the deployment of three airborne divisions to secure these imperiled flanks. General Miles Dempsey's British and Canadian ground forces would be supported by the British 6th Airborne Division while Bradley's Americans would be shielded by the U.S. 82nd and 101st Airborne Divisions. Therefore, including infantry and airborne divisions, the Allies would deploy eight divisions plus substantial auxiliary units on D-Day with the expectation of landing about 175,000 men either by air or sea on the first day of the operation. This was a formidable force to oppose the Germans but its effectiveness would be significantly influenced by three potential problems, none of which were totally resolved by the initiation of the invasion.

The first problem was logistics and this challenge would continue to haunt Allied planners until the last day of the war. The initial major prize for the invaders was the port of Cherbourg, located at the top of the Cotentin Peninsula. However, even optimists among the British and American staffs admitted that it was unlikely that the heavily defended city would be captured in much less than a month and that meant that a rapidly growing Allied army would have to be supplied from some other source. The solution to this problem was the initiation of the Mulberry project, the construction of two massive artificial harbors that would be towed across the Channel and then floated into place in the American and British beaches. This solution was costly, time consuming, and difficult but it did provide invaluable initial

Larger landing craft vehicles were capable of carrying men and equipment, such as this LCT loading a half-track antitank machine-gun vehicle.

service and was an effective response to a seemingly insolvable problem. The two other issues produced far more controversy and second guessing both then and later.

The second challenge was the problem of naval fire support. By the spring of 1944 United States forces in the Pacific theater had become accomplished experts in the conduct of amphibious campaigns and navy, marine, and army commanders had learned invaluable lessons in seaborne invasions. By the measuring stick of these Pacific campaigns the prospective naval support for Overlord was hardly lavish, although from the overall perspective of total vessels employed in Operation Neptune, the naval component of Overlord, the Allied flotilla was truly impressive. There were 2,727 vessels capable of independent sailing operations ranging from battleships to patrol craft. The transport ships also carried an additional 2,606 landing craft on their cargo holds making a grand total of 5,333 vessels, probably more ships than existed in the whole world at the time of the Spanish Armada. However, while contemporary news accounts and later films and books emphasized the awesome power of this formidable fleet, veterans of Pacific campaigns detected some serious gaps in this armada.

The availability of 287 minesweepers and 221 light escort vessels seemed sufficient to counter the challenge of German mines and torpedo boat attacks. However, the number of gunfire support ships was relatively meager by Pacific campaign standards. Since the United States Navy preferred to keep most of its warships in the Pacific and the Royal Navy still feared German surface raids on the home islands, the initial Neptune plan called for a miserly commitment of three British battleships and zero American battlewagons. Finally, after an intense round of wrangling among Allied leaders, three of the oldest American battleships in the Pacific were deployed to the Atlantic Ocean and the Royal Navy contributed two shallow draft monitors. These heavy ships were supplemented by seventeen British and three American cruisers, thirty-seven British and thirty-one American destroyers, and a dozen French, Norwegian, Dutch, and Canadian warships.

This was a modestly impressive fleet but considering that Neptune-Overlord was the most decisive Allied operation of World War II, the fleet was not overloaded with firepower. For example, during Operation Iceberg, the American invasion of Okinawa, naval gunfire support was provided by a formidable array of eighteen battleships, several dozen heavy and light cruisers, and two hundred destroyers. Also, while the Neptune operation would be supplemented by a powerful armada of land-based aircraft, the ships that would have provided the most versatile, effective air support, the aircraft carriers, were totally absent from the invasion armada. The leaders of the Overlord operation tamely accepted Admiral Ernest King's blustering refusal to subject any of his flattops to the confined waters of the Channel. However, given the maximum importance of this operation, President Roosevelt should have overruled his bellicose senior admiral and deployed at least some carrier units for Overlord. While Roosevelt and King should be faulted for the failure to provide more substantial naval support to Neptune, the American naval commander must be placed in tandem with the British head of government for complicating the third major challenge facing the Overlord invasion. Dwight Eisenhower realized from the very beginning of his tenure as supreme commander that the odds of success for the invasion of Normandy would escalate significantly if the German defenders were forced to look over their shoulders at a threat from behind. Eisenhower's ideal operational plan was designed to create a "fire in the rear" of the German defenders, but his strategy was threatened by forces outside of his control.

Eisenhower's plan envisioned the Overlord operation being

launched in conjunction with a simultaneous invasion of southern France, code-named *Anvil*. Eisenhower, heavily supported by General Marshall, proposed a landing in the Toulon-Marseilles area by three or four American and six or seven French divisions that would thrust northward and threaten the German defenders with a huge pincers movement while also capturing ports that would expedite the landing of additional American divisions that were scheduled to embark from the United States during the summer and fall of 1944. Anvil was an excellent, workable plan but soon Ike's hopes would be threatened by an unlikely coalition of opponents.

One part of the anti-Anvil pincers was Winston Churchill. The British prime minister had long been a proponent of the Allied strategy to strike at the "soft underbelly" of Fortress Europe by thrusting northward through Italy into the Balkans and Austria and invading the Reich from the flank. Anvil threatened to weaken significantly this entire campaign as most of the initial forces used for the invasion of southern France would come from an Allied army already crawling excruciatingly slow up the Italian boot. Churchill and Eisenhower represented the epitome of Anglo-American cooperation during World War II, but on this issue they remained on opposite sides of the fence.

Churchill had an unlikely ally in the cantankerous, anti-British senior admiral of the United States Navy, Ernest J. King. The chief of naval operations largely saw the European war as a sideshow to the "real" conflict, the struggle against the Japanese in the Pacific. Since landing craft were indispensable to the prosecution of an amphibious war against Japan, King viewed any transfer of Higgins boats to the Atlantic as tantamount to the destruction of the craft. The admiral deftly sidestepped pleas from Marshall and Eisenhower for ever more landing craft for Overlord and by the spring of 1944 it was apparent that there simply were not going to be enough boats for a simultaneous Overlord-Anvil operation. The best that Eisenhower could manage was delay of Overlord from early May to early June to provide an extra month's factory production of Higgins boats with a concurrent postponement of Anvil, renamed Dragoon, to sometime later in the summer. Since the eventual landings in southern France would be spectacularly successful and absolutely vital to the continuation of the Allied drive toward Germany, Dwight Eisenhower may certainly be forgiven for sharing Ulysses S. Grant's exasperation with outside interference with carefully considered strategies to win a decisive campaign.

The postponement of Overlord for a full month in order to obtain sufficient landing craft for the invasion meant the operation would now take place in June at the earliest. Each service had its own unique requirements for a successful landing and these often contradictory needs narrowed dramatically the window of opportunity to initiate the campaign. The navy, responsible for transporting the invasion force across the Channel and then landing the troops in Normandy, wanted to make the sea crossing in daylight and also land the soldiers in daylight in order to maximize naval gunfire support. Air force officials wanted a daylight assault in order to provide optional conditions for bombing runs. However, most senior army commanders insisted that it would be much better to cross the Channel at night, open naval fire at first light, and then begin landing the ground forces shortly afterward in order to have a full summer day to push as far inland as possible before the first night spent in enemy territory. While the admirals reluctantly agreed to this reasoning, they countered with an insistence that the landings should be made on a rising tide so that the landing craft would have maximum force to push onto the beach while also permitting them to float free shortly afterward. The air leaders added their own priority for a minimum of a half moon to provide

Prior to the invasion, a wide assortment of landing craft were gathered in many English ports to await the invasion day when they would carry troops and equipment across the Channel. The small craft shown in this photograph are British landing and assault crafts known as LCAs.

at least some level of illumination for the vital airborne drops. When all of these factors were calculated, June invasion dates were reduced to five possibilities, the 5th, 6th, 7th, 19th, and 20th. Eisenhower thus agreed on a tentative D-Day of June 5, 1944, and then inaugurated the final countdown for this decisive day.

The men who would be responsible for the invasion of France were soon gathering in the vicinity of a stately mansion near Portsmouth Harbor. Southwick House, Admiral Bertram Ramsay's headquarters for Overlord, included a vast parkland which soon became filled with the command trailers and tents of Eisenhower, Montgomery, and the other senior commanders of the invasion. As June 5 approached, the focal point of attention was one dour Scottish meteorologist, Group Captain J. M. Stagg. Stagg and his staff of weather forecasters provided Eisenhower and his lieutenants with twice-daily weather briefings beginning on June 1 and the spirits of these leaders often rose or fell depending on the divinings of these relatively low-ranking weathermen.

At 4 A.M. on Sunday June 4, Eisenhower was shocked by Stagg's insistence that weather patterns were developing more like December than June and the next several days were predicted to be enormously stormy. Eisenhower reluctantly cancelled the Monday invasion and called for another meeting at 9:15 Sunday evening to digest any new meteorological data. By that hour the whole channel area was being lashed by a major storm and Ike could now see a Tuesday landing begin to unravel. However, Stagg insisted that there was at least a chance of a twenty-four-hour hiatus in the storm centered on June 6 and Eisenhower agreed to postpone a final decision until 4 A.M. Monday.

When Eisenhower awoke in his headquarters on Monday, June 5, at 3:30 A.M. "the whole camp was shaking and shuddering under a wind of almost hurricane proportions with accompanying rain that seemed to be traveling in horizontal sheets," he would later recall. On the one hand, the general breathed a sigh of relief that he had cancelled a Monday invasion; it would have taken place under appalling conditions. However, now Tuesday was the main concern as he rode through the wind in a careening jeep toward the dignified conference room at Southwick House. At just past 4 A.M. Stagg entered the room, gave just a hint of a smile, and confirmed that the storm would blow itself out in time for a Tuesday morning landing. Marshal Leigh-Mallory, ever the pessimist, read the full report and insisted that conditions would still be below the acceptable minimum for air operation.

Late in the afternoon of June 5, Eisenhower went out to talk with the troops of the 101st Airborne shortly before they took off on their dangerous mission behind enemy lines.

Marshal Tedder tacitly accepted the reasoning of his RAF colleague, but Admiral Ramsay and General Montgomery emotionally urged the assault to be initiated.

Eisenhower began pacing around the room realizing now more than ever that the decision, and its consequences, was his and his alone. Finally, at 4:15 A.M., Ike issued a short, clear directive as he quietly shook his head and said, "O.K., let's go!" As the general admitted later, once the order was given, events began to develop of their own accord and "that's the most terrible time for a senior commander. He has done all that he can do, all the planning and so on. There's nothing more that he can do." As soon as it was light Eisenhower left the Southwick House grounds and went down to Portsmouth Harbor where he walked up and down the docks and watched throngs of soldiers clamber aboard transport ships. Then, in a dramatic gesture that confirmed that the choice of an invasion date was entirely his own responsibility, he jotted down a short press release that would be issued if the invasion failed: "Our landings have failed and I have withdrawn the troops. My decision to attack at this time and place was based upon the best information available. The troops, the air and the Navy did all that bravery and devotion to duty could do. If any blame or fault attaches itself to the attempt, it is mine alone."

One of the few men who could empathize with Eisenhower's overwhelming sense of loneliness at this moment in time was Winston Churchill. The prime minister knew that he shared heavily in the responsibility for approving this venture and admitted that Allied success seemed to be far from certain. Now, Britain's head of government reverted to his bulldog image of senior military commander and Churchill requested that Eisenhower secure him a spot on a Royal Navy bombardment ship to observe the landings firsthand. Eisenhower admitted "his request was undoubtedly inspired as much by his natural instincts as a warrior as by his impatience at the prospect of sitting quietly back in London awaiting reports." Eisenhower challenged Churchill's demand to sail with the fleet on the basis that the prime minister's death would cripple the war effort, but the feisty Briton countered, "It is not part of your responsibility, my dear general, to determine the exact composition of any ship's company in His Majesty's Fleet." When Churchill insisted that he would go to sea, if necessary, as a common seaman, Eisenhower acquired a new ally, King George VI. The monarch, in a brilliant piece of theater, calmly informed his first minister that he had no intention of challenging Churchill's plans, but insisted that the concept was so brilliant that His

Just before loading onto transports, many Allied soldiers, some shown here wearing inflatable life belts, attended religious services.

Majesty himself intended to join the invasion fleet and land on one of the invasion beaches at the head of his troops. The king's suggestion quickly dampened Churchill's enthusiasm and the prime minister reluctantly agreed to remain in London until Overlord was more fully developed.

While king, prime minister, and supreme commander each wrestled with their own responsibilities and duties for the decisive campaign, thirty-eight British and twenty-one American convoys steamed out of British harbors and sailed for the Calvados coast and Cotentin Peninsula. The tip of this twentieth-century armada was a flotilla of thirty-six Royal Navy minesweeping launches which divided into groups of three or four and made a highly dangerous skim sweep of the sea in an attempt to locate German minefields. These 112-foot craft were soon followed by 255 conventional minesweepers that cleaned out a circular area south of the Isle of Wight from which each convoy would be routed to its assigned beach area. This five-mile zone was promptly nicknamed Piccadilly Circus and featured ten channels that varied in width from four hundred to twelve hundred yards. Each channel entrance was equipped with a sonic buoy to direct convoys along the cleared lanes while dan buoys floated every mile to mark the edges of the approaches. As Admiral A. G. Kirk, commander of the American Western Task Force, insisted, "Minesweeping was the keystone of the arch of this operation. The performance of the minesweepers can only be described as magnificent." As the first minutes of Tuesday, June 6, 1944, approached an invasion fleet carrying 65,000 sailors, 150,000 soldiers, 2,000 tanks, and 12,000 vehicles began closing in on the Normandy coast. As sailors and soldiers peered through the night formations of Allied planes flew overhead, running lights flickering in a coded letter "V" for Victory. These aircraft were carrying the men who would constitute the first invasion force on Hitler's Fortress Europe, the troops of the British and American airborne divisions.

CHAPTER V

Assault from the Air

The invasion fleet that approached the Normandy coast on the night of June 5–6, 1944, carried almost twice as many assault troops as the initial Overlord plan envisioned. Eisenhower and Montgomery had insisted adamantly on the need for five assault divisions to land on five separate beaches over a fifty-mile stretch of French coastline. This was a much more formidable invasion than the original plan which called for a three-division landing on a thirty-mile front limited exclusively to the Calvados coast of the Bay of the Seine. However, the 150,000 ground troops about to land on this June morning would remain dangerously exposed to counterattack unless their vulnerable flanks could somehow be secured. One possible way to confront this challenge was to employ one of the most technologically advanced yet controversial weapons of World War II, a massive airborne assault by parachute and glider troops.

The development of relatively large capacity transport planes on the eve of the war provided Axis and Allied strategists with the tantalizing opportunity to circumvent the age-old problem of formidable frontal defenses by simply adding a third dimension to the equation and dropping troops behind the enemy's fortifications. However, by the spring of 1944, the report card on airborne operations was decidedly mixed. The Germans had used parachute and glider forces with considerable success in their blitzkrieg through western Europe in the spring of 1940. However, when they undertook a massive airborne assault on the British and Greek defenders of the island of Crete a year later an entire parachute division was nearly annihilated even though the attack did ultimately succeed.

Allied airborne units were given a significant role in Operation Husky, the invasion of Sicily in the summer of 1943. The initial results were a near disaster. Dozens of planes carrying paratroopers were shot down by mistake by antiaircraft batteries on the Allied invasion fleet. Planes veered so far off course that they had to return to base fully loaded. Other aircraft, assuming they were over their drop zones, dropped scores of men into the sea. On the other hand, when the Mediterranean offensive moved into the Italian mainland there were several instances in which dramatic parachute drops of reinforcements into the battle saved tenuously held beachheads.

When Overlord finally became a reality, Eisenhower had access to a powerful airborne force of two British and two American divisions plus additional units of Canadian and Polish paratroopers. This air army represented a powerful trump card in the Allied arsenal and the main problem was how to most effectively use it. General "Hap" Arnold, senior commander of the Army Air Force, wanted to use the paratroopers in a bold, risky venture in which over thirty thousand men would be dropped close to the Seine River near the town of Dreux, about half-way between the Normandy beaches and Paris. This force would then form a huge airhead that would threaten the German coastal defenses from the rear and add a whole new dimension to Overlord. George Marshall was equally enthused about the plan and he sent a strongly worded cover letter to Eisenhower when AAF staff officers were sent to Britain with the proposal.

Eisenhower exhibited a rare annoyance with his mentor's interference and courteously informed both Arnold and Marshall that the deployment of airborne forces that far from possible ground support was an invitation to disaster. Instead, Ike and Monty were in full agreement that the airborne divisions should be dropped much closer to the coast to provide flank security for the invasion.

The plan that was agreed upon at SHAEF headquarters envisioned using Major General Richard Gale's British 6th Airborne Division in a series of parachute drops and glider landings that would secure the vital bridges over the Caen Canal and Orne River, destroy a powerful German artillery fortification at Merville, and create a barrier to a German counterattack from the region between the Dives and Orne Rivers at the eastern edge of the Overlord landings. Meanwhile, the right flank of the Allied line would be secured by the American 82nd and 101st Airborne Divisions. These units would facilitate the 4th

Infantry Division's drive inland from Utah Beach over the few causeways not already inundated by Rommel's engineers. The American paratroopers would be expected to hold open the inland segments of the beach exit roads and in turn prevent the Germans from rolling up the seaborne attack with massive counterattacks. Another target for the paratroopers would be the crossroads town of St. Mère Église, which sat astride the main Paris-Cherbourg road, and in American hands could seriously disrupt enemy activities on the Cotentin Peninsula.

Eisenhower was obliged to intervene in a major dispute in his official family regarding the justification for using airborne assaults. Both Bradley and Montgomery believed a massive air drop was absolutely vital to the success of the seaborne invasion. On the other hand Marshal Leigh-Mallory was convinced that the airborne divisions would be annihilated with 70 to 80 percent casualties probable. Eisenhower sided with his ground commanders but admitted privately that his air deputy might be accurate concerning the losses that would be suffered in the operation.

The first stage of the airborne assault on Normandy began just before 11 P.M. on Monday night, June 5, when six Halifax aircraft took off from a Dorset airfield towing six enormous Horsa gliders carrying 180 men from the Oxford and Buckinghamshire Light Infantry. The Ox and Bucks colors had flown proudly in bloody charges against Americans at Bunker Hill in 1775 and New Orleans in 1815, but now these descendants of the redcoats were the spearhead of an operation that depended on unparalleled Anglo-American unity for success.

Major John Howard, a former factory worker and policeman, had risen from the ranks to command one of the most crucial operations of the campaign. He watched the dark void of the Channel slip by as his men sang, joked, and tried to balance equal parts of euphoria and fear. Despite some cloud cover, visibility was fairly good and the pilots could clearly recognize the coast of France in the distance. At just after midnight, the planes banked over the mouth of the Orne River and the separation process between tow planes and gliders lurched into motion. Navigators in the Halifaxes briefed the glider pilots on exact position, height, and wind speed and provided a course to steer. Tow ropes were cast off as the wooden gliders eased into their soundless descent. Within seconds, boisterous troops became silent spectators as the ground loomed ever closer. While three Horsas glided toward the Orne River bridge near Ranville, Howard personally commanded the other three aircraft headed for the Caen Canal bridge at Benouville. The invasion of Western Europe was now fully underway and the

Allies were entering Hitler's fortress in a twentieth-century version of the Trojan horse.

At almost exactly 12:15 A.M. on Tuesday, June 6, 1944, the lead glider bumped across a series of fields as its undercarriage showered sparks and its pilot desperately tried to avoid hitting a tree or a stone wall. In one of the most impressive feats of the Normandy campaign, the lead Horsa smashed through barbed wire guarding the approach to the canal bridge and came to an abrupt halt at the exact spot designated in model exercises back in England. As Major Howard recalled, "Suddenly there was what was to be the last screeching God Almighty crash amidst smashing plywood, dust and noise like hell let loose followed by sudden silence as we came to a halt. The dazed silence did not seem to last long because we all came to our senses together on realizing that there was *no* firing! There was *no* firing and it seemed quite unbelievable, but where were we? We were precisely where I had asked the glider pilot to put us during briefing. The sense of complete exhilaration was quite overwhelming. I look at my watch, it had stopped at 0016 hours."

Howard was out the door shouting, "Up the Ox and Bucks!" as the first platoon began swarming over the bridge. The two remaining gliders screeched to a halt a few yards away and dazed but functioning troopers poured from exits with guns at the ready. A startled German sentry gasped at this shocking intrusion on a quiet summer night and fired a flare pistol to warn his comrades that the enemy was on them. A fusillade of bullets flashed from both sides and the sentry and British platoon leader Lieutenant Dan Brotheridge went down within seconds of one another, the first two combat fatalities of D-Day.

A confused but fierce engagement erupted as three platoons of British troopers dueled with perhaps fifty German defenders for control of the Caen Canal bridge and the adjacent village of Benouville. Wehrmacht troops who had been dozing in foxholes and trenches lining the bridge approaches sprang into action as Howard's men sprinted along dropping grenades into the ditches. German riflemen holed up in local houses and stores picked off glider troops as they attempted to disconnect demolition charges under the bridge. Howard threw in his last reserves, the just-arriving platoon from the badly damaged third glider commanded by Lieutenant Sandy Smith. Smith, who had been injured in the landing, hobbled along firing his Sten gun, leading his men in a charge against German machine-gun pits located near Benouville's café. A small force of German parachute troops happened to be driving through the town when the glider troops landed and they were quickly caught up in the swirling melee. Sergeant Heinz Hickman deployed his men near the bridge and engaged the British in a furious firefight. But, his men had no ammunition reserves and as Hickman later recalled, "If you see a Para platoon in full cry they frighten the daylights out of you—the way they charge, the way they fire, the way they ran across the bridge. I gave the order to go back." The glider troops made one final rush into town and German resistance collapsed. In an incredible six-minute battle at a cost of sixteen casualties the Allies had liberated the first community in Nazi-occupied France and secured the first priority objective of D-Day. The canal bridge's counterpart spanning the Orne River proved to be an even easier target as the very small German garrison retreated from Ranville before they could be overwhelmed.

While the capture of the Orne bridges seemed to go according to plan, the other prime objective for the British airborne troops emerged as a textbook example of how every possible thing that can go wrong very well might go wrong. The Norman town of Merville was a picturesque village that was too far inland to be a shore resort and too small to be a manufacturing or transportation center. However, barely three hundred yards south of the community the Germans had built a formidable artillery fortification that Allied intelligence suspected might deploy a battery of 150mm guns that could fire 96-pound shells over eight miles onto the British landing zone on Sword Beach and the Channel beyond.

It was obvious that the Germans intended to use the Merville battery as a major link in their defense of the Norman beaches. Casemates were constructed in a broad arc facing the coast just over three miles away, and were protected by one-foot, steel-reinforced concrete walls. Earthen banks provided additional cover while the entrance to each casemate featured a steel door to discourage unwanted intruders. German engineers had also constructed an imposing outer defense including a ten-foot-deep, fifteen-foot-wide, antitank ditch, and an extensive minefield encircled by two belts of barbed wire, the outer one eight feet high. The fortification was defended by about two hundred German troops divided between artillerymen and infantry manning fifteen machine-gun and mortar pits. A nearby orchard was utilized to deploy a battery of dual-purpose 20mm guns that could be used against either planes or tanks.

While Major Howard was given only a reinforced company to secure the Orne bridges, Lieutenant Colonel Terrence Otway was given command of a reinforced battalion of 750 men to capture

Merville. The 29-year-old mission leader divided his command into a number of subgroups, each with a specific mission in the assault. A ten-man "redness party" was charged with beaming five different colored signals to each of five different assault forces approaching five points of the German defense perimeter. Two "reconnaissance parties" were ordered to scout the enemy fortifications and report by radio which parts of the fort seemed most vulnerable to attack. A "taping party" was assigned to cut gaps in the barbed wire, locate a clear path through the minefield, and string white tape through the safety zone. A special storming unit of fifty-seven men, including seven sappers, was asked to actually crash land in gliders on top of the casemates and then stun the defenders with Sten guns and flamethrowers just as the main assault force burst through the wire. Meanwhile, another auxiliary unit including a number of German-speaking troops would scream commands in German to distract enemy attention from other threats and then open fire with rocket launchers and Sten guns when the charade was no longer useful. Finally, a mobile column equipped with jeep-towed antitank guns would cover the flanks in case of an early German counterattack. If this powerful force failed to totally destroy the German guns, an accompanying party of naval personnel would use radios and flares to signal the British warship *Arethusa* to open fire on the Merville battery at 5:30 A.M.

This complex plan seemed to take into consideration a number of possible foul-ups, but the actual case was far beyond what the most pessimistic planner could possibly have comprehended. The assault plan began to unravel only moments after Major Howard's textbook success at Benouville. At 12:30 A.M., one hundred RAF bombers pounded the Merville fortifications in a raid that some Allied optimists hoped would negate the need for a ground assault. The bombers created dozens of crater holes around the strongpoint and devastated a number of local apple orchards but had almost no impact on the battery itself. Then the paratroop drop fell apart. When the transport planes arrived over the drop zone, German flak batteries opened a lethal fire that forced pilots into massive evasive action that scattered the paratroopers over dozens of square miles of Norman countryside. Colonel Otway landed on top of a building that served as a German headquarters, and his assistant, Lance Corporal Wilson, fell through the glass roof of an adjacent greenhouse. The two men dodged a hail of bullets and made their way to the rendezvous point only to realize that they were almost alone. Otway located his second in command who exclaimed, "The drop's a bloody chaos; there's hardly anyone here!"

Two hours after the drop only a scratch force of 110 men had arrived and nearly every machine gun, mortar, radio, antitank gun, jeep, and mine detector was still missing. Finally, as Otway's watch crept toward 3 A.M., the colonel welcomed an additional thirty men and a single machine gun and ordered this skeleton force to move out toward Merville, a ninety-minute march away. When Otway's small party arrived near the enemy fort, the paratroopers met a few men from the reconnaissance force which had managed to cut a narrow approach path through the outer perimeter. The colonel assigned men to guard the approach roads, deployed his single machine gun, and then ordered his second in command, Major Allen Parry, to form an initial storming party of about fifty men who would go after the enemy guns while Otway and the rest of the force diverted the defenders. The gliders carrying the force that would crash land on the battery flew over Merville right on time, but an exasperated Otway had no signal gun to confirm the invasion. As the gliders circled, looking in vain for the affirming signal, the small ground force prepared to charge the emplacements totally on their own.

At just before 5 A.M., as dawn was about to break across the lush Norman countryside, a paratrooper blew a hunting horn and the single machine gun and a few lighter Bren guns opened fire. The assault party clambered up and over the inner stretch of wire as German mortars and automatic weapons poured a deadly fire into the invaders. One British company commander marveled at the intensity of the German fire as he recalled, "I saw a stream of machine gun tracer which appeared to be uninterrupted. Through this gap were pouring assault troops. I do not know how it happened, but they seemed to be going through." While Otway's main force engaged in a bloody shootout with the German infantry, the surviving members of the storming party split into four squads and pushed into the casemates. The defending gunners were not trained for this sort of close in, hand-to-hand combat and in each successive compartment the Germans threw up their hands and surrendered their guns. Otway's assault force had destroyed the Merville battery, captured about one hundred and fifty enemy soldiers and killed or wounded another fifty defenders. But, as the colonel signaled his success to the invasion fleet, he quickly counted the bodies of almost half of his force sprawled dead or seriously wounded around the fort. Even more exasperating, the guns that had been captured were not the potent 150mms but much less formidable Czech made 100mm howitzers that had been apparently deployed in an emergency until the regular guns arrived.

Despite the unraveling of the Merville assault and the wide drops that would plague the 6th Airborne Division the rest of the night, the men with the winged Pegasus patches on their sleeves had accomplished their primary mission and severely weakened enemy ability to smash the British ground assault before it fully developed. Now, if the men of the All-American and Screaming Eagle Divisions could meet with the same success on the opposite end of the invasion area, the prospects for Rommel's promise to push the invaders back into the sea would grow dimmer during each hour of "the longest day."

At almost the same moment that Major Howard's Horsa careened to a halt near Benouville, a schoolteacher in the town of St. Mère Église, nearly sixty miles away, trudged out into the garden to investigate strange noises coming from the air. Sixty-year-old Angele Levralt looked up and saw a boy not much older than some of her students floating down in a parachute and tumbling head over heels through her yard. Private Robert Murphy, an 18-year-old member of the 82nd Airborne Division, was armed to the teeth and had a face painted much like an Indian going into battle but he simply put a finger to his lips in a gesture of silence and disappeared into the trees. Murphy, who would someday become a prominent Boston attorney, was a Pathfinder, a member of the advance force of American paratroopers charged with marking the drop zones for the main contingent of over thirteen thousand men who would be dropping on the Cotentin Peninsula on this early summer night. However, only 38 of 120 of these scouts landed directly on target, and their scattered deployment was merely the first act in a frustrating drama that would play itself out for most of the men of the All-American and Screaming Eagle Divisions.

The men of the American airborne contingent were expected to secure the exits to the Utah beaches, capture the important crossroads town of St. Mère Église, seize bridgeheads on the Douve and Merderet Rivers, and block access roads that would permit the Germans to move armored units north into the Cotentin Peninsula from major bases around the city of Carentan. However, the paratroopers were dropping into a region held by over forty thousand German defenders, and their only hope of success was to concentrate rapidly and hold the enemy at bay until ground troops pushed inland to support them.

The carefully constructed plan of action for the airborne divisions began to unravel almost as soon as the nearly nine hundred C-47 planes of Troop Carrier Command crossed the Channel and approached the Cotentin. The pilots had been instructed to begin their drops at six hundred feet and at a throttled back speed of ninety miles an hour. However, as the seemingly endless squadrons droned on through the night toward their release points, the mostly very inexperienced pilots were subjected to a series of unexpected shocks. First, almost as soon as they reached the coast of France most of the planes hit a huge cloud bank and lost their already tenuous visibility. As aircraft veered either left or right to avoid mid-air collisions, planes became hopelessly separated and the tight formations simply disintegrated. Then, as the jump point approached, dozens of German flak guns cut loose with a formidable barrage. As brilliant, multicolored tracers lit the sky, alarmed pilots headed either higher or lower to avoid the enemy shells. Planes weaved, jinked, rose, or dove while green lights winked on in the passenger cabins and startled paratroopers attempted to disembark from the reeling transports. More than a few times a plane full of troopers simply disappeared in a huge fireball as a German shell hit the aircraft. Other men slumped lifeless in their parachutes as enemy machine guns ripped through them. A terrifyingly large proportion of the men who exited safely from the planes dropped into watery graves in the Channel, a French river, or in the innundated fields covering vast stretches of the Cotentin.

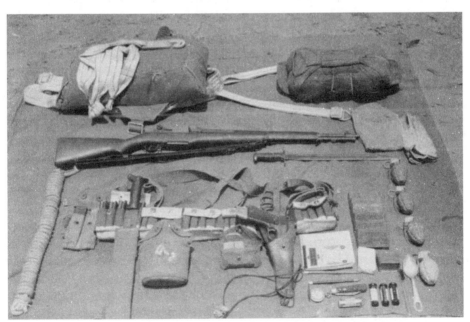

As heroic American paratroopers made their jumps the night of June 5–6, 1944, they carried plenty of equipment with them. This photo shows some of what each paratroop rifleman carried on his back as he landed on the deadly fields of France.

Large numbers of paratroopers died without ever firing a shot and a majority of the survivors were hopelessly lost and would play little or no role in offensive operations for the first forty-eight hours of the battle. The success or failure of the airborne assault would ride on a shockingly small number of men who had just parachuted into a region that Hitler had heavily reinforced in the last few weeks as his famous intuition told him that even if the Allies landed at Pas de Calais as he expected, they also would launch a huge airborne lunge at Cherbourg. German units had been marching steadily into the Cotentin and the American parachute troops soon faced a challenge to their very existence. The flashpoint that would soon come to symbolize this clash of arms was the crossroads town of St. Mère Église.

The quaint road center, just over four miles from the dunes of Utah Beach, was far more strategically important than the size of the community would suggest. The main road from Paris to Cherbourg ran through town and both opposing armies wanted control of that highway. The contest for the town began soon after midnight when German tracers firing at the American transport planes fell back into the town square and ignited the home of M. Hairon across the way from the mayor's house and store. As bored German soldiers from the town garrison stood guard over dozens of civilians called out to fight the flames, a detachment of the 506th Parachute Regiment was fluttering to earth, six miles from their intended drop zone. One startled, and lucky, trooper, Sergeant Ray Aeibischer, hit the ground just out of sight of the German sentries and hid behind a stone wall adjacent to the church. The American watched in horror as the Wehrmacht troops aimed pistols, rifles, and submachine guns at other members of his unit who had come down in the middle of the town square. One trooper's parachute caught in a tree and he slumped dead from dozens of bullets from a German machine pistol. Three men were killed in mid-air before they even hit the ground. Another American landed in the town square and played dead while a distracted defender rolled his body over and then rushed off to shoot at other paratroopers. In a few minutes the first confrontation over St. Mère Église was over and the Germans returned to prodding the townspeople to extinguish the raging fire.

A half hour later a platoon of the 505th Parachute Regiment began fluttering downward into the town square and realized to their horror that the defenders were aiming dozens of weapons skyward. Tracers from antiaircraft guns added surrealistic illumination to the grisly drama. Paratroopers gasped as they were shot in mid-air; others drifted low enough to become entangled in trees or telephone poles producing virtual target practice for the men in field gray and coal-scuttle helmets. An even worse fate awaited one or two men who were sucked into the burning building and incinerated by the leaping flames and the explosion of their own ammunition and grenades. A few troopers managed to hit the ground firing and traded their lives dearly in shootouts that would rival the gunfights of Dodge City or Tombstone.

A member of the French Resistance living in St. Mère Église was among the firefighters in the town square when the shooting began. Raymond Paris recalled:

> We were able to see that the doors of the airplanes were open. We suddenly saw men jumping … and their parachutes opening. I was standing on the edge of the square shouting, that's it, it's the invasion! Some of the parachutists landed as close as four or five meters from where I stood. All the Germans who were there on the spot with us began to fire at the boys who were coming down. I saw a parachutist fall into the trees, where he remained hanging helplessly, and before he could make the slightest movement, he was shot by some German soldiers. Almost immediately afterward another parachutist became tangled up in the trees; and once again, the Germans shot him. There was the sound of the bell, the noise of the airplanes, the bursts of automatic gunfire, the shouts and cries of the German soldiers, the cries of the French and the screams of the women who obviously were terrified. It was Dante-esque.

Among the lucky survivors of this chaotic, one-sided battle were Private Ken Russell, who caught his risers on the church steeple and then slid off the roof just before a German soldier spotted him, and Private John Steele, who flinched in terror as his parachute wound around the steeple and he watched the rest of the engagement dangling precariously from the spire with the bell tolling only a few feet away. A few other paratroopers managed to slip into nearby orchards and, almost incredibly, as the fire was finally extinguished, the members of the garrison attended to their casualties and returned to bed in their billets around the village. The Germans had won the first round but the contest for St. Mère Église was far from over.

Lieutenant Colonel Edward Krause of the 505th Regiment had managed to concentrate 180 paratroopers from a wide assortment of units and this energetic officer was determined to use this pick-up force to capture St. Mère Église and its vital highway. Krause placed ambush parties across each road leading into town, divided his remaining men into two assault companies and eagerly accepted the services of a local citizen to act as a guide to the German-held buildings. The paratroopers were incensed at the sight of their helpless comrades dangling from trees and poles, obviously gunned down without a chance to surrender. The airborne troopers smashed their way into enemy strongpoints and initiated a wild melee in which fists, knives, and rifle butts swung viciously in a series of mini-battles. The German resistance soon collapsed and Krause produced an American flag that the regiment had raised over Naples a few months earlier. The colonel had promised his men that "before dawn on D-Day this flag will fly over St. Mère Église" and in the pre-dawn darkness of June 6 the emblem was raised up the flagpole of the local town hall. The American paratroopers had liberated their first town in the Normandy campaign—but the Germans would be back in the morning.

Large numbers of British and American airborne troops were still cut off from their units as the first hint of daylight appeared in the Norman sky. However, contrary to Marshal Leigh-Mallory's gloomy prognosis, most of the troopers were still alive and, even if disorganized, were confounding German attempts to discover the "real" location of this invasion. German commanders were receiving reports of Allied parachutists all over Normandy and staff officers did not have a clue to which positions were really most jeopardized. The Allied high command had cheerfully added even more uncertainty to the enemy response by dropping hundreds of cleverly designed dummy paratroopers that wore battle dress and helmets and ignited impressive fireworks displays when they hit the ground. Between the widely scattered drops of real paratroopers and the clever deployment of bogus parachutists the pre-dawn hours of D-Day were becoming chaotic for the defenders. Suddenly, the "fog of war" was becoming even foggier. Now, as isolated firefights raged up and down the Norman countryside, German officers became ever more perplexed as to where they should commit their formidable reserves of men and tanks. As this deadly game of tag erupted over and over in farmyards, hedgerows, and villages, a vast force of over 150,000 young Britons, Frenchmen, Canadians, and Americans were clambering down nets and ladders and preparing to launch a beachfront invasion that might very well determine much of the future course of the twentieth century.

CHAPTER VI

Utah Beach
The Right Invasion at the Wrong Place

Most American soldiers who grew up near the eastern seaboard of the United States would have felt very much at home if they had walked along Utah Beach any time before 1940. This part of the Cotentin coast was about nine miles long, roughly the same extent of beachfront as popular American shore resorts such as Atlantic City, New Jersey; Ocean City, Maryland; or Virginia Beach, Virginia. The beach featured a span of wet sand which children in peacetime might have utilized to build sandcastles; a stretch of dry, yellowish beach perfect for the chairs and towels of sunbathers; and a final rim of drift-wood, seashells, and seaweed that would have been very familiar to American bathers. Beyond the beach proper was a 100-yard-wide stretch of low sand dunes partly covered with grass; another familiar touch for American vacationers entering or leaving their favorite shore resorts. Thus, in peacetime, visitors from the United States would have been able to experience sights, sounds, and smells that were tantalizingly familiar. However, on the morning of June 6, 1944, by a quirk of tidal schedules, the coastline code-named Utah would be the site of the first seaborne invasion of Fortress Europe and the festive activities of a summer holiday were nothing more than distant memories to the thousands of GIs about to wade ashore.

As the American paratroopers fought their scattered battles with German defenders in the interior of the Cotentin, VII Corps commander General "Lightning Joe" Collins and Task Force commander Rear Admiral Don Moon, stood side by side on the bridge of the USS *Bayfield* twelve miles off shore and watched the final preparations for the embarkation of over 21,000 assault troops and 1,700 vehicles. Collins and Moon made an excellent team as the army commander had become deeply impressed with the value of naval support in his Pacific campaign and the nautical chief was determined to provide maximum fire support to the absolute limit and range of his biggest guns. Now the two leaders made a final checklist of the enemy capabilities to oppose the landing. Allied intelligence had identified twenty-eight German coastal batteries in this region and it appeared that they could deploy about 110 guns ranging from 75mm army cannons to naval weapons of up to 170mm. This formidable array was supported by eighteen additional batteries deployed further inland which included a powerful section of 210mm guns near Saint Marcouf. Finally, a third tier of defense would be provided by dozens of mobile 88mm guns which could pop up anywhere along the invasion front.

Collins and Moon would have felt more confident if the Allied high command had provided naval firepower on a level with Pacific

D-Day landing forces met ferocious fire from batteries of German artillery including mobile German 88mm guns such as this one.

amphibious campaigns but the ships that were available were still moderately formidable. The only battleship allotted to the Utah landings was the venerable USS *Nevada* which had been resurrected from the disaster of Pearl Harbor after being severely damaged on December 7, 1941. The American cruisers *Quincy* and *Tuscaloosa*, the Royal Navy monitor *Erebus,* and the British cruiser *Black Prince* would join the *Nevada* in laying down gunfire at 11,000 yards offshore; while the British cruiser *Enterprise* and a squadron of destroyers would maneuver in much closer to the beach and pummel the German fortifications with rapid-fire guns. Then, as the landing craft approached the beaches, rocket ships would saturate enemy positions with five thousand five-inch rockets while an armada of American bombers flew in low and attacked the defenders from above.

At just past 4 A.M. the transports began to debark the assault force. On each ship fifteen to sixteen hundred anxious, excited, overloaded men in olive drab scrambled down cargo-net ladders into landing craft. The first sensation for many assault troops was that they seemed to be nowhere near the invasion beaches. For a number of reasons, the Overlord planners had decided to begin the run on the Utah Beach almost twelve miles out to sea, a ridiculously long trip for men crowded aboard a thirty-foot craft pitching uncontrollably on a choppy English Channel. This stretch of water that had to be covered in Higgins boats was almost two-thirds of the *entire* distance across the Channel between Dover and Calais and provided for too many opportunities for the almost helpless landing craft to be destroyed. Equally important, the long run-in virtually guaranteed that the majority of assault troops would be substantially incapacitated by seasickness, a major handicap in a probably desperate battle. As Private Bruce Bradley, a radio operator in a field artillery battalion, insisted afterward, "The sea was rough and it was dark. The navy guys had remarked that they were glad they were navy at this point. I'm sure they were. We got V for Victory signs from them as they helped us over the side. Victory didn't seem possible at this time to me. Survival, maybe."

As the landing craft circled the mother ships waiting for the order to head toward Utah Beach, the bombardment ships made their final adjustments and prepared to fire. Most naval experts felt that the forty minutes allocated for the pre-invasion bombardment was ludicrously brief by the standards of the Pacific campaigns, but army planners favored a short bombardment in order to achieve an initial shock effect and surprise over the more extensive damage that a longer bombardment would produce. While the bombardment ships made final adjustments to their guns, the onset of daylight revealed the armada's presence to German defenders. At just past 5 A.M. a shore battery was able to target the destroyers *Fitch* and *Corry* and a salvo bracketed both ships. When another battery scored several near misses on Allied minesweepers, the HMS *Black Prince* let loose with her heavy guns and in turn attracted the attention of dozens of German weapons. Finally, Admiral M. L. Deyo, commander of the naval bombardment group, lost patience at this still mainly one-sided duel and at 5:30, fourteen minutes ahead of schedule, ordered every available ship to open fire.

As the defenders dove for cover, their faces pressed into the ground, the naval guns created a man-made inferno on this peaceful Cotentin beachfront. Lieutenant Colonel Frederick von der Heydte, the commander of the German 6th Parachute Regiment was driving from his headquarters to the coast when he heard the furious bombardment and he quickly climbed the church tower of a nearby village. Through his fieldglasses he could see, stretching out to infinity, a huge invasion fleet protected by hundreds of festive looking barrage balloons. He saw the flashes of the naval guns and detected the movement of countless small boats sailing between the larger vessels and the coast.

The spectacular panorama that impressed von der Heydte as a gigantic theatrical production seemed far more malevolent in the frontline defenses. A German officer who had huddled in a coastal bunker remembered, "The shells screamed like a thousand express trains as bunkers and casemates shook furiously." Nothing but smoke and dust could be seen from the sea as the first wave of landing craft finally sailed within sight of the beaches. Then, as the naval bombardment lifted temporarily, the defenders could see the reason for their brief reprieve from the guns; squadron after squadron of Allied bombers appeared over the beaches and added their own special brand of terror to the drama on the seashore.

By the first week of June, the AAF and RAF had clearly gained not just air superiority but actual air supremacy over the skies of northern France. The round-the-clock bombing missions had forced the Luftwaffe high command to pull more and more fighters back inside the Reich for home defense and by June 6 virtually no German fighter squadrons were available to challenge the Allied invasion. When Eisenhower confidently told his troops that if they looked up in the sky on D-Day they would only see Allied plans he was hardly exaggerating as only two Luftwaffe fighters penetrated far enough to actually strafe the invasion beaches. Meanwhile, the Allies were deploying 3,500 heavy bombers, 1,600 medium bombers, and 5,400 fighters to

Smaller landing craft vehicles (LCVPs) were designed to hold up to thirty-five men or they could be used to carry one vehicle. These would be the craft the Allied forces would use to storm the Normandy beaches but many of the men who crowded onto them would never make it ashore.

cover every aspect of the invasion process including this first landing at Utah.

As the Higgins boats throttled up for their final run toward the beach, about three hundred IX Army Air Force B-26s swooped across the water and began to pummel the enemy fortifications. Each Marauder was carrying twenty 250-pound bombs and the planes were flying in fast and low. While much of the heavy bomber force would operate at nearly twenty thousand feet on D-Day, the B-26s were racing across the beach only five hundred feet above the dunes. While German antiaircraft guns sent a few Marauders spiraling into the dunes or the sea, the defenders were taking a terrible pounding. One key German strongpoint lost two 75mm guns, two 50mm antitank guns, several mortars, and several flamethrowers in less than five minutes and their single surviving 88mm weapon was damaged.

Allied planners had decided to enhance the naval and air support of the attackers with an experimental weapon called a dual-drive tank. This vehicle was a Sherman tank fitted with accordion pleated canvas screens that, when raised, were expected to float the tank ashore and provide close-in fire support simultaneous with the infantry assault.

The "DD" tanks were expected to be launched from transports five thousand yards off shore and then "swim" toward the beach in unison with the riflemen on the Higgins boats. The plan was a good one, but the operation began to unravel almost immediately.

Eight LCTs, each carrying four amphibious tanks, began their run nine miles out in the Channel, dividing into four vessel contingents. Each squadron was guided by a patrol craft responsible for shepherding the boats into the launch zone. However, about halfway to the beach, PC-1261 struck a mine, rolled over and sank, leaving half the transports without a control vessel. Then, fifteen minutes later, LCT-597 hit a mine, exploded, and sank with all four tanks. At this point the quick thinking of a young naval officer salvaged the rapidly deteriorating situation. Lieutenant (j.g.) John Ricker, skipper of the only surviving control vessel, ignored the order to launch the tanks from five thousand yards out and instead escorted the seven surviving LCTs to within a mile of Utah Beach. The sinking of two ships of the flotilla caused enough delays that the tanks were not able to land before the first infantry splashed ashore, but Ricker's quick thinking at least put the Shermans on shore only moments behind schedule, still capable of providing vital support to the riflemen.

For the D-Day landing, the Allies used amphibious vehicles, such as the DUKW ("Ducks") shown here.

A truck disembarks from an LCT (landing craft, tank). The LCTs carried men and large vehicles onto the beaches of Normandy.

As the tank transports were regrouping in the Channel, the Higgins boats were making their dramatic dash for the beaches. Private Bradley recalled, "Making the run in to shore was intermittently lit by explosions, some of them of tremendous force. Bombs, shells from the battleships standing out to sea, rockets whooshing overhead, ack-ack from German positions and tracers were coming and going. An awesome display." The defenders may have undergone a mind-numbing bombardment, but German batteries were not all silenced and, one by one, seven Higgins boats sank or blew up from enemy fire. Scores of men in surviving landing craft watched in horror as dead bodies floated around them and the screams of still-living men pierced the early morning air. Private George McIntyre of the 4th Engineers recalled, "The water around us was cluttered with debris— crates, life belts, knapsacks, books, several K-rations and several bodies. They were face downward and were Americans."

Despite these disconcerting scenes, most of the landing craft were still more or less seaworthy and at almost exactly 6:30 A.M. members of the 2nd Battalion, 8th Infantry Regiment of the U.S. 4th Division scrambled out of their boats and either waded or dogpaddled onto Utah Beach. Lieutenant Arthur Jahnke, commander of one of the German fortifications, watched men throw off lifejackets and run across the wet sand. One of Jahnke's few surviving machine guns cut loose and bullets thumped into the soft sand, hitting at least some of the advancing Americans. Then his gunners managed to partially repair their single damaged 88mm gun and a just-landed Sherman tank ground to a sudden halt just beyond the shore. However, a moment later another amphibious tank lurched forward, fired a well-placed shell, and silenced Jahnke's strongpoint.

As dozens of these gunfights erupted up and down the beach a few American officers urged their men to push toward the dunes and over a concrete seawall that stood between the beachfront and a road that paralleled the coast. One of the officers urging the men forward was the 4th Division's assistant commander, General Theodore Roosevelt Jr., the son of the hero of San Juan Hill and legendary occupant of the White House. He had experienced a rollercoaster career during World War II and had been a significant presence in the Mediterranean campaign as assistant division commander of the Big Red One, the 1st U.S. Division. However, he and his superior, General

The German Army manned 50mm antitank gun emplacements along the shoreline at Utah and Omaha Beaches.

Terry Allen, had incurred the wrath of Omar Bradley for their relatively lax attitude concerning discipline and both men had been relieved. Roosevelt was given a second chance with his posting to the inexperienced 4th Division and, despite arthritis and a heart condition that would kill him a few weeks later, he lobbied incessantly to lead the first wave ashore. Now, on this crucial day of battle Roosevelt had clambered ashore with the first assault troops and organized the sodden, confused troops into a battleworthy attack force. Within a few minutes after he had scrambled onto the beach, the feisty, controversial general would be faced with one of the most crucial decisions of D-Day.

The Allied invasion plan assumed that the first wave of invasion troops would land near the village of La Madeleine, opposite exit three on the maps of Utah Beach. However, tidal currents had carried most of the surviving Higgins boats over a mile south of this area and the Americans were now pouring ashore opposite exit two. Roosevelt, who had spent several days poring over maps of almost every feature of the landing zone, quickly realized that the landing craft had deposited his men over two thousand yards from their target and subsequent units would simply keep landing on that same incorrect zone as they were largely following the initial assault force. As senior officer on the beach, Roosevelt was faced with the decision of either re-embarking the troops and staging a new landing up the coast or attempting to push inland from where they were.

Roosevelt called an impromptu conference on a beach swarming with soldiers dodging significant, but not overwhelming, German artillery fire. Regimental commander Colonel James Van Fleet, naval beachmaster Commodore James Arnold, and the two assault battalion commanders considered their options. As Van Fleet recalled, "We faced an immediate and important decision; should we try to shift our entire landing force more than a mile down the beach and follow our original plan? Or should we proceed across the causeways immediately opposite where we had landed?" The regimental commander and his superior both noticed that enemy small-arms and machine-gun fire was relatively light, a possible sign that the Germans had stacked their main defenses elsewhere. Van Fleet exclaimed, "We've caught the enemy at a weak point, so let's take advantage of it." Roosevelt agreed, declaring, "We'll start the war right here!"

This decision would save scores of American lives as the two officers had made a very correct guess. The Germans had deployed more men and more guns opposite exit three and this more formidable force would have taken a much heavier toll of assault troops landing on the "right" beach. The "new" Utah landing zone was not exactly a pushover but was not a slaughter pen either. Teams of army engineers and navy demolition units converged on the beach removing the tiers of obstacles that could thwart the landing of heavy equipment and more tanks. Strongpoints such as the one commanded by Lieutenant Jahnke were overrun in combined infantry-tank assaults and dozens of Germans became prisoners of war. Now the next objective was the seawall and the road beyond.

As the ground troops prepared to push off the beach the men became exhilarated by the level of naval fire support that was preceding their advance. Flying over the beach were squadrons of RAF Spitfires and Mustangs and Royal Navy Seafires, calling in targets to the warships below. Specially trained British and American pilots, supplemented by naval shore fire control parties on the beach, allowed the infantry and tanks to move forward under a massive umbrella of naval gunfire. The American destroyers *Herndon*, *Shubrick*, and *Glennon*, the British destroyer *Hawkins*, the Royal Navy cruiser *Enterprise*, and the Dutch warship *Soemba* angled ever nearer to the invasion beaches to provide close-in fire support while other Allied cruisers and battleships dropped shells farther inland in a deadly minuet of naval bombardment activities. The *Nevada* fired three hundred 14-inch shells and three thousand 5-inch projectiles during the day, an intensity of fire that the defenders simply could not fully challenge.

As the assault troops scrambled inland to secure the coastal road, the airborne troops pushed toward the sea from inland in order to link up with their infantry counterparts. A short distance from the coast a tiny force of fifteen paratroopers under Sergeant Harrison Summers slammed into an enemy artillery base held by ten times as many Germans. The airborne sergeant, aided by one or two men providing cover, staged a spectacular one-man assault as he barged into a succession of enemy-held buildings, spraying the Germans with his tommy gun and lobbing grenades in sprints punctuated by a hail of opposing gunfire. When Summers was finished, nearly an entire German company had surrendered or died and another barrier to the airborne-seaborne linkup had fallen. Lieutenant Robert Cole organized a larger scratch force from the 502nd Regiment and other assorted units and led an assault on Audouville and St. Martin, the towns straddling the causeways leading from exits three and four of Utah Beach. The operation snared dozens of German prisoners and threw another wrench into enemy plans for a massive counterattack.

Germans captured at Utah Beach were quickly rounded up and shipped to England as POWs.

Despite these successes and the safe arrival of the 4th Infantry Division, the Germans could still deploy far more troops on the Cotentin Peninsula than the Americans and at least some of them belonged to crack combat units. Yet hour by hour the American forces inexorably gained momentum and the Germans were never quite able to organize a really successful counterthrust. The paratroopers may not have suffered the 70 to 80 percent casualties feared by some Allied leaders, but they paid steeply in blood for securing the flanks of the seaborne landings, losing twenty-five hundred men in this single day of fighting. Their sacrifice was far from wasted. Utah Beach was secured with an amazingly light casualty list of 197 men from the landing forces and by the end of D-Day, thirty thousand troops would land and push into the interior of Normandy. The Americans had secured the Allied right flank and created a pivot on which the attack on Cherbourg could advance. However, the capture of Utah Beach alone was useless unless the Americans could link up with the British and Canadian assault forces to the east. The bridge between Utah and the other Allied sectors was a stretch of Calvados coastline that would evoke memories of sacrifice and triumph in future generations. Its simple code name was Omaha.

CHAPTER VII

Omaha Beach
The Perilous Shore

*T*he American landings on D-Day produced essentially two separate battles that featured enormous contrasts in their conduct and outcome. While the operations at Utah Beach have become notable for their minimal casualties and early prospects for success, Omaha Beach evokes memories of poor intelligence, command foul ups, and casualties that were alarmingly similar to some American Civil War battles. The events of June 6, 1944, would earn glorious reputations for the men of the Big Red One, the Blue and Gray Division, and the Rangers, but their accomplishments were largely despite, not because of, the plans developed by senior American commanders. Eighteen-year-old privates, twenty-five-year-old company commanders, and even a few middle-aged colonels and brigadier generals turned a potential fiasco into a significant, if costly, American victory. However, the inflexibility and lack of imagination of more senior leaders seriously jeopardized the most extensive American operation of this climactic day.

Utah Beach may have spawned images of east coast seashore resorts among many GIs, but the stretch of Norman coastline between the Carentan estuary and the small fishing village of Port-en-Bessin evoked images of the more intimidating beaches of the Pacific shore of the United States. This expanse of the Calvados coastline featured a distinctive and formidable high plateau formed by alternating stretches of rocky cliffs and sandy bluffs. The beaches over which the cliffs towered were narrow and stony while the strand adjacent to the bluffs was wide and sandy and peppered with a series of passes or ravines connecting the shoreline with the lush fields and orchards of Normandy on the far side of the coast road.

Quite simply, this tract of Norman coastline code-named Omaha was a dreadful place to begin an invasion of France. The defenders would enjoy almost every advantage over the attackers. Assault troops would be forced to advance over either extremely wide beaches covered by Germans perched on moderately high bluffs or narrow beaches covered by defenders situated on even more daunting cliffs. Neither prospect was very appealing for the landing forces. In normal circumstances, it would have been better to simply go around Omaha altogether, but as long as Allied plans emphasized the need to capture both Cherbourg and Caen early in the operation, seizing Omaha was vital. Capture of Utah Beach on the right and Gold, Sword, and Juno Beaches on the left flank would still leave a gaping hole between the Allied armies and allow the enemy to generate a massive counterattack against the invaders. The capture of Omaha, no matter how costly, was essential to any hope of cobbling together an unbroken line along the over fifty miles of coastline that formed the Overlord target.

In fairness to senior Allied commanders and planners, they did not really expect this operation to become another Charge of the Light Brigade or assault on Cold Harbor. Allied intelligence had initially identified the defenders of Omaha as two understrength battalions of the second-rate 716th Division, a unit manned substantially by over-age Germans and reluctant *"Ostruppen"* gleaned from the prison camps of the Eastern Fronts. Beyond the expected marginal nature of the defenders, the Americans would enjoy the three-tiered support of massive air bombardment, naval gunfire, and amphibious armored support. This awesome chain of offensive firepower appeared to be irresistible against the modest weaponry the Wehrmacht could deploy on the morning of D-Day.

Omar Bradley, the senior American ground commander, and Leonard Gerow, commander of V Corps, had no intention of needlessly sacrificing the lives of their men, but Bradley may have been optimistic about the nature of their opponents and Gerow had reservations about the effectiveness of the Allied support forces. It appeared the GIs would be facing outnumbered and overmatched German defenders. However, several months before the invasion, General Friedrich Dollman, commander of the German Seventh Army, had dispatched the 352nd Division to the region and deployed most of two regiments in the vicinity of Omaha Beach. This meant that in the first stage of the landings the Germans would actually outnumber the Americans, a gross violation of the standard rule of thumb that a successful attack should be based on a three to one advantage of attackers over defenders. Second, each element of the plan for the utilization of air, sea, and armored support contained flaws. The air bombardment was scheduled to be carried out by strategic bombers not designed for close air support; the naval bombardment was scheduled for only a half hour; and no one was certain that the amphibious tanks actually were capable of swimming through rough seas.

Another important decision by the Allies that some say was potentially disastrous was their refusal of Montgomery's offer of a large number of specially designed British tanks nicknamed the "funnies." General Percy Hobart, the British ground commander's brother-in-law, had supervised the development of a variety of special operations armored vehicles including flail tanks designed to destroy enemy mines, "crocodile" tanks equipped with flamethrowers, "bobbin" tanks outfitted with road building capabilities, mortar-equipped tanks designed to smash concrete emplacements, and another vehicle

British General Percy Hobart supervised the development of a wide variety of specialized tanks called "funnies," such as this one equipped with a folding bridge for navigating difficult terrain. Many felt these specialized tanks were underutilized in the D-Day invasion.

equipped to carry bridging materials. Montgomery ordered Hobart to provide the American assault forces with one-third of all "funnies" available but Bradley brusquely refused the offer citing vague concerns that his troops would have problems learning to use such strange equipment.

Between them Bradley and Gerow had thus underestimated enemy strength, overestimated the effectiveness of Allied air and armored support, and spurned the offer of potentially valuable British weapons. Instead, these two generals offered the assault troops the opportunity to engage in a battle that very well might resemble the bloodbaths of the Western Front of World War I. The army and corps commanders had eschewed tactical subtleties and ignored the possibility of seizing the vital beach exits by maneuver. Gerow had no other option but to hurl his men frontally against the most strongly defended positions along the invasion. The recipe for disaster had been created and it was at Omaha that the Germans had a genuine opportunity to throw the invaders into the sea.

Wooden poles angled toward the sea and topped with mines were part of the many impediments constructed under Rommel's plan to stop the invasion on the beaches. Layers of these obstacles met the Allied soldiers debarking onto Omaha Beach.

Field Marshal Erwin Rommel had insisted that the only hope of parrying an Allied invasion was to utterly annihilate the landing forces on the beaches. Thus the Desert Fox had used thousands of his own soldiers and large numbers of relatively well-paid French workers to construct layers of obstacles on Omaha's shores. These impediments included an outer tier of "Belgian gates" seven-by-ten-foot steel frames studded with mines; "hedgehogs," six-foot steel bars welded together at right angles to look like giant sets of toy jacks; and sharpened wooden and concrete poles angled toward the sea and laced with mines. Rommel knew that if the Allies chose this particular section of the Calvados coast as a landing point they could only advance inland if they could gain possession of the sandy ravines that fronted the villages of Vierville, Les Moulins, St. Laurent, and Colleville. Therefore, a dozen or so of the most formidable stone villas in each hamlet were filled with riflemen, machine gunners, and light artillery crews while the nearby bluffs were fitted with heavily camouflaged gun emplacements.

Rommel had insisted that the landing phase was the only period that the probability of German success was high as "the enemy will be at his weakest just after the landing. The troops are unsure and possibly even seasick. They are unfamiliar with the terrain. Heavy weapons are not yet available in sufficient quantity. This is the moment to strike at them and defeat them." However, Bradley and Gerow were equally confident that the formidable combination of air power, naval gunfire, and amphibious armored support could nullify the defenders' advantages and permit the GIs to penetrate into the Norman countryside. Their theory would soon be put to the supreme test.

One of the German officers responsible for ensuring that the Allied troops never got off the beaches was Major Werner Pluskat, an artillery officer in the 352nd Division. Pluskat commanded a formidable array of twenty long-range cannons that could sweep much of Omaha Beach with their deadly projectiles. The major's command bunker provided a remarkable view of the Normandy coast as his fieldglasses could detect the panorama from the tip of the Cotentin Peninsula to the huge port of Le Havre. Just before dawn on June 6, Pluskat swept his binoculars up and down the coast and peered intently at the inky blackness of the Channel. Then, just as the first hint of daylight streaked the sky, the Wehrmacht officer gasped in horror and amazement as he detected hundreds of ships emerging from the mist like nautical phantoms. He breathlessly put in an emergency call to the 352nd Division's headquarters, blurting out that he had spotted perhaps ten thousand ships spread across the length of the horizon. An artillery corporal attached to one of the forward batteries detected the enemy fleet at almost the same moment. He later recalled, "When the fog finally disappeared there was what looked like a city out there; ship upon ship upon ship. You could not see the water between them. It defied description; there was no word for it."

As Pluskat and his gunners watched the warships deploy into firing positions, the silence of the early morning was shattered by the drone of thousands of airplane engines. Flying high above the Germans were nearly five hundred B-24s that had made pre-dawn takeoffs from dozens of airbases in southern England to pulverize German coastal defenses along Omaha Beach. At just past 6 A.M. the huge aerial armada approached the Calvados coast at below twenty thousand feet, more than ten thousand feet below normal bombing altitudes. This low approach allowed armorers to stuff the planes with 100-pound bombs, making their arsenal one-third higher than normal missions.

This explosive power was intended to annihilate German gun emplacements and drive the defenders into a terror induced stupor. Unfortunately, strategic bombers would hardly qualify as precision weapons and and the weather was overcast. Pilots and bombardiers feared bombing short and hitting friendly ships; they were instructed to bomb targets at least one thousand yards inland. The fear of short bombing became so pervasive that most pilots gradually shifted that safety margin further and further inland until the bomb line ranged between two and three miles from the actual invasion beaches. The Liberators and Flying Fortresses produced a visually stunning aerial bombardment in which thousands of bombs produced massive explosions as the ground quaked with their impact. Apple orchards were turned into kindling wood; dozens of haystacks caught fire; scores of cows dropped to the grass with fatal injuries. However, damage to German emplacements was minimal and virtually no Wehrmacht guns were knocked out of action. One of the major trump cards in the Allied arsenal had produced no measurable effect on the enemy's ability to defend the coast and it was now up to the naval and armored weapons to provide the shield against a disaster on the beaches.

The Allied naval bombardment had been timed to work in unison with the strategic bombing raids, and as the huge bombers droned overhead, the 14-inch guns of the *Texas* and *Arkansas* boomed across the gray-green waters of the Bay of the Seine. The two old battlewagons, supported by the cruisers *Glasgow, Montcalm,* and *Georges Laygues,* and a bevy of destroyers were able to silence some enemy batteries.

However, the Allied bombardment started far too close to H-hour to be really effective and while naval support would prove decisive before the day was over, the American infantrymen would be confronting a still largely intact Wehrmacht on the shores of Omaha and a relatively small force of amphibious tanks was now the final hope for the enormously vulnerable landing troops.

The sixty-four duplex-drive Shermans assigned to support the Omaha assault were expected to swim several miles through the choppy channel and clamber out of the water just before the first riflemen waded ashore. A contingent of eight LCTs were deployed to support the landing of the 16th Regiment of the 1st Division on the eastern edge of Omaha while a similar force was expected to bolster the landing of the 116th Regiment of the 29th Division. The transport vessels were expected to approach to within six thousand yards of the beaches and then the senior armor officer in each contingent was expected to decide whether the DDs should be driven into the sea for a swimming approach or should be landed directly from the LCTs onto the beach. Unfortunately, army officers had little perception of the dangers of the Channel and this oversight would soon lead to disaster.

The LCTs designated to support the landing of the lead units of the 1st Division steamed to the six-thousand-yard point and the army captain commanding the Shermans squinted over the rail of the landing ship and decided to at least postpone the debarkation of the Shermans. However, as the vessels closed another half mile closer to shore, the armor officer suddenly became convinced that the sea had become less choppy and ordered the tanks to enter their swimming mode. On seven of the eight transports groups of four olive-drab vehicles hoisted their canvas "bloomers" and drove slowly from the ramps into the chilly water. However, as naval crewmen looked on in shock and horror, the Shermans did not swim towards shore but plummeted like brownish rocks toward the bottom of the Channel. In moments nearly the whole support force for the 16th Regiment had foundered while only the quick thinking of a junior naval officer who held back three swimming vehicles after the first tank sank allowed a skeleton force to be landed directly on the beach.

The men of the 29th Division would fare a little better as Lieutenant D. L. Rockwell, commander of the control ship for the western flotilla, managed to convince the senior army officer aboard to cancel the debarkation due to the rough seas. A startling number of Shermans would still end up as flaming wrecks when they were landed directly on the Omaha shore but at least a few DDs survived long enough to

Soldiers waited in fear and seasickness for the front of the landing craft vehicles to open. Once they left the landing craft vehicles, they had to fight their way through chilly water and German machine-gun fire before making the shoreline. This photo was taken at Omaha Beach.

provide a semblance of support for the men who were about to stumble ashore.

Considering the millions of Allied soldiers, sailors, and airmen involved with the execution of Operation Overlord, the success or failure of the pivotal Omaha landings was actually in the hands of a remarkably small number of men. The first assault wave assigned to capture this vital beach was a mere eight companies fielding just under fifteen hundred men. Those soldiers of the 16th and 116th Regiments would be opposed by three frontline Wehrmacht battalions fielding just over two thousand men, eight heavy guns, thirty-five antitank guns, and eighty-five machine guns. The attackers could expect to enjoy a modest numerical superiority when the follow-up waves began landing, but in the crucial opening phase of the battle the Germans would have more men, more guns, and far more protection than their American adversaries and a gruesome and bloody assault was far from unlikely.

As H-hour approached, the first wave of Higgins boats lurched through the rough Channel waters as many of the assault troops bailed furiously with their helmets trying to keep the small landing craft afloat until they reached the shore. Not all of these efforts were successful as ten of the LCVPs either slipped under the waves as they foundered or simply disappeared when a German shell found its mark. Ten of the boats, carrying over three hundred men from the assault force, sank or were destroyed whittling the GIs modest numbers even further. Finally at 6:30 A.M. the first of the surviving landing craft lowered their exit ramps and a scene worthy of Dante's Inferno quickly unfolded. For a few seconds time seemed suspended as a few men in the front of the Higgins boats plunged into the chilly water while the defenders adjusted their gunsights. Then, an instant later, the fury of the German machine-gun fire was unleashed. American assault troops, overloaded with equipment, groggy from seasickness, and shocked almost to numbness by the deep, cold water either

Throughout the day, June 6, a variety of landing craft vehicles off-loaded American GIs and equipment onto the Normandy coastline.

Allied assault troops had to carry unusually heavy packs and equipment through the water in order to reach the beach.

waded or paddled toward the wet sand ahead of them. All along four miles of beach, almost by signal, a fusillade of deadly metal met the almost helpless assault troops.

The torment of the 116th Regiment began only seconds after the landing craft lowered their ramps. As the official unit account stated:

> This was the signal for which the enemy waited, all boats came under criss-cross machine gun fire. As the first men jumped, they crumpled and flopped into the water. Then order was lost. It seemed to the men that the only way to get ashore was to dive head first in and swim clear of the fire that was striking the boats. But, as they hit the water, their heavy equipment dragged them down and soon they were struggling to keep afloat. Some were hit in the water and wounded. Some drowned then and there. But some moved safely through the bullet-fire to the sand and then, finding they could not hold there, went back into the water and used it as cover, only their heads sticking out. Those who survived kept moving forward with the tide, sheltering at times behind under-water obstacles and in this way they finally made their landings.

The survivors were now reasonably safe from the threat of drowning, but there was very little cover from the awesome combination of German 88s and 1,200-shot-a-minute Spandau machine guns, and the damp gray sand was soon streaked with red and covered with dead or dying men in olive-drab uniforms. As a battalion account noted, "Within ten minutes of the ramps being lowered, A Company had become inert, leaderless and almost incapable of action. Every officer and sergeant had been killed or wounded. A Company had ceased to be an assault company and had become a forlorn little rescue party bent upon survival and the saving of lives." As the pitifully few survivors lunged and staggered toward the stormy shelf that formed a seawall beyond the sand, another barrage of cannon and machine-gun fire pushed A Company dangerously near to total annihilation. Only eight of two hundred men would survive the assault unwounded and much of the life blood of several American towns was seeping out onto the Normandy beaches.

A little more than a mile east of this slaughterhouse, two other companies of the 29th Division were drifting ashore and preparing to meet a reception only marginally less harrowing than the doomed company on Dog Green. The assault troops from F and G Companies were supposed to land on two different beaches, but tidal currents dragged most of their landing craft toward the same landing point, the boundary between Dog Red and Easy Green. Unfortunately for the GIs, this zone was opposite the vacation hamlet of Les Moulins whose formidable stone villas were now well-defended with Germans. When the Americans tumbled ashore, every weapon in Les Moulins opened up deadly fire. Americans struggling under the weight of cumbersome flamethrowers vanished in a blinding flare as an enemy shell or bullet found its deadly mark. Men lost arms or legs as they sprinted toward the small shelf of shingles that offered a tiny amount of protection from the ceaseless firing. Higgins boats floated listlessly at the shoreline, filled with the corpses of now dead assault troops.

The final unit of the 116th Regiment's first assault wave, E Company, completely missed its landing zone and the men found themselves on Easy Red and Fox Green, areas totally outside their anticipated zone of operation. Here again, the shingle seawall was the first objective for the GIs who managed to reach the beach alive and more or less uninjured. The six Higgins boats carrying the men of E Company were dispersed over almost two miles of coastline so that each small group of about thirty men faced the fury of the German defenders with little or no support from other units. Company commander Captain Laurence Madill urged forward the tiny band of assault troops that were under his personal supervision but had his arm blown off seconds after he set foot on the beach. As he staggered forward to lead a ragged charge by the pitifully few survivors a hail of

American GIs wade ashore near the dunes of Omaha Beach late in the afternoon of June 6.

machine-gun fire cut him down and he gasped, "Senior non-com, take the men off the beach!" At this moment in time, heroism was not in short supply but prospects for victory appeared to be increasingly ominous for the men of the Blue and Gray Division.

While the men of the 29th Division were enhancing a grim legendary status that had begun some eighty years earlier along Bull Run, the troops of the Big Red One were embellishing a reputation tempered by actions on the beaches of North Africa and Italy. The GIs of the 1st Division were still justifiably bitter at the failure of the high command to rotate them out of combat duty after their heavy losses in the Mediterranean campaigns, but their courage was undiminished and their combat experience would be a vital asset on this bloody Tuesday morning. Along with their counterparts in the 29th Division, the men of the 1st Division would undergo a mind-numbing unraveling of the assault plan almost from the moment the first soldier clambered down the rope netting into the waiting landing craft.

A flotilla of twelve vessels carrying E and F Companies of the 16th Regiment was supposed to put the troops ashore on Easy Red beach but only two boats managed to find this elusive target. Some of the remaining craft found themselves intermingled with even more off course vessels carrying part of the Blue and Gray contingent and the joint force quickly encountered the formidable German defenses around the beach exit at Colleville. Enemy 75s and 88s hidden near the ravine turned the landing beach into a shooting gallery as E Company lost 105 men before the invaders could even reach the relative safety of the shingle seawall. One German gun decimated F Company when a shell scored a direct hit on a Higgins boat, hitting twenty-three of the thirty men aboard. As a single surviving amphibious tank fought a lonely, unequal duel with dozens of German guns, the few unwounded survivors of the first assault wave huddled grimly behind the shingled wall waiting for the arrival of the follow-up units that were their only hope of avoiding complete annihilation. Meanwhile, a few miles to the west another bloody drama was just beginning to unfold in front of an ominous looking precipice called Pointe du Hoc.

Allied intelligence may have failed to detect the crack 352nd Division that was now tormenting the assault troops on Omaha, but reconnaissance units were certain they had identified a major threat to the landings atop a formidable cliff not far from the Carentan estuary. Aerial photographs revealed a heavily casemated fortification that seemed to deploy a battery of long-range 155mm guns; weapons that could spray deadly projectiles over a vast sweep of the landing beaches. Since this structure atop Pointe du Hoc seemed impervious to either aerial bombing or naval gunfire, a select force of men from the

Wounded soldiers of the 16th Infantry Regiment at Fox Green on Omaha Beach were eventually evacuated back to England. They were among the "lucky" ones who made it ashore at all.

2nd Ranger Battalion was assigned to what might become a suicide mission.

Lieutenant Colonel James Rudder, commander of the Ranger detachment assigned to the mission, had put his men through vigorous exercises on similar terrain in various parts of Britain and the thirty-three-year-old leader was convinced that these elite troops were capable of carrying out this dangerous task. Rudder had borrowed several of the London Fire Brigade's longest extension ladders and then fitted the upper part of the devices with light machine guns in a unique integration of medieval and modern warfare. The energetic colonel then sidestepped his superior's orders to appoint a subordinate officer to lead the actual assault. Instead, in the early morning hours of June 6 Rudder was leading a small flotilla of ten British-built armored landing craft and two heavily laden supply vessels on a final run toward the looming cliff.

This hazardous operation began to unravel almost as soon as the vessels approached the Norman coastline. One boat promptly foundered after being hit by a large wave. The craft was soon followed

Soldiers of the 2nd Ranger Battalion were assigned to scale the cliffs at Pointe du Hoc to take out the heavily casemated fortification there.

to the bottom of the Channel by one of the supply vessels which went down with much of the scaling equipment. Then the surviving boats drifted so far off course that it took nearly thirty minutes to shift direction back toward the correct landing zone. Finally, at just past 7 A.M., two Allied destroyers steamed close to shore to provide covering fire while the Rangers climbed out of their landing craft and sprinted across the tiny, six-foot-wide shingle beach. German defenders dodged naval gunfire to lob hand grenades down on the attackers while the GIs struggled to obtain their footing on the treacherous, wet stones. The beach was so slippery that three of the four Fire Brigade ladders could not be manhandled into position, but one of the devices was lifted upward with an intrepid Ranger perched on the top spraying the cliff top with wild machine-gun fire. While the Germans tried to silence the American automatic weapon, rocket-propelled grappling hooks began clanging onto the summit and dozens of ropes soon dangled toward the beach.

Rudder and Colonel Travis Trevor, a British commando accompanying the Rangers, led the troops across the shingle and directed the scaling operation. Wehrmacht defenders managed to cut some ropes and dislodge some of the grappling hooks but most of the Rangers were inching their way to the summit. The Germans challenged the ascension with rifles, grenades, and even rocks but enough of the men in olive drab were able to haul themselves over the edge of the cliff to engage their tormentors in a vicious firefight. The naval gunfire and aerial bombardment had filled the plateau on top of Pointe du Hoc with dozens of craters, and these holes provided instant cover for both defenders and assault troops. The result was a deadly game of jack-in-the-box as men in field gray and olive drab popped up from cover and sprayed their adversaries with automatic-weapons fire or pitched grenades at their nearest opponent.

The Rangers had suffered appalling casualties in their ascent, but they sensed that they were driving the enemy inland and kept edging closer and closer to the casemates. Finally, in one final wild rush, the remaining defenders either fled or were captured, and the GIs scrambled into the fortification to deal with the heavy guns. A moment later shock set in as the badly mauled Americans realized that they had not captured deadly 155mm guns but a battery of cleverly painted telephone poles. The Germans, fearful that Allied air attacks might penetrate the casemates, had moved the real guns to a heavily camouflaged apple orchard and substituted wooden dummies in their place. A group of daring Rangers would deal with those weapons a little later in the day, but, for the moment, the survivors of the Pointe du Hoc assault could only shake their heads in wonder and disgust that so many men had been killed or wounded to capture a battery of telephone poles.

Despite the relatively hollow nature of their victory, the Rangers at least stood poised to push across the coast road and penetrate inland through the orchards and fields of Normandy. Unfortunately, their counterparts back down on Omaha Beach were still restricted to a narrow strip of shingle between the lapping waves of the Channel now choked with dead assault troops and a stretch of dunes and bluffs with very live German defenders. As follow-up waves of assault troops scrambled ashore, they simply added that many more targets for enemy sharpshooters and machine gunners. The men huddled on Omaha had already suffered ten times as many casualties as the troops on Utah and they had virtually nothing to show for their terrible losses. As each newly arriving landing craft lowered its ramp, a new group of men would wade ashore leaving a trail of casualties behind them. The survivors would then converge behind the seawall, joining the remnants of earlier assault parties. The invasion of Omaha had bogged down almost completely and Bradley and Gerow, observing the operation from the relative safety of naval vessels, were moving

Low tide revealed the stretch of obstacles erected by Rommel's troops that made them a menace to ship bottoms as well as the shallow-draft landing vehicles and the men they carried.

inexorably toward abandoning the attack and shifting the follow-up units to Utah. Then, at this moment of crisis, a crusty one-star general and a small group of young junior officers began to turn the tide of the American experience on D-Day.

General Norman "Dutch" Cota, assistant division commander of the 29th Division, arrived on the beach at 7:30 A.M. accompanied by 116th Regiment commander Colonel Charles Canham and some reinforcements. A spray of German machine-gun fire killed several of the men around the general, but Cota managed to wade ashore only to confront a scene of utter chaos. As Sergeant Robert Slaughter remembered, "It was all very disorganized, because we lost nearly all our officers and people just lay around, not knowing what to do. If the Germans had counterattacked we could not have held them. We threw our hand grenades away or lost them ... so we didn't really have any weapons at all!" Private Harry Parley noted, "What I found when I finally reached the seawall at the foot of the bluffs is difficult to describe. I can only call it disorganized chaos. Men were trying to dig or scrape trenches or foxholes for protection against incoming fire. Others were carrying or helping the wounded to shelter. We had to crouch or crawl on all fours when moving about. To communicate, we had to shout above the din of the shelling from both sides, as well as the explosives on the beach. Most of us were in no condition to carry on. All we could do was try to stay alive for the moment."

Cota realized that these huddled soldiers were only thinking in terms of holding their position rather than advancing, but if they were going to survive much longer they would have to break clear of the beach and the deadly fire raining down on them. Unlike World War II generals who tended to lead from the rear, Cota exposed himself to a fusillade of bullets as he jumped over the seawall and charged forward with a small group of followers. Bangalore torpedoes were pushed into place, the next batch of enemy defenses was breached, and an open, if deadly, route to the interior was pried open. Cota then bellowed, "There are two kinds of soldiers on this beach. Those who are dead and those who are about to die. So let's get the hell off the damned beach!" The feisty general then personally took charge of a spirited fire and maneuver operation in which one section of men would lay down covering fire while another group sprinted towards the nearest enemy position. The American infantrymen lurched forward between the passes at Vierville and St. Laurent and then split into two assault groups prepared to hit the Germans from the rear at both positions.

The casualties were high at Omaha Beach, and many brave men, such as these from the Big Red One U.S. 1st Division, did not live to see another day.

While Cota maneuvered to get at the enemy flank and rear, his advance was provided with vital support from the naval bombardment units. Captain Harry Sanders, commander of Destroyer Squadron 18, closed his lightly armored ships to the point of nearly grounding them and was appalled at the scene of wrecked tanks, burning vehicles, and bodies of assault troops bobbing up and down in the water. He ordered the rest of his squadron to steam as close to the shore as possible and open fire with every weapon they carried. When bombardment group commander Admiral C. J. Bryant saw the destroyers' gambit, he called over the radio, "Get on them men! Get on them! They are raising hell with the men on the beach and we can't have any more of that! We must stop that!"

Commander Robert Beer maneuvered his ship, the USS *Carmick*, to within nine hundred yards of the beach, established visual communication with the assault troops, and fired salvos that covered the soldiers as they advanced toward the German-held high ground. The USS *Thompson* pounded the Les Moulins strongpoint that was pinning large numbers of Americans behind a nearby seawall. Lieutenant Commander Edgar Powell's USS *Baldwin* engaged in a wild duel with German batteries, took two hits, but suppressed some of the most dangerous enemy weapons. As the destroyers' deadly fire began to take effect, the ground troops huddling behind cover finally had the level of fire support necessary to advance inland without being annihilated. More and more units were able to push over the coastal highway and penetrate inland transforming a near disaster into a successful, if costly, operation.

While both the 1st and 29th Divisions were still more or less functioning combat units at the end of D-Day, a number of their assault companies had taken casualties reminiscent of the bloodiest Civil War battles. The 2,500 American casualties at Omaha Beach were most heavily concentrated among the first two or three assault waves, many of which lost over half of their men in a single day of fighting. Company A of the 116th Regiment entered the battle with two hundred men and ended the day with eight soldiers still standing. In the single town of Bedford, Virginia, nineteen families would replace the blue star in their window symbolizing a person on active service with the gold star announcing the tragedy of death in action. The American assault force had lost altogether 6,600 men to secure the western flank of the Normandy invasion beaches but this loss would be futile if the British and Canadian troops storming ashore on Gold, Juno, and Sword Beaches could not defeat the enemy in the center and eastern flank. As the GIs stormed through a hail of German steel at one end of the enemy defenses, soldiers from Birmingham to British Columbia were about to test the mettle of the Wehrmacht at the other end of the Overlord beaches.

An American soldier lies on a bloody beach of Normandy in the aftermath of June 6, 1944.

Omar Nelson Bradley

The man who would become known as the "GI General," was born the son of a local schoolteacher and principal in Clark, Missouri. The family's already marginal prosperity was shattered by the death of Omar's father, and an appointment to West Point became the young Missourian's only path to higher education. Bradley graduated in the same class as Dwight Eisenhower in 1915 and, like his future commander, essentially missed World War I through a series of training assignments in the United States. After spending much of the 1920s teaching at West Point and serving with an infantry unit in Hawaii, Bradley was selected to attend Command and General Staff School which prepared him for assignments as an instructor at the Infantry School at Fort Benning and another stint as a tactical instructor at the Military Academy.

Bradley's first significant move toward army command occurred in 1938 when he was assigned to duty with the general staff in Washington, an assignment that he handled well enough to gain a brigadier general's star and an appointment as commandant at the Infantry School. After Pearl Harbor, Bradley was given successive command of the 82nd and 28th Divisions and then, at the end of 1942, was sent to North Africa as Eisenhower's deputy commander.

The organizational shake-up in the wake of the less-than-spectacular performance of the Americans in their first full-fledged encounter with the Germans at Kasserine Pass in February 1943, found Bradley as commander of the U.S. II Corps, a position he held for the remainder of the Tunisian campaign and through Operation Husky, the invasion of Sicily. Just prior to the Allied invasion of mainland Italy, Bradley was called to England to take part in planning the invasion of France and soon found himself as the senior American ground commander for Operation Overlord.

After the capture of Paris, Bradley directed the southern wing of the massive Allied advance across France, the Low Countries, and Germany and, by the end of the war, Bradley was a four-star general commanding 1.3 million men, the largest ground force ever assembled under an American general. He succeeded Eisenhower as army chief of staff in 1948 and became chairman of the joint chiefs of staff in August 1949 with a promotion to five-star general the next year. When the Korean War ended, Bradley retired from the army to pursue business interests and write his memoirs, including the bestselling *A Soldier's Story* which enhanced his public stature even further. Bradley outlived most of the other senior commanders of World War II and was able to produce an updated memoir *A Soldier's Life* just before his death in 1981.

Infantry Weapons in the Normandy Campaign

The numerous vicious, close-in fire-fights during the battle for Normandy provide excellent illustrations of the contrasting strengths and weaknesses of the weapons provided to Allied and German infantrymen at this stage of World War II. On the level of the most basic infantry weapon, the rifle, the British and German soldiers were fighting on a virtually even basis as the British Lee Enfield and German Mauser were both five-shot, bolt-action weapons that were reliable and accurate but represented no great leap forward from the Great War. On the other hand, the American GI was equipped with a rifle that really was an enormous step forward from the musketry of 1914-1918. The army's M-1 rifle, developed by John C. Garand, was a revolutionary weapon that represented the American army's biggest effort between the wars. The M-1 was a nine-pound, .30-caliber, semi-automatic rifle that fired an eight-round clip that could fire forty rounds a minute in the hands of an average infantryman and one hundred rounds a minute in the hands of an expert. It had only half the recoil of a bolt action rifle and was amazingly simple to service and repair.

However, while the Americans held a substantial edge in the most basic weapon, the Germans responded with an equally effective gambit. While most of their soldiers were still equipped with the relatively slow-firing bolt-action rifle, a substantial minority of men in each company were issued a variety of machine pistols and sub-machine guns that produced an awesome amount of firepower in the aggregate of the whole unit. Then the Germans added a trump card, the MG-42 machine gun. This weapon had a firing rate of a fantastic twelve hundred rounds a minute and dramatically out-gunned American and British counterparts that could fire only five hundred rounds in the same time frame. Thus a relatively small group of Germans, using a few MG-42s and a lavish number of submachine guns, could prove to be an awesome defensive force, especially in the hedges of the Norman bocage country.

The Germans also had varying edges in two other commonly used infantry weapons. The famous German hand grenade, the "potato masher," had a stick handle that allowed the weapon to be thrown further and more accurately than the American "pineapple" grenade. While the American weapon did carry almost twice the explosive charge as the German version, the superior throwing accuracy of the "potato masher" probably gave that weapon the edge in most close-contact situations. The German infantryman enjoyed an even more substantial advantage over his Allied counterpart in the area of individual antitank weaponry. The British-made PIAT was a spring-loaded, heavy weapon that packed a formidable punch against an enemy tank. But the weapon was both fairly complex and had a relatively short effective range that earned it a reputation as a "suicide weapon" among Tommies who were hardly lining up to get their hands on the device. On the other hand, the relatively few soldiers who were willing to ignore these limitations were able to inflict considerable damage on the panzers.

The American "bazooka" was actually named after a long tubular instrument used during the 1930s by comedian–big band leader Bob Burns. Otherwise known as the M-1 Launcher, or Rocket, or Antitank, the bazooka was a five-foot-long, 18-pound weapon that fired a 2.36 rocket. This weapon had greater range than any of its counterparts in other armies but had relatively modest penetrating power and required two men to operate. On the other hand, the German panzerfaust, despite shorter range, was the most coveted antitank weapon of the Normandy campaign. This weapon was operated by a single soldier who required no special train- ing. The German weapon launched a charge that had far more penetrating power than the bazooka and became so deadly in the hedgerow fighting that GIs scoured the battlefield to "liberate" panzerfausts for their own use. Thus, outside of the notable exception of the M-1 rifle, the Germans tended to employ superior infantry weapons throughout the Normandy campaign and for much of the rest of the war.

CHAPTER VIII

Gold Beach
The First Allied Link-Up

The Wehrmacht had conducted a spirited defense of Omaha Beach and exacted a high price for each yard of ground the Americans had captured. However, the German High Command insisted that even in the unlikely event that the main Allied invasion route was through Normandy instead of Pas de Calais, the battle would be won or lost at the gateway to Paris and the heart of Germany, the city of Caen. Thus while the main crisis moment for the American landings occurred on the beaches and sand dunes of Omaha, the British and Canadian troops of General Miles Dempsey's Second Army, would most likely meet their most daunting challenge several miles inland as they approached the university city and its vital network of highways and railroads. The outcome on Omaha Beach had been largely decided within a few hundred yards of the lapping waves of the English Channel; the men landing on Gold, Juno, and Sword Beaches would encounter their stiffest resistance in village streets, apple orchards, and wheatfields beyond the immediate reach of the sea.

The plan developed by Generals Montgomery and Dempsey for the landings on the eastern flank of the Overlord operation had the same attention to detail as the American invasion of the western beaches. However, the British assault had its own unique structure that differed in several important aspects from its American counterpart. First, the key American objective of the port of Cherbourg was so far away from Utah and Omaha Beaches that no one really expected the capture of the city in less than a week or even a month. On the other hand, the primary British prize, Caen, was located a tantalizingly close eight miles from the Channel. If an intricate balance of infantry-tank cooperation could be orchestrated on June 6, it was not beyond the realm of possibility that the city could be in Allied hands by nightfall on D-Day.

A second major difference between American and British planning involved the contrasting nature of the landing areas in each sector. The region around Utah and Omaha Beaches was sparsely populated and the communities straddling the beach exits were only tiny hamlets of about a dozen buildings each. However, the eastern end of the Calvados coast had developed as a much more popular vacation site for French tourists and there were also a number of fishing ports dotting the coastline. Thus while the American assault troops would experience a very rapid transition from sand dunes to inland hedgerows and orchards, the British and Canadian forces would probably find themselves engaged in extensive street fighting before they emerged into the relatively open countryside between the coast and Caen. This would produce a rather different kind of battle than the one experienced by the GIs on D-Day.

Finally, Montgomery and Dempsey were far more intrigued with the capabilities of the special armored units than Omar Bradley and his corps commanders and they insisted on maximum use of the vehicles generally designated "the Funnies." DD amphibious Shermans, "Flying Dustbin," and "Crocodile" Churchills, and many other variations of special tanks were viewed as absolutely vital elements of the British landing operation and their use was heavily endorsed by most British generals.

While the focal point of the landings was the capture of Caen, only one of the three Anglo-Canadian assault forces was directly assigned to the capture of the city. Dempsey's complex invasion plan envisioned General Brian Bucknall's XXX Corps utilizing its landings on Gold Beach to cover the extreme right flank of the British advance by cutting German access to the main Bayeux-Caen highway and linking up with the extreme left flank of the Americans on Omaha Beach. Meanwhile, a largely Canadian force based on the Canadian 3rd Division would advance on the western suburbs of Caen and capture the vital airfield at Carpiquet while discouraging German counterattacks from that direction. Finally, the most easterly assault force centered around the British 3rd Division, British commandos, and French naval fusiliers, who would capture Ouistreham at the mouth of the Orne River, link up with the 6th Airborne Division around Benouville, and finally, lunge toward Caen in a massive infantry-tank operation.

The British advance on Caen was an integral part of Montgomery's plan to attract every available German armored unit to the eastern end of the Allied line in a desperate battle for the city while the Americans captured Cherbourg and then, after landing their own powerful armored forces, wheeled eastward for a massive drive on the Seine River and Paris before the enemy fully realized what had hit them. This was an ambitious plan loaded with numerous opportunities and dangers. However, Montgomery was convinced that he had planned for almost any contingency and the Allied ground forces commander was confident that the British advance, even if it failed to capture Caen as quickly as he hoped, would so distract the Germans that Bradley's forces would have a clear shot at the heartland of France and the Reich beyond.

The entire British assault coastline extended for about twenty-five miles from Port-en-Bessin in the west to Ouistreham at the mouth of the Orne River. The western edge of the landing zone was designated Gold Beach and featured about three miles of coast centered on the port town of Arromanches. The assault force included the 231st and 69th Brigade Groups of the 50th (Northumberland) Division support-ed by tanks of the famed Desert Rats of the 7th Armoured Division and a number of commando units all under the overall command of Lieutenant General Brian Bucknall, senior officer of the XXX Corps.

At just past 5:30 A.M. on June 6, the naval gunfire vessels of Force "G" under Commodore Cyril Douglas-Pennant, R.N., wheeled guns into position and prepared to open fire on the target beaches. This sector's naval support included the Royal Navy cruisers *Orion*, *Ajax*, *Argonaut*, and *Emerald*, the Royal Netherlands Navy's gunboat *Flores*, twelve British destroyers, and the Polish destroyer *Krakowiok*. Due to local tidal conditions, the first assault wave was not due to hit the beaches until 7:25 A.M., nearly an hour after the first American troops splashed ashore. One significant result of this delay was that the Tommies would enjoy a far more extensive naval bombardment than their counterparts on Utah and Omaha.

The British troops chugging toward Gold Beach in their relatively frail landing craft may have received more naval support than the GIs, but many would have eagerly traded the additional naval fire for calmer landing conditions. The sea off this part of Normandy was the roughest at any point in the Neptune-Overlord operation as a Force 5 wind whipped waves over four feet high crashing over the landing craft and turned even the staunchest troops into miserable, vomiting passengers. Private Dennis Bowen, an 18-year-old rifleman in the East Yorkshire Regiment, recalled, "The ship was rolling, the landing craft were bouncing right up in the air and back down again, probably twenty feet, and you had to time it so that you could step down from the netting onto the landing craft when it came up on a wave." However, one fortunate result of the heaving waves was that the commanders of the DD tank squadrons decided to either launch their tanks at seven hundred yards out or even land their Shermans right on the beach rather than the seven-thousand-yards launching point initially envisioned. Some tanks still went to the bottom of the Channel, but a much higher percentage of DDs were able to intervene on Gold Beach than Omaha.

The naval bombardment seemed endless to both assault troops and defenders but the landing units could take some comfort in the volume of fire sailing over their heads as they neared the beaches. Sergeant Major Jack Brown of the 147th Essex Yeomanry marveled at the intensity of fire coming from both sides: "Everybody opened up, the noise was horrific; it was ear shattering. It was bad enough with our own people firing, but there were rocket things on either side, there were capital ships, destroyers dashing backwards and forwards; we'd never experienced anything like it." Private Joseph Minogue of the Desert Rats was particularly impressed with the spectacular fury of the rocket boats as "they turned largely to one side and fired vast numbers of rockets at the beach, then maneuvered to fire on the other side," which resulted in a seemingly endless stream of fiery projectiles crashing on the German positions. Several men in the landing craft noted the awesome firepower of the vessels that were conducting the close-in bombardment. One soldier noted, "There were destroyers right in close to the beach, firing like mad. They must have been almost aground. Rocket ships and self-propelled guns firing from LCTs added to the general din. Smoke hung over everything and we could see the flashes of exploding shells on land. We couldn't tell which way they were arriving."

The defenders of this sector, the men of the 736th Grenadier Regiment of the 716th Division belonged to a unit with little mobility and far too many of them were either middle-aged or recovering from wounds suffered on the Eastern Front. However, they were fronted by one of the most heavily mined sectors of the entire French coast and they did have reasonably ample machine-gun and artillery support.

As the first landing craft approached, the Germans watched with grim satisfaction as vessel after vessel exploded or had its bottom ripped out by the difficult to detect underwater obstructions. Then the Germans watched in both horror and fascination as the first amphibious tanks lumbered up on shore like giant mechanized alligators. Corporal Fritz Behrendsen, commander of a skillfully concealed machine-gun post, ordered his gunners to fire and watched the British infantry "keel over like trees." He noted that "they shouted. They flung themselves to ground." A 75-mm cannon joined the barrage and a newly beached landing craft was suddenly wreathed in flames and capsized as burning soldiers rolled in the water or scrambled up onto the wet sand. However, more and more tanks emerged from the water "creeping up on us like tortoises" and the British armor provided desperately needed cover for the shrinking band of riflemen. As the Shermans lurched forward, the infantry dashed toward a seawall that offered at least some hope of protection. A member of the Royal Hampshire Regiment, I. G. Holley, recalled, "The beach was filled with half bent running figures, and we knew from experience that the safest place was to get as near to Jerry as we could. A sweet rancid smell, never forgotten, was everywhere; it was the smell of burned explosives, torn flesh, and ruptured earth."

The German defenders of Gold Beach may have been second-line troops deployed on less advantageous terrain than their counterparts on Omaha, but they were supported by one of the most formidable strongpoints on the entire Normandy coast, the powerful fortification adjacent to the town of Le Hamel. This position was manned by the troops that had decimated the American landings on Omaha, and these defenders would wreak havoc on their British adversaries as well.

The men of the 1st Hampshire Regiment faced the fury of Le Hamel's guns as they waded through chest-deep water. Struggling through the waves in an extended line, the Hampshires were caught by heavy mortar bursts and machine-gun crossfires that steadily whittled the number of combat effective riflemen as nearly two hundred men were killed or wounded in the agonizingly glacial advance. Sergeant Major H. W. Bowers of the Hampshires noted, "Terrific fire was coming from our right from a pillbox we didn't know was there. I decided that it was impossible for me to attack the pillbox on my own and so I picked up a couple of naval commandos who asked if they could come along for a bit of fun." The three men crawled through a dense minefield and found themselves at the edge of a trench system that extended all the way to a sanitorium building that housed the deadly pillbox. Soon grenades and automatic-weapon fire filled the early morning landscape with an appalling racket and the tiny group of attackers found themselves accepting the surrender of a large bag of *"Ostruppen"* prisoners. However, the Germans still had their best troops and best guns defending the main fortifications at Le Hamel and it would be an agonizing eight hours later before the town was finally cleared of enemy troops.

While the Hampshires were engaged in a slugfest over Le Hamel, a strike force of Royal Marines was pushing westward past Arromanches in an attempt to link up with the American landing forces at the rear of Port-en-Bessin. That town, which featured a formidable array of fortifications originally designed to discourage British pirates, had been designated as the terminus for Pluto, an underwater pipeline designed to carry fuel from England to the Continent in order to supply the Allied advance into France. The Allies

German prisoners were taken daily during the campaign. In this photograph, a British soldier guards two Germans from a Luftwaffe division.

needed a quick capture of this port town and the Royal Marines had set out on a ten-mile, cross-country trek carrying almost ninety pounds of equipment and ammunition per man. Their objective was to join forces with American troops advancing inland from Omaha to launch a combined attack on a town that had harbored ships preparing for William the Conqueror's invasion of England in 1066. As the marines passed through the ripening fields of Normandy, they began encountering a succession of German strongpoints that had to be overcome one at a time in vicious and often costly assaults. When twilight descended on the region, the commandos had won a series of bloody skirmishes and closed to within a thousand yards of Port-en-Bessin, but darkness and a series of looming cliffs bristling with enemy guns postponed the final engagement for the town. Port-en-Bessin would be the scene of a major battle, but it would occur on June 7 not on D-Day.

While the Hampshires battled for possession of Le Hamel and the Royal Marines drove for Port-en-Bessin, a territorial regiment from Yorkshire embarked on one of the most demanding and ambitious assignments on this first day of Overlord. The 6th Green Howards constituted a unit of citizen soldiers not unlike an American National Guard regiment and the unit was now entrusted with a key role in the Gold Beach landings. Lieutenant Colonel Robin Hastings, a handsome twenty-seven-year-old battalion leader, had been ordered to use his unit to neutralize a series of enemy pillboxes, capture a prominent villa expected to be crammed with enemy troops, overrun the Mont Fleury fortifications bristling with powerful 150mm guns, and then thrust further inland and seize Meuvaines Ridge which was suspected of concealing an enemy rocket battery. Once the Yorkshire men had pushed past this high ground they were expected to advance another nine miles and capture a ridge near the town of St. Leger, a community that straddled the main Caen-Bayeux-Cherbourg highway.

Colonel Hastings was placed in command of a diverse task force which included four companies of infantry, a supporting heavy weapons company, a machine-gun platoon from the Cheshire Regiment, a squadron of Royal Dragoon Guards, amphibious Shermans, a force of flail tanks, and a detachment of Royal Engineers. Hastings allocated specialized assignments to each unit in his command with the understanding that all forces would rendezvous on Meuvaines Ridge for the drive on St. Leger.

When the Green Howards landed on a nine-hundred-yard front of the King section of Gold Beach, they immediately encountered at least six pillboxes and an assortment of German artillery units. Private Francis Williams, a 22-year-old rifleman in the assault force, recalled, "As we came in close to the beach, some of the occupants being killed, drowned; others, good swimmers, were picked up or managed to struggle ashore, not many managing this. The doors of the ramp went down, belts were fastened … and Sergeant William Hill followed by two privates were the first to go… that was the last I saw of them." Private Williams waded ashore in water up to his chest, carrying a Bren guns above his head. "There was a small, sandy ridge just off the beach. On our left a flail tank went forward and blew up. Just fifty or sixty yards in front of me were a Spandau firing to our right. I jumped up and ran at the machine gun post, firing short bursts from the hip. I was on them before they knew what was happening." Private Williams shot two of the defenders and captured six others, noting with some interest the badges that indicated that these men were adversaries from the old Afrika Korps of the Desert War.

Williams was not the only Green Howard to make a spectacular attack against an enemy strongpoint. Corporal Albert Joyce had spent part of his last leave getting drunk and hurling bricks through shop windows in Glasgow, Scotland. Only the timely intervention of Colonel Hastings had prevented a jail term and now the corporal repaid his commanding officer handsomely for his favor. Joyce crawled up to the firing slits of an enemy pillbox and tossed grenades through the openings, then burst through the rear entrance of the strongpoint and sprayed automatic-rifle fire until the survivors surrendered. Another group of Germans was added to the P.O.W. list by the efforts of a single Tommy.

Soon after Williams and Joyce pierced the crust of German defenses, a company of Green Howards advanced slowly toward a prominent stone villa looming above the sand dunes. Major Robert Lofthouse directed two platoons of Company D to bypass the house and maneuver toward Mont Fleury while the rest of the command sprinted across the manor's huge circular driveway and began a furious firefight with the villa's defenders. The British troops were dismayed to find themselves caught in a crossfire between the house and a carefully concealed pillbox nestled among the bushes and hedges of the backyard. As most of the men dashed for cover and opened fire, Company Sergeant Major Stanley Hollis charged the pillbox with a Sten gun, threw a grenade at the door, and then dashed into the stronghold killing two defenders and capturing the rest. He then sprinted toward a nearby supporting trench and shot or captured several more startled Germans. In one bold action, a single Green Howard had eliminated over thirty Wehrmacht troops from the battlefield and saved his own unit from substantial casualties.

While Lofthouse's men were dealing with the villa, a task force of C Company infantrymen and Royal Dragoon tanks were advancing toward the crest of Meuvaines Ridge. The suspected rocket batteries had been moved but the ridge was the location of a German head-quarters complex which was bristling with desperate defenders. A vicious slugging match added another substantial bag of prisoners to the Green Howards's total and the victorious Tommies reorganized for a lunge at the village of Crepon, which straddled the main route between the coast and the objective of St. Leger. Hastings had been forced to patch together a jury-rigged command structure as almost half of his key officers were either dead or wounded, and the new platoon and company commanders now earned their spurs in one of the first major street battles of the Normandy campaign. Almost every one of Crepon's buildings seemed to conceal German snipers or machine gunners and a firefight swirled through cobbled alleys out into the farm buildings adjacent to the villages.

The ever-present Sergeant Hollis became a focal figure in the battle as he directed a ferocious duel between a British antitank gun and a well-concealed German cannon and then rescued several Tommies who were trapped by the enemy barrage. By the end of the duel, Hollis was on his way to becoming the only British soldier awarded the Victoria Cross on D-Day and the Green Howards were once again pushing inland. At a cost of ninety casualties, Hastings's command had pushed to within a mile of St. Leger by dusk and set in motion an operation that would find Bayeux in British hands by Wednesday afternoon.

At a cost of just under four hundred dead and wounded, the men of XXX Corps had driven a deep wedge into the German defenses at Gold Beach and provided vital flank protection for the Americans at Omaha to the west and the Canadians on Juno to the east. The British, Canadian, and French assault troops of General J. T. Crocker's I Corps were now beginning their massive thrust at Caen and the struggle over that university town would determine the course of the Normandy campaign for weeks or months to come.

Sir Bernard Law Montgomery

This controversial yet successful commander was born in London but his family moved to Tasmania, Australia, when his clergyman father was promoted to bishop. He returned to England to attend the Royal Military Academy at Sandhurst and in 1908 joined the Royal Warwickshire Regiment. Lieutenant Montgomery was sent to France at the outbreak of World War I and was nearly killed at First Ypres. After winning a DSO, he was posted back to Britain as a training officer but was soon back in combat as brigade major for the 104th Brigade in early 1916. Montgomery was heavily involved in the slaughterhouse of the great Somme offensive of that summer and served as a staff officer for the 33rd Division at Arras in April 1917. The future field marshal was elevated to staff duties in the IX Corps for the battles around Passchendale in the autumn of 1917 and saw another ferocious round of bloodletting at close quarters. When Montgomery finally returned to England at the end of the war he was determined that if he ever held a senior command in a future war, he would do everything in his power to avoid the needless slaughter of British soldiers.

Montgomery spent the inter-war years alternating between instructional duties at the staff college at Camberly, where he singlehandedly revised the army's main infantry training manual, and assignments with overseas units, mainly in Palestine. His ascetic lifestyle was briefly interrupted by marriage and the birth of a son, but when his wife died due to a freak allergic reaction at a seaside resort Montgomery attempted to reduce his grief by plunging even more heavily into studying military operations and theory. When Britain entered World War II, Montgomery had

risen to major general in command of the 3rd Division and this unit distinguished itself by serving as the rear guard in the evacuation of the B.E.F. at Dunkirk. Montgomery returned to England as a hero and was assigned to command the V Corps which was expected to bear the brunt of a German invasion of the United Kingdom. By the end of 1941, as the probability of an enemy invasion gradually lessened, Montgomery had risen to command of the Southeastern Army.

When the entrance of the United States into the war allowed more extensive consideration of offensive operations, Montgomery was slated to command the British First Army in the proposed Allied invasion of North Africa. But when the new commander-designate of the British Eighth Army in Egypt, General W. H. Gott, was killed in an air crash, Monty was switched to that post in the wake of the disaster at Tobruk. Montgomery almost immediately instilled new confidence in an army that was reeling from successive hammer blows by Rommel's Afrika Korps and the new commander ignored Churchill's demands for an immediate counteroffensive. The new desert commander meticulously built up large reserves of men, tanks, and supplies, and only attacked when the odds strongly favored a British victory. The result of the general's planning was the significant victory at El Alamein which allowed the Eighth Army to chase Rommel back to the Tunisian border. In late March and early April, Montgomery outflanked the German Mareth Line position and then linked up with the Americans to trap a large Axis army and force the surrender of most of it.

Montgomery followed the victory in

North Africa with a successful but hard-fought campaign in Sicily which was used as a springboard for the invasion of mainland Italy. The British commander launched a well-executed operation to capture the important Foggia airfields, but became bogged down in attempts to provide decisive support for the Fifth Army's plan to move inland from Salerno. As the Italian campaign sputtered into a winter stalemate, Montgomery was recalled to England to become commander of Allied ground forces for Overlord and, along with Eisenhower, exercised considerable influence on the direction of the campaign. On September 1, 1944, as Eisenhower assumed direct command of operations in western Europe, Montgomery relinquished his position as overall ground forces commander but received a promotion to Field Marshal on the same day. Montgomery's activities during the next eight months included a hugely disappointing attempt to push across the Rhine in Operation Market-Garden, a significant role in blunting the German Ardennes offensive, and an ultimately successful thrust into the heart of the Third Reich culminating in the capture of several large German armies.

Montgomery was rewarded for his wartime service with the title Viscount Montgomery of Alamein, assignment as chief of the imperial general staff, and command of NATO forces in 1948. Monty exerted considerable influence on the development of that organization during the next decade, and produced a memoir that was widely read on both sides of the Atlantic. The viscount's version of the Allied victory in his book and subsequent television and radio interviews seemed to exasperate Eisenhower. Yet they apparently did not dissolve genuine bonds of professional admiration between the two former commanders and the two men maintained correspondence and personal visits until late in their lives. As Monty lived out a long life for over three decades after the end of the war, he came to personify Britain's sacrifice and ultimate triumph in one of the most critical moments in the nation's long history.

CHAPTER IX

Juno Beach
Payback for Dieppe

While the men of the XXX Corps dueled the Germans on Gold Beach, a rough and ready force of soldiers with North American accents and British uniforms splashed ashore on Juno Beach. These troops were the assault units of the 3rd Canadian Division and they carried with them a unique status in the Allied invasion force. Of all the major forces fighting over the Normandy beachfront on this chilly June morning, the troops fighting under the Canadian colors were under the least compulsion to be there. The American and British assault units and the Wehrmacht forces that opposed them were the products of a conscription process that assigned men to combat units as the need arose. On the other hand the rosters of the Royal Winnepeg Rifles, the North Shore Regiment, and the Regiment de la Chaudiere were composed of men who had volunteered to leave the peaceful shores of Canada in order to fight in a war three thousand miles on the other side of the Atlantic Ocean. Not only were these troops volunteers, they were among the most intrepid men on either side as their ranks included large numbers of lumberjacks, fishermen, hunters, and construction workers who had not exactly left the relative comfort of an office desk or store counter to serve in the Canadian overseas forces.

The Canadians who were about to land on Juno Beach served in the tradition of American volunteers in the Civil War and British

Tommies in the Great War who had joined local regiments with groups of friends and relatives, trained together, and volunteered for combat because of a belief in a cause that transcended their personal safety and comfort. The men of the 3rd Canadian Division were also deeply committed to avenge the fate of their comrades in the 2nd Division who had been virtually annihilated two summers earlier during the disastrous Allied raid on Dieppe.

On August 19, 1942, the Canadian 2nd Division supported by a modest force of British commandos and a small contingent of American Rangers attacked the French port of Dieppe in one of the most reckless schemes of the war. The assault force, landing with no air cover and minimal naval support, smashed into German defenders deployed on almost inaccessible cliffs and armed to the teeth with automatic weapons and artillery. A few hours later only a third of the Allies were still alive and uncaptured and every Canadian battalion commander was dead or wounded. Of the 4,963 Canadians taking part, 3,367 were killed, wounded, or taken prisoner—the equivalent to an American loss of 40,000 men in a single day, a carnage never matched by any single day in United States military history. Now the men of the 3rd Division were going back to France and they waited anxiously to settle accounts with the defenders in field-gray uniforms.

The Canadian landing on Juno was to be supported by a relatively long bombardment supplied by a fleet of two British cruisers, the HMS *Belfast* and the HMS *Diadem*, and eight British destroyers, a French destroyer, and two Canadian warships, the *Sioux* and the *Algonquin*. Short-range fire support included eight small monitors mounting four 7-inch guns, four landing craft bristling with automatic cannon, and eight rocket vessels each carrying a complement of eleven hundred 5-inch rockets. As the landing craft were about to hit the beach, eighteen special landing vessels would fire clusters of twenty-four 60-pound bombs into the beach obstacles while twenty-four LCTs, each carrying four 105mm field guns mounted on Sherman chassis, would pound identified enemy strongpoints. Next, two squadrons of Royal Marine Centaur tanks would emerge from the sea firing 95mm howitzers at the edge of the water. Finally, seventy-six DD Shermans would storm ashore just ahead of the infantry to cover the advance to the seawall. Each element in the formidable arsenal had a carefully designated assignment. The big guns of the cruisers were intended to crack the concrete fortifications of the coastal batteries; the destroyers were expected to knock out enemy cannons deployed along the beach; the rockets were designed to create blast waves at the machine-gun nests; and the self-propelled guns were expected to keep the enemy infantry's heads down during the landing.

The Canadians were provided with extensive fire support but they were also assigned a number of ambitious tasks in the face of formidable enemy impediments. The Canadian troops were expected to pierce a string of German strongpoints centered on Courseulles, which was considered the most powerful fortification in the entire eastern sector of Overlord. The 3rd Canadian Division troops would then advance through a gently rolling plain of meadowland and wheatfields which abounded in small woods, orchards surrounding dozens of hamlets of solidly constructed stone houses, and farm buildings crammed with German riflemen who were in turn supported by well-concealed 75mm and 88mm guns. The most optimistic scenario was that the Canadians would somehow punch through or bypass these obstacles and then seize a vital airfield in the Caen suburb of Carpiquet. This airport was one of the most valuable pieces of real estate in the coastal area of Normandy as it would allow the Allied air forces to conduct support operations almost literally at the front line of the fighting thus allowing maximum impact of British and American air superiority.

General Wilhelm Richter, commander of the German 716th Division, was responsible for defending a long stretch of Norman coastline that included the Canadian landing sites. His two frontline regiments, the 736th and the 726th, could deploy a total of four battalions of regular Wehrmacht troops and an additional two battalions of captured "volunteers" and were responsible for nineteen miles of coastline. Richter wanted to maintain enough reserve units to mount some form of counterattack so he placed only twelve companies astride the beaches, only three of which, the 5th, 6th and 7th Companies of the 736th Regiment were directly in the path of the Canadians. Thus about four hundred defenders would face an enemy assault force of twenty-four hundred men, a ratio that on the surface seemed to provide overwhelming superiority to the attackers. However, what Richter lacked in riflemen he partially compensated for in artillery. The Germans had twenty batteries of 75mm and 155mm guns deployed to enfilade almost every square foot of the landing beaches. Sixty-seven guns, including German, Polish, French, and Czech weapons, were positioned in a series of bunkers, casemates, and redoubts along the invasion points. Two dozen machine guns and nearly as many mortars provided close-in support for the heavily entrenched German infantry. Finally, if the defenders could hang on long enough, the tanks and panzergrenadiers of the 21st Panzer Division would emerge from their lairs about six miles inland and swoop down on the invaders before they could fully deploy their own armor. All in all, the German position was far from impregnable but could prove a very tough nut to crack, especially if the Canadians encountered large forces of enemy panzers before their own tanks could effectively intervene.

At just past dawn on June 6, the *Belfast* and the *Diadem* sent their first shells arching over the invasion beaches toward the German fortifications beyond the dunes. Soon the big guns of the cruisers were joined by destroyers maneuvering close to the beach and adding their own deadly barrage to the spectacle. However, while the assault troops' spirits were lifted by the stupendous display of firepower, they were quickly sobered by the grim prospect of moving towards shore in the teeth of high winds and four-foot waves rolling over the relatively fragile landing craft. One company commander lamented, "I had been in small boats off the coast of British Columbia many times and never been seasick; this was the first and only time in my life I was sick." The less than ideal maritime conditions caused more than seasickness as the wind and high water concealed many of the mines and obstructions that Rommel had ordered deployed. Landing-craft skippers could not detect many of the deadly contraptions bobbing just below the frothing waves and the men of the 7th and 8th Brigades watched in horror as obstructions ripped the bottoms out of their vessels or mines turned the craft into a deadly funeral pyres.

As an ominous number of assault troops disappeared into the murky channel or floated lifeless over the waves, the survivors swam or waded ashore just in time to be greeted by Richter's enfilading artillery. Captain Dan Flander, adjutant of a unit of British commandos, was accompanying the Canadian assault units. He later described the landing: "The shore was under bombardment, craft were sinking, and from where I stood it certainly didn't look as if the Canadians had secured the beaches. The tide was high and we had craft hitting the beach obstacles. The beach was covered with casualties, some Canadian and some ours. The surf was incredible with beached and half sunken craft wallowing about in it." Captain L. N. Clark of the Canadian assault force noted, "Those last moments were pretty awful. We were coming under intense small arms fire and everyone was down as much as possible. Many of the lads on our LCI never got ashore; a Spandau opened up just when the water was full of men struggling to get ashore."

The initial armored support was far below expectations as only six of the forty Royal Marine Centaurs made landfall and most of the surviving Shermans were delayed by the high waves. As machine-gun and mortar fire peppered the beaches, the first wave of the Regina Rifle Regiment began sprinting for the seawall fronting the town of Courseulles. The men had conducted numerous training exercises in England based on the information provided by extensive aerial photographs of the town. The village and harbor were broken down into twelve sectors with an assault platoon assigned to each one. While units from B Company pushed through the streets with only minor harassing fire, the men of A Company landed under the guns of the harbor fortifications and were subjected to a withering crossfire. Each platoon split up into mobile, ten-man fire teams and advanced under the cover of light machine guns, but the Germans had faster-firing weapons and more of them. The stakes in this gunfight were raised when the defenders opened fire with carefully concealed 88mm guns while the attackers employed the Shermans of the 1st Hussars. While the big guns engaged in a noisy duel, the Reginas worked their way through a maze of trenches and dugouts, losing nearly fifty men killed and dozens of others wounded as the Germans were gradually pushed back from their strongpoints.

As the Reginas worked their way through town, their counterparts in the Royal Winnipeg Rifles were advancing on Courseulles from another direction and facing equally intense opposition. Company B of the Winnipegs had borne the brunt of the most vicious German machine-gun fire of the Juno front and wave after wave of charging Canadians were cut down while wading ashore and picking their way through the beach obstacles. The survivors then plunged into a bloody street battle that gained key segments of the town but left only twenty-six men from B Company uninjured and able to march inland.

The assault troops of the Queen's Own Rifles underwent a similar trial by fire as they approached the seawall in front of Bernieres sur Mer. One company's landing craft had been carried off course by the strong winds and high tides and the vessels ended up landing in front of the town's most formidable strongpoint. While the supporting tanks of the Fort Garry Horse were attempting to land, German automatic-weapons fire cut a wide swath through the Rifles' B Company, killing or wounding sixty-five men in a few minutes. Then Lieutenant W. G. Herbert led a small party of survivors in a wild dash for the seawall. The Canadians used covering fire from their Sten guns to support engineers attempting to punch a hole through the obstacle with explosives. The riflemen then sprinted over the wall and shot their way into the nearby streets where they engaged in a heavily contested fallback of the Germans through the cobbled alleys.

That same frustrating experience of surviving an initial landing only to confront a bloody street battle confronted the New Brunswickers of the North Shore Regiment. The Reverend R. M. Hickey, chaplain of the regiment, chronicled the heavily contested landing: "The noise was deafening; you couldn't even hear our huge tanks that had already landed and were crunching their way through the sand; some men, unable to hear them, were run over and crushed to death. A blast shook the air like an earthquake; it was the engineers blowing the wall. All the while, enemy shells came screaming in faster and faster; as we crawled along, we could hear bullets and shrapnel cutting in the sand around us."

As more than one hundred defenders let loose with every weapon at their disposal, tanks equipped with "Flying Dustbins" lumbered forward and fired their 25-pound shells, cracking the concrete and eliminating about half the garrison while the others surrendered. However, new dangers awaited the New Brunswickers as they advanced through the streets of St. Aubin-sur-Mer. The whole town seemed to be turned into a gigantic shooting gallery as Germans used windows, ledges, and rooftops to pour a galling fire into the Canadians and whittle their numbers before the North Shore men could fix a target. Once again, as in the other coastal towns, the price of capturing the community was that a high proportion of the attackers lay bleeding or dead on the ancient cobblestones.

While the troops of the first assault wave grappled with the defenders over the string of strongpoints between Bernieres and St. Aubin, follow-up units initiated a series of thrusts aimed at capturing Carpiquet airport before the Germans could launch an armored counterattack. The North Nova Scotia Highlanders had been ordered to "break through immediately after hitting the beachhead, stop at nothing, do not fight unless you have to, but get to Carpiquet airport and capture and consolidate the position." However, the Highlanders and their counterparts from the Regiment De La Chaudiere were hardly outfitted for rapid marching. The men from Nova Scotia and Quebec were burdened with ninety pounds of equipment, a ridiculously heavy load for a rapid advance. In addition, communications between infantry battalions and tank squadrons remained erratic all day as foot soldiers and armored support units drifted too far apart to be effectively integrated. The Canadian riflemen often found themselves advancing through fields of wheat that had grown almost as tall as the troops which added enormously to the feeling of isolation and imminent danger. Meanwhile as the foot soldiers pushed their way through fields that would have made American Civil War troops feel quite at home, the tank units began outrunning their infantry support. One troop of 1st Hussar tanks actually pushed across the main Caen-Bayeux highway and sent scout vehicles poking around near Carpiquet airport, but when the infantry battalions failed to appear, the Hussar's commander ordered his tanks to pull back to a defendable position north of the road. The battle for Carpiquet would have to wait at least one more day.

By nightfall on June 6 units of the Canadian 3rd Division had advanced to within a tantalizingly close distance to their primary target of Carpiquet. At a cost of 335 dead and just over 800 wounded, the Canadians had not only staged a successful landing but were poised to thrust deeply into the Norman countryside if only tanks and infantry could be properly linked. However, much of the future timetable for these hard-fighting Canadian troops would be determined by the attempt of their British counterparts on Sword Beach to pierce the eastern end of the German line and capture the most significant prize of this "longest day," the city of Caen.

CHAPTER X

Sword Beach
First Lunge for Caen

While the long-term success of Overlord was dependent on the rapid linking of the five separate landing zones, only the assault on Sword Beach offered the possibility of delivering a potentially mortal blow to the German position in Normandy on the very first day of the battle. If the infantry and tanks of General J. T. Crocker's I Corps could push eight miles inland and capture the city of Caen, Rommel and von Rundstedt would be forced to deploy every available armored unit in the vicinity of that university town in order to challenge a possible breakout toward Paris. Once the panzergrenadiers had been fully committed to a massive battle on this eastern flank, the Americans would be free to launch a huge armored assault of their own which would eventually threaten to obliterate the defenders from flank and rear. Thus an early capture of Caen seemed to be the key to the campaign, and the men about to land on Sword Beach were about to become caught up in one of the most exciting and frustrating battles of D-Day.

Sword Beach was a stretch of Norman coastline that extended for about three miles from the outskirts of Lion sur Mer in the west to Ouistreham at the mouth of the Orne River in the east. General Crocker was acutely aware that the 21st Panzer Division was in or around Caen and that the 12th SS Panzer Division was deployed relatively close to the city. If these two powerful armored units reacted quickly enough, the British landing force would be overwhelmed by

About three hundred IX Army Air Force B-26s bombed enemy fortifications during the invasion. Each Marauder flew very low during the landing-support bombing runs because of the weather and the extra armaments they carried.

German tanks and thrown into the sea. Thus it was vital that the assault troops break through the enemy defense crust quickly and move rapidly inland to challenge a German armored counterattack as far from the vulnerable beaches as possible. Major General T. G. Rennie, commander of the initial assault unit, the British 3rd Division, decided to attack on a single brigade front on the White and Red sectors of that part of Sword designated Queen landing zone. Part of the 8th Infantry Brigade, spearheaded by the DD tanks of the 18th Hussars and the infantry of the South Lancashire, East Yorkshire, and Suffolk Regiments would secure the landing area and relieve the 6th Airborne Division at the Benouville span that was now being called Pegasus Bridge. Meanwhile, a force of British commandos and French naval fusiliers would capture Ouistreham, a Royal Marine force would link up with the Canadians near the village of Langrune, and 1st Special Service Brigade troops would move east across Pegasus Bridge to discourage a German counterattack from that direction. Then, if all went according to plan, the 185th Infantry Brigade Group would land, pass through the 8th Brigade's position, and seize Caen before nightfall.

Each landing point of D-Day seemed to present some special problem or challenge to the invaders, and Sword was no exception. This landing zone was very much in range of the powerful German coastal batteries at Le Havre, while the presence of the Merville sandflats extending a mile out into the Channel gave another reason for the Allied naval commanders to keep a wary eye on their easternmost flank. The Allies responded to these threats with a particularly powerful naval bombardment including the battleships *Warspite* and *Ramillies*, the monitor *Roberts*, four Royal Navy and one Polish navy cruisers, and twelve destroyers including the Norwegian warship *Svenner*. As this formidable flotilla maneuvered into position, the ships encountered the only major German naval attack of D-Day.

The approach of the Allied invasion fleet had not gone completely undetected, and before dawn a squadron of German torpedo boats operating from Le Havre had steamed out of port looking for enemy prey. The fast-moving E-boats closed on "Force S" in the first moments of daylight and let loose with guns and torpedoes. The British battleships narrowly avoided disastrous hits but one or more torpedoes caught the *Svenner* and a series of explosions ripped through the Norwegian warship as the vessel broke in two and went to the bottom of the Channel. Then, as the German raiders headed back toward Le Havre, the coastal batteries from that port joined in the attack and sent huge shells straddling the *Warspite*. The enemy guns prompted a massive barrage from the Allied warships and opened a duel that would last much of the morning. In many respects this engagement was an advantage to the Allies as the powerful coastal batteries ignored vulnerable targets among the landing craft and engaged in a duel with the battleships that produced no decisive result on either side.

The landing area confronting the British 3rd Division consisted of a number of resort beaches filled with vacation homes and tourist hotels straddling wide promenades that somewhat resembled the boardwalks along many American seashore resorts. Rough seas and high waves smashed against the landing craft as they advanced toward the barely visible shoreline. Captain Robert Neave, an assistant squadron commander in the Royal Hussars, was in a lead unit of DD tanks participating in the Sword landings: "Once in the water, to our surprise, all went well despite the rough sea. The morning was dark and black, rough but not cold. Standing up on the turret I could see the light coming up over the Le Havre peninsula and the lights of the French coast and I noticed the bows of sunken ships away to the left. The coast in front of us looked dark and forbidding—a few straggling houses behind dunes."

Those dunes were already developing into an obstacle for the infantrymen as they featured German pillboxes bristling with machine guns. As the riflemen seemed stopped in their tracks, the tanks intervened. Captain Neave noted, "Having pulled out of the water, we fired at all before us, partly to revive our confidence, partly to scare the other side. There was a big concrete pillbox in front of me. I fired at it and quite suddenly I saw four or five little chaps in enormous helmets coming off the beach running towards me with their hands up."

One of the major obstacles to the British advance was a series of German strongpoints around Lion sur Mer on the extreme western end of the landing zone. Two leading companies of the South Lancashire Regiment were mauled by successive echelons of enemy mortars, machine guns, and 75mm guns until the Polish destroyer *Slazak* maneuvered close-in toward the beach and unleashed a barrage of over one thousand shells from her four-inch guns. The Lancashires used the heavy covering fire to bypass Lion and push inland by a parallel road, but this shift of direction left a dangerous gap in the Allied lines and allowed the Germans to maintain a beachfront presence throughout the remainder of the day.

Meanwhile, at the other end of Sword Beach, a combined Anglo-French commando force was just encountering opposition from the enemy at the outskirts of Ouistreham. The joint assault force, designated Number 4 Commando, had landed at 8:30 A.M. at Beach Red and promptly lost forty men, including commanding officer Lieutenant Colonel R. W. Dawson, dealing with a well-concealed German pillbox. When the survivors edged their way toward town, the senior French officer, Commandant Philippe Kieffer, took charge of the operation and exploited the vital information gleaned from a cooperative local police official. The gendarme had slipped out of town to contact the advancing Allies and furnished Kieffer with the deployment of the enemy defenders. The French officer led a multipronged assault on German positions until only the formidable casino building remained in Wehrmacht hands. The Germans had turned this former gambling hall into a powerful fortress featuring reinforced concrete casemates and several powerful artillery positions, and the first French assault force suffered severe casualties before the attack was temporarily halted. Kieffer quickly called for armored support which was provided by Royal Marine Centaur tanks that initiated a furious duel with the casino's defenders. The Centaurs scored several vital hits and a swarm of cheering French fusiliers soon overran the position to produce the first Free-French victory on their own soil.

While one segment of the Special Service Brigade was battling for Ouistreham, that unit's commander, Lord Lovat, was leading the rest of his command on a rapid march toward the hamlet of Benouville. Major Howard's small contingent of glider troops was encountering mounting German pressure to retake Pegasus Bridge and the British commander knew his men were badly outgunned by the enemy attackers. At just past 8 A.M. Lovat, followed by his ever faithful bagpiper, scrambled ashore on Sword Beach and began the march inland toward Benouville. The dashing brigadier, wearing a decidedly nonregulation white turtleneck sweater, pushed his commandos to the limit, always fearful that an enemy counterattack would annihilate Howard's men before he arrived. However, when Lovat arrived Pegasus Bridge was still firmly in British hands and the sound of the approaching bagpipes ensured that any future German counterattacks would meet a formidable reception.

By 11 A.M. on D-Day, the British foothold on Sword Beach was firmly established, and the 185th Brigade was being assembled near the village of Hermanville in preparation for its lunge at Caen. The men of the King's Shropshire Light Infantry finished gulping down cups of cocoa and tea and then formed up for the march into town. As they entered Hermanville they observed two uplifting activities; the local inhabitants were eagerly welcoming them as liberators and an extended file of German prisoners was being escorted back to Sword Beach. The commander of the brigade's three infantry battalions, Brigadier K. Pearce-Smith, was confident that he had enough riflemen to deal with enemy foot soldiers on the way to Caen, but he was more than a little concerned that his supporting armor, the tanks of the Staffordshire Yeomanry, were nowhere in sight. Actually Pearce-Smith would have been even more uncomfortable had he known that the vital Shermans were caught in a monumental traffic jam back on Sword Beach, the result of far too many vehicles crowding onto far too little dry ground. The extremely high winds whipping across the Channel had reduced a normal thirty-yard-wide beach to a mere thirty feet wide, and the landing craft carrying the Staffordshires were stacked up behind dozens of other vessels carrying cargoes that were far less vital in a decided failure of logistic discipline.

Pearce-Smith sent the commander of the Shropshires cycling back to the beach to find the missing tanks and that officer, Lieutenant Colonel F. J. Maurice, took one look at the chaos on the beach and climbed back on his bicycle and informed Pearce-Smith that there was no telling when the tanks might link up with the foot soldiers. The brigadier decided that some progress at foot speed was better than no progress at all and at just past noon gave the order to begin the march to Caen.

The men of the 185th Brigade moved in three parallel columns through the cornfields, wheatfields, and apple orchards that lined the roads between Hermanville and Caen, just over five miles to the south. Then disaster struck unexpectedly. One of the most formidable obstacles to the British advance on Caen was a German fortification designated "Hillman" which loomed just south of route D-35. This superbly constructed defensive network covered twenty-five hundred square yards and was protected by mines, barbed wire, and concrete bunkers ringed around an inner fortification that included the head-quarters of the 736th Regiment and several powerful guns. A detach-ment of the Suffolk Regiment had been assigned to capture the strong-point before Pearce-Smith's force arrived in the vicinity, but the Suffolks had become entangled in the wire and minefield and were being mauled by accurate mortar fire. Even the arrival of limited British armored support produced little more than a frustrating stale-mated shootout that was still going full tilt when Pearce-Smith's columns marched into the area. Germans in Hillman's observation posts quickly detected the lead elements of the Norfolk Regiment advancing down the road and adjacent wheatfields and shifted some of their guns to this new and inviting target. Within moments, 150 Norfolks were sprawled dead or wounded on the road and in the fields while the survivors were ordered to keep marching and let other units handle the deadly enemy post.

At this point in time the Shropshires were facing their own trial by fire in front of Hill 61, another enemy strongpoint a little more than a mile south of Hillman. Major Hof, the German commander of this position, observed the British troops advancing through the fields and immediately telephoned Lieutenant Rudolf Schaaf, commander of a battery of self-propelled guns, and asked him to move his weapons to support the major's infantrymen. As the Shropshires pushed through a field of tall standing corn, the German guns backed into action and tore through the front ranks of the Tommies. A few minutes later the first of the Staffordshire Yeomanry's Shermans came lumbering for-ward and opened a vicious counterfire on Schaaf's mobile guns. Hof ordered his riflemen to leapfrog back toward Caen and the stuttering British drive lurched forward once again.

The combined infantry-tank advance managed to get as far as Bieville before the next serious obstacle developed. This small town, three miles from Caen, was guarded by Germans who had deployed in numerous homes and stores and positioned carefully concealed guns in the woods adjacent to the community. The 185th Brigade soon found itself engaged in a wild street battle in which enemy troops seemed alternately everywhere and nowhere and large numbers of attackers suffered death or wounds with relatively little payback to the Germans. Then when the Shropshires finally cleared the town and advanced through the wheatfields beyond, they encountered an even more sinister presence—the first hint that the panzers were about to be unleashed. The lead unit in the British advance, Y Company, found itself facing the advance panzergrenadiers of the powerful 21st Panzer Division who were pushing north from Caen. The Shropshires backpedaled warily to the relative safety of the town and waited for the first German counteroffensive to begin.

Although the Shropshires were not aware of it at the moment, the panzergrenadiers who threatened to outflank them in the fields beyond Bieville were merely one element of a multipronged counterattack orchestrated by the talented and energetic commander of the Wehrmacht's LXXXIV Corps, General Erich Marcks. The colorful general, who now hobbled around his headquarters in St. Lô with an artificial limb to replace a leg lost on the Eastern Front, had just celebrated his fifty-first birthday at midnight on June 6 but had spent much of the morning trying to make sense of the Allied paratroop and shore landings. Marcks was one of the few German generals who believed that the Allies's main thrust would come towards Normandy and he agreed with Rommel that the battle would probably be won or lost in the first twenty-four hours. Therefore with the Desert Fox absent in Germany, the LXXXIV Corps commander became the leading proponent of a massive armored counteroffensive to be initiated almost immediately. Three armored divisions, the 21st Panzer, the 12th SS Panzer, and the Panzer Lehr were within striking distance of the Allied beachhead and Marcks was determined to organize these units into a powerful phalanx of steel that would attempt to throw the Allies back into the Channel.

Unlike many of his colleagues who seemed incapable of acting without specific orders, Marcks interpreted his authority very broadly and ordered 21st Panzer Division commander General Edgar Feuchtinger to prepare his regiments for a massive armored attack. However, Feuchtinger was a cautious, only marginally competent commander and he dithered hours away as his most energetic regimental commander, Major Hans von Luck, paced around his own headquarters waiting to put his vehicles into the battle. As von Luck insisted, "If Rommel had been with us instead of in Germany, he would have disregarded all orders and taken action—of that we were convinced." Finally, while Feuchtinger temporized, Marcks climbed into a fast-driving staff car and headed for the division commander's headquarters south of Caen to expedite the attack.

While Marcks was on the road, Feuchtinger gave the commander of the division's tank regiment, Colonel Hermann von Oppeln-Bronikowski, permission to throw his armor against the British troops advancing toward Caen. However, the 22nd Panzer Regiment was deployed south of the city and Allied bombers had turned Caen's streets into a shambles of piled up debris that was impossible for heavy vehicles. Von Oppeln raced around the city in a small command car searching desperately for a clear road for his tanks while encountering thousands of French people who were desperate to get out of town before the bombing resumed. The panzer commander finally ordered his battalion commanders to pull their tanks out of the south end of Caen and detour around the city over narrow country roads that were still free of debris.

By late afternoon von Oppeln had shifted his panzers to the town of Lebisey, just north of Caen, and General Marcks drove to that point to supervise the counterattack. The corps commander had just received a call from army headquarters in Germany that released the 12th SS Panzer and Panzer Lehr Divisions to join the offensive, but it was now 4 P.M. and these units were too far away to have an impact on the battle on June 6. Marcks climbed a hill beyond town where von Oppeln had formed his regiment and counted a total of ninety-eight tanks ready for offensive operations. While the Germans could deploy over fifteen hundred tanks on the Western Front, the success or failure of their first counterattack would depend on fewer than one hundred panzers and the crews who manned them. Marcks limped over to his regimental commander and said softly, "Oppeln, if you don't succeed in throwing the British into the sea we shall have lost the war!" The young colonel was already famous in the Reich for his medal-winning exploits in equestrian events in the 1936 Olympics and he could sense the drama of the movement. He uttered a simple response, "General, I shall attack now; I intend to do my best," and acknowledged his superior's exhortation to "press on to the coast."

Reports from the front revealed that the Germans continued to hold a number of strongpoints on the coast between Luc sur Mer and Lion sur Mer near the seam between Juno and Sword Beaches. Marcks's plan was to use von Oppeln's tanks and the mobile riflemen of 192nd Panzer Grenadier Regiment to link up with the German units remaining on the coast and use their strongpoints as pivots for attacks on the British and Canadian flanks. This plan began to gain some dividends when a column of half-tracks carrying panzergrenadiers charged directly onto the beach near Lion and the company commander sent a dramatic confirmation that "we've made it!" The grenadiers dug in around the beach and waited for the tanks to arrive to begin an attack on the vulnerable Allied flanks.

Meanwhile, Colonel von Oppeln had divided his modest force into armored columns that would lunge for the high ground at Periers and Bieville, capture a series of key ridges, and then begin a downhill thrust toward the sea. However, the panzer colonel must have had his confidence severely tested when he encountered the commander of the 716th Division, General Wilhelm Richter, leading a retreat of remnants of his units away from the coast. Von Oppeln insisted that Richter was "almost demented with grief" as tears filled his eyes he exclaimed, "My troops are lost. My whole division is finished!" When von Oppeln suggested that his tanks might yet turn the tide, the division commander just shook his head and insisted that the day was lost.

One column of panzers rumbled across the fields toward the British defenders holding recently captured Hill 61. Unknown to the Germans, the Tommies had turned the ridge into a killing ground bristling with 17-pounder antitank guns supported by a group of Sherman Fireflies that featured upgraded weapons far more lethal than their conventional counterparts. The German tanks had to advance over rising ground featuring very little cover while the British vehicles and guns were deployed on high ground that dominated the area. Ten minutes of vicious action proved which side had the advantage as thirteen German tanks exploded or caught fire and the survivors backpedaled to get clear of the deadly crossfire. A short distance away another panzer formation rumbled up the rise at Bieville and faced another torrent of fire from a mix of Shermans and antitank guns that seemed to be virtual phantoms. Enemy fire was coming from several directions at once and one by one five Panzer IVs blew up with no discernible damage to the British.

A little further west, Captain Wilhelm von Gothberg was leading a column of thirty-five of von Oppeln's tanks toward a ridge outside of the town of Periers. The British defenders watched the panzers approach the ridge in the fading late spring twilight and commanders of antitank batteries dropped their arms and ordered their gunners to shoot. Within ten minutes of furious firing, ten panzers were left burning furiously and von Gothberg ordered a rapid fallback to save his now badly mauled command, an action that was now occurring all along the line between Periers and Bieville. The panzergrenadiers watched twilight turn to night from their positions on the beach and continued to wait in vain for their tanks to appear over the nearby dunes. As darkness engulfed the Germans holding onto strongpoints along the beach there was still enormous optimism that the panzers would arrive at first light. However, they now shared Sword Beach with over 29,000 British soldiers who were busy landing their own tanks and guns at a furious pace in preparation for a D+1 that would offer little let up in the violence and confusion.

CHAPTER XI

The Road to Villers-Bocage

During the early morning hours of June 7, 1944, leaders of Allied and German forces reviewed the first twenty-four hours of the Normandy invasion and considered their options for future operations. Eisenhower, Montgomery, and Bradley were encouraged by the fact that over 150,000 troops had been landed with generally lower than expected casualties. A total of 6,500 Americans, 3,000 Britons, and 1,000 Canadians had become casualties on D-Day and included just under 2,500 killed in action. The Allies had advanced as far as six or seven miles inland in several places and now held a reasonably defendable, if not yet continuous, front from a point above Carentan to Ouistreham. British ground units had linked up with their airborne counterparts east of Caen and Americans driving inland from Utah Beach were beginning to converge with paratroopers operating on the Contentin Peninsula. However, there were two gaps in the Allied line that provided inviting targets for German counterattacks. The extreme left flank of the Omaha beachhead was not fully connected to the British flank on Gold Beach, and there also remained a wide gap at the mouth of the Vire River between the American V Corps and VII Corps. While most senior Allied commanders were cautiously optimistic about the general state of affairs on D+1, they were bracing for what seemed to be an inevitable German riposte and they did not know exactly when or where the formidable panzer reserves would make their first significant appearance on the battlefield.

On the other hand, the German High Command had been surprised by the timing and location of the Allied landings and there was a wide divergence of opinion regarding the long-term impact of the invasion. General Erich Marcks, commander of the frontline forces of the LXXXIV Corps, was convinced that Normandy was the main Allied landing site and that the best that could be expected was a holding action to keep the line from crumbling. Field Marshal Rommel, who had gone back to Germany for a meeting with Hitler and to celebrate his wife's birthday, seemed unsure as to whether Normandy was the main invasion or not but he asked the high command for the bulk of available divisions in Brittany and the Channel Islands to be deployed in Normandy in order to have some prospect of delivering a major counterblow to the invaders. Finally, Hitler seemed almost jubilant at the news of the landings. He smiled and chuckled to his entourage, "The news couldn't be better. As long as they were in Britain we couldn't get at them. Now we have them where we can destroy them." Despite these substantial differences of opinion all three men agreed that the Allied beachhead must be liquidated as soon as possible and the key to securing that victory would be the power behind the armored divisions that were either in Normandy or were in striking distance of that region.

Two examples of the young, energetic officers that the German High Command depended upon to drive the Allies back into the sea

Once it was clear that the long-awaited Allied invasion was taking place, German units rushed to reinforce the Normandy front.

were Colonel Kurt "Panzer" Meyer and Captain Michael Wittmann. Both of these men would play an enormous role in the struggle between the Allies and Germans for control of Caen in the first week of Overlord. Kurt Meyer was a thirty-three-year-old SS officer who had become a member of Hitler's bodyguard regiment despite having to wear orthopedic shoes due to a severe injury as a child. By 1944 he had been decorated in France, Greece, and the Soviet Union for heroism under fire. In Greece, when his soldiers had seemed reluctant to attack enemy machine guns, he had rolled live hand grenades from behind in order to encourage them to keep charging. Now he commanded a regiment in one of the most ruthless, fanatical units of the German armed forces, the 12th SS Hitler Youth Division. This force was a potent mixture of the teenaged young toughs of the Hitler Jugend movement and non-coms and officers sent over from the elite Leibstandarte Division, which served as the Führer's bodyguard. Meyer was a swaggering, arrogant Nazi fanatic who also happened to have great tactical skill and almost no sense of personal fear and he was at the head of elite troops armed with the best weapons the Third Reich could produce. He would quickly get an opportunity to display his skills against the invaders.

On the morning of June 7, Meyer found himself in command of Battlegroup Meyer, a composite force of three battalions of his own 25th SS Panzergrenadier Regiment and a battalion of the division's Panzer IV tanks. His force was to be paired off with the 21st Panzer Division on his right and the two units were expected to drive side by side until they reached the invasion beaches and then wreak havoc on the disembarking Allies. A little before noon Meyer climbed to the top of one of the turrets of Ardenne Abbey, which overlooked Caen from the west, and carefully surveyed the ground over which he would launch his attack. General Fritz Witte, commanding officer of the Hitler Youth Division, had given Meyer a terse order that "the Division will attack the disembarked enemy together with 21st Panzer Division and throw him back into the sea!" Meyer carefully focused his fieldglasses on a panorama that almost looked like the scenery of a model train layout with its perfectly spaced roads, orchards, fields, and villages. He could see the distant channel shore where ships were unloading men and equipment under the cover of dozens of barrage balloons floating in the sky, carrying steel cables to protect the fleet and beaches from low-flying German planes.

As Meyer maneuvered his glasses to the right and left he suddenly detected enemy tanks nosing their way forward through an orchard about two hundred yards away. Then he spotted an advance force of North Nova Scotia Highlanders pushing through a tall field of wheat, apparently oblivious to the danger in front of them.

Meyer's panzergrenadiers were carefully concealed behind a series of hedges fronting the abbey while Lieutenant Colonel Max Wünsche was standing in the hatch of his armored car, ready to unleash a force of tanks that were deployed inside the abbey grounds and on a rearward slope near the road. The somewhat startled Meyer quickly picked up his field telephone and called down to Wünsche ordering him to hold his fire until the Canadians approached closer. It became obvious that the plan for a slightly later offensive was now useless and the SS colonel sent a dispatch rider to 21st Panzer head-quarters requesting an immediate coordinated attack of both units. Then Meyer uttered the single word "Attack!" into his phone and Wünsche signaled, "Attention! Tanks advance!"

The Highlanders and their supporting armor of the 27th Tank Regiment were advancing toward the Caen-Bayeux highway headed for Carpiquet and its valuable airfield. However their drive halted abruptly as tank after tank burst into flames and then the black-clad teenagers of Meyer's regiment charged through the wheatfields and engaged the Canadians in furious hand-to-hand combat. The High-landers were no less eager for a brawl than the panzergrenadiers and a bloody shootout erupted up and down the line. However, in this first phase of the battle the Germans had surprise on their side and the tough Nova Scotians were forced to backpedal toward the nearby vil-lage of Authie while Meyer's troops snapped up the rear guard as prisoners. Many of these captives never saw the inside of a P.O.W. camp as the young toughs dressed in black uniforms promptly dragged nearly two dozen Highlanders back to the abbey and shot them all in cold blood, an action that would be repeated several times in the next few days. The eighteen- and nineteen-year-old troops of the Hitler Jugend now emerged as the most detested unit among the Allies of the whole Normandy campaign.

While his panzergrenadiers were pushing through the wheat-fields, Meyer charged down the turret steps and climbed on his favorite command vehicle, a high-performance motorcycle. As he roared over the roads and fields urging his tanks and riflemen for-ward, the charging SS troops suddenly came within range of the awe-some spectacle of a perfectly coordinated Canadian artillery barrage which ripped through the black-uniformed ranks like avenging scythes. Then a newly arrived formation of the Sherbrooke Fusiliers mounted a ferocious counterattack that sent the stunned Germans reeling back through the fields as one battalion commander slumped over with a fatal wound and several company commanders dropped from lesser injuries. As one admiring British soldier exclaimed as he watched the bloody confrontation, "the strength of the Canadian army is as close in fighters. They go at it like hockey players." When Meyer received word that the 21st Panzer's attack had also bogged down in front of the town of Epron, he reluctantly broke off the action and pulled his surviving troops back to the abbey. He was convinced that help was on its way and the next day would bring a far better outcome.

Early the next morning, Thursday, June 8, General Bernard Montgomery disembarked from the HMS *Faulknor* and set up his headquarters in a comfortable trailer parked near the town of Cruelly, while his staff set up a string of tents in the adjacent fields. The Allied ground forces commander was convinced that the Germans had been dealt a severe blow in the first two days of Overlord as "the speed, power and violence of the assault carried all before it." Montgomery was pleased that the Allied line was almost continuous and that forces were pushing inland relatively fast. However, he was worried that the proportionally high casualty toll among experienced officers would soon begin to disrupt the chain of command. He was also determined to avoid turning a struggle for Caen into a bloodbath of First World War proportions as he emphasized to one friend, "I have decided not to have a lot of casualties by butting up against the place so I have ordered Second Army to keep up a good pressure at Caen and then make its main effort towards Villers-Bocage and Evrecy and thence towards Falaise."

While the British general was convinced that it was vital to the morale of Allied troops that they should consider themselves to have as good weapons as the Germans, he was increasingly apprehensive about the qualitative advantages of enemy panzers over British and American tanks. Intelligence reports estimated that the Germans were deploying about eight hundred tanks in the Normandy region and of these eighty were powerful Tigers and two hundred and fifty more were formidable Panthers. Most of the Allied collection of Churchills, Cromwells, and Shermans simply could not match the best German tanks in any kind of equal engagement while the British still deployed a relatively limited number of upgunned Shermans Fireflies and the Americans did not have any of these upgraded models. Therefore, a major German counterattack against British defenders equipped with their 17-pounder antitank gun and a small force of Fireflies could spell trouble, and an enemy armored thrust against the Americans could end in disaster, at least for the moment.

Montgomery's Desert War nemeses, Erwin Rommel, spent the early morning of June 8 reestablishing his command presence at his La Roche Guyon headquarters after his breakneck journey back from the Reich. As the Desert Fox studied the situation maps, a number of attractive prospects seemed available to him. The American beach-heads were still relatively shallow and widely separated with a number of their most-advanced positions still held by lightly armed para-troopers. The troops holding the Omaha sector had been badly mauled on D-Day and there was a chance that the survivors might unravel in the face of a really determined panzer attack that could send Tigers and Panthers lumbering over the sand dunes onto the crowded beaches. However, the Utah-Omaha gap was over forty miles from the nearest major panzer units and an attack in that direction would leave the tenuously held defenses around Caen extremely vul-nerable to a British attack for several days while the armored regi-ments were absent. Therefore, Rommel and the commander of Panzer Group West agreed to send all three available armored divisions on a concentrated drive against the Allied beach positions between Bayeux and Caen. This plan offered the advantage of allowing the 21st Panzer Division, the Panzer Lehr Division, and the 12th SS Panzer Division to attack side by side while permitting at least some units to backtrack to Caen if the British threatened to break through the defense lines manned by remaining infantry and artillery units.

The recent arrival of General Fritz Bayerlein's Panzer Lehr Division gave the defenders a vital third armored unit to use in a counterattack, but this formation had been badly mauled in its trek into Normandy. Allied planes had left a grisly trail of burned out trucks, smoldering gun tractors, and dead soldiers in field-gray uni-forms for miles below the rendezvous point at Falaise. All but five tanks had survived the aerial gauntlet, but Bayerlein counted the destruction of forty fuel trucks, ninety supply trucks, and eighty-four half-tracks and self-propelled guns during the march. Vehicle losses of this magnitude would soon become a major feature of the German struggle to hold Normandy.

Late on this warm early summer afternoon, General Leo Geyr von Schweppenburg arrived at Ardenne Abby and climbed the steep steps to an upper turret already occupied by "Panzer" Meyer. Geyr was commanding general of Panzer Group West, a command directly responsible to Hitler and for most of the armored forces on the Western Front. Geyr was on hand to personally supervise a renewed attempt to use the panzers to break through to the channel coast and drive the Allies into the sea. Meyer had just returned from a violent localized engagement in which his panzergrenadiers had ambushed four companies of the Royal Winnipeg Rifles near the town of Putot on the Bayeux road. When the Canadians's advanced positions were overrun, the fanatic Nazi teenagers dragged nearly fifty prisoners back to headquarters and gunned them down almost to a man. Then a company of Panther tanks, accompanied by Meyer's ever-present motorcycle, charged into Bretteville and captured most of the town including the headquarters of the Regina Rifles. However, the surviving Canadians retreated to a final stronghold and blasted away with their antitank guns as the panzers clattered around in a huge circle, looking for a weak point to ram into the midst of the defenders. In a scene eerily reminiscent of Western movies of the era, the Canadians carefully picked off six of the Panthers and prompted Meyer to call off the attack until he could return with reinforcements. Now, as Meyer chronicled the bloody engagement for Geyr on the abby turret, the two discussed a much larger-scale operation scheduled for the next morning.

On the morning of June 9, the tanks of three panzer divisions clanked past their start points and began their thrust to the sea. The most successful initial penetration was accomplished by the 2nd Battalion of Panzer Lehr's tank regiment commanded by a member of the old German nobility, Prince Schonberg-Waldenburg. By late morning this aristocratic major's tanks were smashing into the town of Ellon while reconnaissance vehicles had pushed as far as Arganchy, only three miles from the center of Bayeux. As General Bayerlein arrived to coordinate the next phase of the assault, one of the company commanders assured him, "It's going to be all right Herr General. It looks as if we might run straight into the gap between the British and American sectors. With a little luck, we'll push through to the coast neatly between Yanks and Tommies and stop them from linking up."

At this point Major Waldenburg personally directed an advance over a stretch of undulating ground that led to the village of Audrieu and the Bayeux-Caen highway a few hundred yards beyond. However, in order to reach the main road, the panzers had to navigate through a narrow trail that wound through a densely wooded area. The tankers thought they had scored a major advantage when they

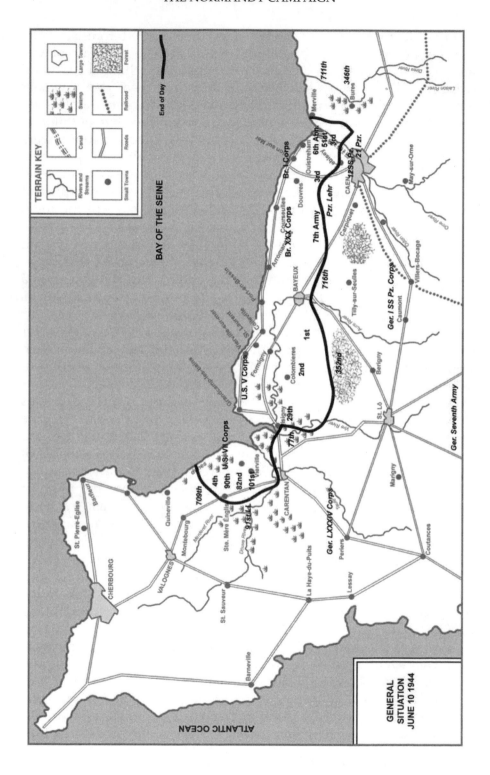

encountered well-camouflaged British positions that seemed to have been abandoned in haste at the approach of the Germans. However, as the Mark IVs lumbered further in the foliage, Allied artillery salvoes pierced the early summer stillness and tank after tank exploded into an orange fireball. Waldenburg was killed in the first salvo and when the Allied cannonfire was joined by shells from British tanks, the surviving second in command of the battalion ordered a fallback to more defendable ground.

Meanwhile, a powerful thrust by Canadian armored columns had checkmated another wing of the German advance and then sliced through a seam between the 12th SS Panzer and the Panzer Lehr in the area around the crossroads town of Tilly. Geyr and Rommel now reluctantly agreed that a thrust to the coast was at least temporarily out of the question and the surviving tanks would be better employed as anchors in a new defense line being formed around the outer suburbs of Caen. The German offensive was now sputtering out and Montgomery, who had been content to merely parry the enemy thrusts until he developed a better feel for the battle now prepared to launch a massive attack designed to take Caen from the flanks and rear.

Monty's basic plan was to follow up the check against the German armor with an advance from the Bayeux area to Tilly, followed by an attempt to gain the even more important crossroads town of Villers-Bocage which straddled one of the main approaches to Caen. While the Desert Rats of the 7th Armored Division maneuvered toward the university city from its western suburbs, the Highlanders of the 51st Division would move along the opposite periphery of Caen and cut off enemy access to all eastern roads. Finally, the 1st Airborne Division, still on call back in England, would be dropped south of the city and be used to link the flanks of the 7th and 51st Divisions in a huge three-sided envelopment. If all went well, the German garrison of Caen would be forced to capitulate and the city would then serve as a pivot for a combined Anglo-American drive to the Seine River.

The first major British thrust against Caen began with a devastating airstrike aimed at creating chaos in the German command structure. General Geyr had established an advance headquarters for Panzer Group West near the town of Thury-Harcourt, twelve miles south of Caen. Geyr and his senior officers had been installed in a comfortable chateau called la Caine while four radio trucks providing communications links for the headquarters were deployed in a nearby orchard. Allied intelligence units soon located the source of the transmissions and were able to pinpoint specifically the location of Panzer West headquarters. On the evening of June 10, squadrons of rocket firing Typhoons and B-26 medium bombers suddenly appeared over the villa and began pulverizing the headquarters and the nearby vehicles. Geyr and one staff officer escaped but with serious injuries while the chief of staff and most of the other senior officers were killed and all of the radio equipment was destroyed. Thus just as the British offensive was about to begin, Panzer Group West virtually ceased to function and command temporarily fell on General Sepp Dietrich, senior officer of I SS Panzer Corps. Dietrich, who had begun his career as a Nazi street brawler and Hitler bodyguard, suddenly found himself in effective command of German armor in Normandy yet holding a rank far below Rommel and von Rundstedt. The RAF raid had inflicted a serious handicap on the functioning of the German chain of command.

While German senior officers scrambled to patch up their command network, two important elements of Montgomery's plan unraveled almost immediately. First, Air Chief Marshal Leigh-Mallory refused to allocate the transport aircraft required to drop the 1st Airborne Division into the region south of Caen, citing unwarranted hazards to his aircrews. Thus there would be no vital linking force joining the extreme right flank of the 7th Armored Division and the extreme left flank of the 51st Division in their quest to envelop Caen.

The second element of the offensive began to frazzle on June 11 when the advance units of the 51st Division began their left hook around the eastern side of Caen. The Highlanders made rapid early progress before the Germans were fully aware of the British plan. Then the Scots pushed through the small town of St. Honorine just in time to clash with Colonel Hans von Luck's powerful panzer force in the far side of the community. The energetic von Luck had been provided with a formidable task force in which his own battalions of tanks and grenadiers had been reinforced with three batteries of assault guns, an antitank company of 88mm guns, and a battalion of multiple rocket launchers capable of firing three hundred 21mm and 30mm rockets in a single nerve shattering barrage. Soon a wild battle was surging back and forth through town as the Highlanders and a reinforcement of Canadian infantry and tanks grappled with some of the best units in the German army. However, as the battle reached its climax, the British forces were able to call upon naval and air support that von Luck could only dream about from the Kriegsmarine and Luftwaffe. As the panzer commander insisted, "Thus began the heaviest naval bombardment we had known so far. We could see the firing of the battleships, cruisers and destroyers. The shells, of calibers up to 38 cm came whistling over like heavy trucks, to burst and rip vast craters in our line. British fighter-bombers swooped down on us unhindered; a veritable inferno broke over our heads." The Highlanders were able to hold onto St. Honorine, but they had suffered such severe losses that the offensive ground to a halt. The last hope for an early capture of Caen now remained in the hands of the Desert Rats of the 7th Armoured Division.

As the Highlanders and panzergrenadiers engaged in a slugging match over St. Honorine, Montgomery sensed that a new opportunity seemed to be emerging on the right flank. Allied intelligence believed it had found a weak spot in the enemy line west of the Aure River, about three miles west of the town of Tilly. If British infantry units could temporarily hold the Panzer Lehr Division in place, there was a good chance that the Desert Rats of the 7th Armoured Division could push through beyond the vital crossroads town of Villers-Bocage, outflank the enemy from the west, and punch a gaping hole in the German line. General Miles Dempsey, commander of the British Second Army, drove out to the headquarters of the 7th Armoured and ordered General George Erskine to disengage from the unit's current front and deploy every available tank and half-track to swoop down on Villers-Bocage before the Germans realized their peril.

Erskine was delighted with a plan that he had already promoted the previous day, and he immediately ordered Brigadier Robert Hinde to lead a powerful armored strike force in capturing the town and thrusting for Caen before the enemy panzers knew what hit them. Hinde commanded the 22nd Armoured Brigade which included the 4th County of London Yeomanry, also known as the Sharpshooters, two tank battalions of the Royal Tank Regiment, and a motorized infantry battalion, all veterans of El Alamein and confident of their ability to wrest an advantage over the Wehrmacht.

At 4 P.M. on June 12, leading elements of Hinde's force reached the Caumont-Villers-Bocage road five miles west of their objective and early the next morning a combined tank-infantry column stormed into town, overwhelmed a small force of German defenders, and established a headquarters post near the town square. The tankers and riflemen were pleasantly surprised by the exuberance of the local citizenry who had changed into their best clothes and thronged the streets to embrace their liberators. The capture of Villers-Bocage was an important coup as the town was the gateway to both the high ground of Mont Pincon to the south and the Odon valley and Caen itself to the

The German Mark IV medium tank was armed with an effective 75mm gun.

east. However, control of the town would be almost useless if the Tommies did not seize a nearby ridge northeast on the Caen-Villers-Bocage highway. Hinde quickly dispatched a strong force of tanks and half-tanks to seize Point 213 less than a mile away from the town square. The commander of the London Yeomanry, Lieutenant Colonel Arthur Cranley, left a headquarters section of four tanks to set up communications around the square while he led a force of over fifty vehicles toward the nearby ridge. Cranley, a British viscount, had received reports that German armored cars seemed to be lurking just beyond the ridge, and he decided to lead a reconnaissance force into the countryside while the bulk of the force parked along the side of the road and awaited further orders. However, as many of the tankers and riflemen clambered out of their hot vehicles and stretched their legs or sprawled under nearby trees, a lone German officer was carefully surveying the peaceful scene from the turret of his powerful Tiger tank.

Captain Michael Wittmann had emerged as the leading tank ace on the Eastern Front and had been transferred to France along with a company of Tigers from the 501st Heavy Tank Battalion that was deployed to reinforce the regular panzer units operating in Normandy. On this hazy, warm June day Wittmann commanded a small but potentially deadly contingent of four Tigers and one upgraded Mark IV Special and was under orders to scout the area around Villers-Bocage and do anything possible to deter the British advance toward the Odon until reinforcements could arrive. Fearing Allied air strikes, Wittmann had deployed most of his command in a nearby woods and set out in a single tank to reconnoiter the road between Point 213 and town. He quickly discovered the British armored column emerging from Villers-Bocage and realized that this powerful force could strike the largely unguarded flank of the Panzer Lehr before that unit fully appreciated the danger. However, Wittmann was also fascinated by the lack of security around the British vehicles that seemed to be almost inviting German ambush. He agreed with his gunner who insisted, "They're acting as if they've won the war already!" The tank ace responded softly, "We're going to prove them wrong."

Wittmann found himself in a serious quandary. He was only eighty yards away from a totally unsuspecting enemy force and could easily launch an attack before the British could respond. However, the remaining four tanks of his unit were still some distance away and could not provide any immediate support. The obersturmfuhrer decided to risk an immediate attack although outnumbered nearly fifty to one and he calmly initiated one of the most spectacular five-minute periods of World War II. Wittmann maneuvered his Tiger along a narrow cart track that paralleled the main road but was separated from the highway by an extended line of hedges. Using this fence line for cover, Wittmann approached the lead vehicle of the British column and sent a shell crashing into the British half-track which promptly blocked any forward movement by the rest of the column. Then the German tanker roared along the hedges and poured shell after shell into a line of tanks and half-tracks that often had no drivers in the vehicle. As the startled British crews scrambled back to their vehicle, Wittmann's gunners methodically picked off each adversary in turn while machine guns sprayed deadly fire on the men attempting to return to the column.

The lone Tiger then roared back onto the main road when it reached the end of the British column and rammed a Cromwell that had driven out from the town to aid the threatened advance force. This British tank now became the last in a long line of burning vehicles as Wittmann lumbered down the road into Villers-Bocage itself. The quartet of headquarters tanks left behind by Colonel Cranley initiated a deadly duel with the oncoming Tiger but Wittmann's tank destroyed three adversaries in quick succession and sent the sole surviving

The Sherman "Firefly" had a superior 76.2mm gun, but was in short supply.

Cromwell scurrying into the cover of a nearby yard. However, as Wittmann stormed through the cobbled streets, his tank met its first serious opposition of the day. An upgunned Sherman Firefly commanded by Sergeant Stan Lockwood nosed around a street corner and slammed four 17-pounder shells into the Tiger's hull while Wittmann's gunner opened fire on the upper story of a nearby house and sent most of the building crashing down on Lockwood. Wittmann then maneuvered his slightly damaged Tiger out of town and linked up with the remainder of his unit to launch a new attack on Colonel Cranley's advance force scouting east of Point 213 on the road to Caen. The combined firepower of the five German tanks ripped through Cranley's undergunned force and the viscount and most of his men were captured and their vehicles destroyed.

Michael Wittmann had singlehandedly turned the course of the battle and demonstrated a remarkable feat of arms. The panzer commander had almost annihilated a column of twenty-five tanks and twenty-eight other vehicles and brought a potentially decisive British advance to a grinding halt. Only the brilliant antitank gunnery of a small number of London Yeomanry prevented an even worse debacle when the Sharpshooters staged a clever afternoon ambush in the town when Wittmann returned to Villers-Bocage with a powerful supporting force of newly arrived 2nd Panzer Division tanks. The cleverly concealed British defenders knocked out seven German tanks including Wittmann's and bought time for Hinde to initiate an orderly fallback toward more defendable high ground to the west. The destroyed British tanks and half-tracks could be easily replaced by the huge number of new vehicles coming ashore daily, but the Allies had lost a splendid opportunity to rip open the entire eastern flank of the German line and Montgomery and Dempsey were forced to search for a new key to enter the city of Caen. As the British generals studied their maps and prepared for a new operation, the hopes for an early tangible Allied success now shifted to the western end of Normandy and the GIs attempting to push inland from Utah and Omaha Beaches.

Genesis of the Waffen SS

Many of the bravest—and most fanatic—troops defending Normandy against the Allied invasion were members of the *Schutzstaffel* divisions, popularly know as the Waffen SS. This dark instrument of Nazi terror began in the early 1920s as the *Stosstrupp*, Adolf Hitler's bodyguard. Five members of this unit were killed during the future dictator's abortive coup of 1923. When Hitler emerged from prison in 1925 he changed the unit's name to *Schutzstaffel* (Defense Squad) and expanded its activities to include protection of party interests in each German city where the National Socialists had a presence.

As late as 1930 the whole SS only numbered three hundred men, but in that year Hitler placed the organization under the command of the man who would come to embody its terror, Heinrich Himmler. Himmler was a young middle-class Bavarian with a mild appearance and bookish glasses, but behind this façade was one of the most bloodthirsty imaginations of the twentieth century. The new SS commander was obsessed with racial superiority, eastward expansion, the cult of the superman, reading of runes, occult and magic arts, and back-to-the-land movements. The SS was increasingly transformed into Himmler's image and accepted volunteers who were not only physically fit, sober, trustworthy, and amenable to discipline, but also able to show untainted (non-Jewish or non-Slavic) ancestry for at least three generations.

During the next four years the *Schutzstaffel* functioned as a semi-autonomous component of the main Nazi paramilitary organization, the *Sturmabteilung* or SA. However unlike Himmler's organization, the SA under Ernst Röhm was a mass movement that its leader envisioned as the successor to the Reichswehr, the current German army. The SS was used by Hitler as a sort of party police force to keep the SA in line while the dictator made the transition to absolute power. Then, once the Führer's power was secured, Röhm and most of his senior lieutenants were murdered while the German army gave its tacit support for the "Night of the Long Knives."

The effective removal of the SA as a major force in 1934 opened up enormous oppportunities for Himmler and his own organization. The membership of the SS was now restricted to volunteers who could document "pure" blood as far back as the seventeenth century. The organization also split into two units, the *Totenhopfuerbande* which was the security element and the Waffen SS which was the more conventional military force. Himmler had convinced the Führer to make him chief of German police and he soon directed an intricate network including the Prussian Secret State Police, the Criminal Police, the ordinary uniformed police from the local districts, and the Gestapo, as well as a personal security service called the Sicherheitsdienst or SD. During the war Himmler expanded his operations to include the notorious extermination units, the *Einsatzgruppen,* and eventually the *Abwehr*, the Wehrmacht's counter-espionage service.

The more conventional military organization, the Waffen SS, had its origins in the Leibstandarte Adolf Hitler, the Führer's personal bodyguard, commanded by one of his old beer-hall cronies, Sepp Dietrich, who would become a corps commander during the Normandy campaign. While SS troops were often far more fanatic than the regular army personnel, their organization was actually much more in keeping with German military tradition. Hitler had deliberately reconstructed the army on a pattern which owed nothing to the past and made no differentiation between one unit and another since he wanted the new army to be wholly and entirely his own. This broke with the kaiser's army which had been built on the principle of strong unit identities and a hierarchy of regiments with the Guards at the top of the list. Himmler had a much better sense than the Führer that German soldiers really wanted to belong to an identifiable and elite formation and the SS commander obliged them by making substantial use of popular German historical memories for the titles of his divisions.

Units such as Hohenstaffen, Frundsberg, Prinz Eugen, Reich, and Leibstandarte were all reminders of either an important episode or hero of Germany's past. The oakleaf and acorn symbols on SS uniforms were emblematic of the First German Empire which Himmler wished to recreate. The Death's Head badge on headgear was the famous badge of four legendary regiments of the kaiser's army—the Brunswick Infantry, the 17th Regiment, and the 1st and 2nd Hussars. Thus while the SS was often seen by Allied commanders and soldiers as a group of bloodthirsty fanatics, a large number of Germans were drawn to the strong identity with the past that Himmler's organization offered them.

CHAPTER XII

The Fall of Fortress Cherbourg

The British drive on Caen may have produced less than spectacular results during the early days of the Normandy campaign but General Miles Dempsey's Second British Army continued to play an essential part in the Overlord plan as the thrusts toward that city induced the German High Command to deploy most available armor in that sector rather than the American zone to the west. This decision allowed General Omar Bradley's First United States Army to advance inland without encountering enemy armored counterattacks that would massively complicate an already difficult mission. Bradley's major units, the V Corps under Leonard Gerow and the VII Corps under Joseph Lawton Collins, were under orders to initiate a series of offensive operations that would link the Omaha and Utah Beaches by capturing the city of Carentan, thrust westward across the Cotentin Peninsula to the Atlantic Ocean to seal off that land mass from further German reinforcements, and wheel northward to besiege and then capture the vital port city of Cherbourg. The capture of that maritime center was the first significant objective of the Overlord operation as the city contained harbor facilities that seemed vital to any hope of launching a major drive toward the Seine and the heartland of the Reich in the foreseeable future.

The Allies had already scored a major technological coup when they transported major elements of a harbor and then constructed two artificial harbors on the invasion beaches. These mechanical marvels code-named "Mulberries" allowed the Allies the luxury of an initial

In a mission code-named Mulberry, large concrete caissons were built and floated into position where they were sunk in order to create breakwater and an artificial harbor for the follow-up landings of the men and equipment that would be needed for the invasion of France.

The harbor at the port town of Cherbourg, shown here in an aerial photograph, was considered vital to Allied success in the Normandy campaign.

landing at a point so far from a major port that the Germans had not fortified the five invasion beaches to the same extent as more likely landing sites near major harbors. However, these man-made ports were vulnerable to the capricious storms that popped up in the English Channel and their facilities were not extensive enough to cope with the sheer mass of cargo that was expected to be landed as the campaign progressed. Therefore, the Allies needed a major port as quickly as possible and Cherbourg was the most likely candidate.

Cherbourg sprawled over several miles of seafront at the top of the Cotentin Peninsula, about thirty miles north of Carentan which marked the divide between the Utah and Omaha invasion sectors. During the early months of 1944 the port was defended by two German divisions but Hitler began to suspect an Allied attack in the area and quickly rushed two additional divisions to the peninsula with contingency plans to add several more crack units if the threat proved real. The American GIs who had survived the D-Day landings were now about to face German units deployed in some of the most advantageous defensive terrain in the history of warfare. Crack units such as the 3rd Parachute Division and the 17th SS Panzergrenadier Division were deploying between St. Mère Église and Carentan and preparing to utilize their powerful weaponry to block the American advance. These first-rate units were equipped with almost ten times as many automatic weapons as a typical American infantry division and also had access to a wide variety of mortars and deadly Panzerfaust antitank weapons that were far more effective than either American bazookas or British Piats.

This formidable array of weapons was matched by the imposing ground on which the defenders were deployed. While the advancing British forces were encountering alternating belts of hedges and open fields in their thrust toward Caen, the heart of the hedgerow country of Normandy was actually more in the American zone of operations. The bocage region around Carentan, St. Lô, and much of the Cotentin Peninsula featured hedges four to six feet high crisscrossed by sunken lanes and roads that allowed the Germans to move from hedgerow to hedgerow largely undetected by the Americans. The standard German procedure was to deploy machine guns in the angles where two fields met so each gun had two fields of fire. Almost every sunken road concealed powerful mortar units that were almost impossible to detect and destroy by American artillery or airplanes. The defenders deployed panzerfaust units along each of the narrow country lanes and threatened to take a terrible toll of the lightly armored Shermans that attempted to support the advancing American infantry. The defensive power of the hedgerows in the Cotentin area was interspersed with both natural and man-made swampland that channeled almost all American advances down a limited number of causeways that were almost always carefully pre-sited by German mortar and machine-gun teams. As Brigadier General Norman Cota, one of the heroes of D-Day, recalled, "What held us up at first was that we originally were organized to assault the beach, suffered a lot of casualties among key men, then hit another kind of warfare for which we were not organized."

The dreadful initiation to the "battle of the bocage" began only hours after the first American troops advanced past the sand dunes into the interior of the Normandy countryside. On Wednesday, June 7, elements of General Matthew Ridgway's 82nd Airborne Division tried to establish a foothold on the western side of the Merderet River, one of the major barriers to an advance toward Barneville and the Atlantic coast of the Cotentin Peninsula. However, the river could only be crossed on a low causeway running near the village of La Fiere, a town

The streets of St. Mère Église were nearly deserted after the 82nd Airborne occupied the town in the days immediately following June 6.

After the D-Day landings, the men of the U.S. 101st Airborne Division, "the Screaming Eagles," continued their assault in France, encountering Germans in nearly every village they entered.

bristling with German artillery batteries. All day long Ridgway's troops tried to rush down the causeway to the other side but German guns mauled each new assault force before the far side could be secured. Finally, on Thursday morning, 4th Division tanks and assault guns arrived at the causeway and provided a covering barrage for a new crossing attempt led by General James Gavin, assistant division commander of the 82nd. Ridgway and Gavin continually exposed themselves to enemy fire as they personally led small units of paratroopers across the causeway into the teeth of the German defenses. While both senior officers miraculously survived the gauntlet of shells and bullets, the carnage began to take on First World War proportions as relatively few GIs survived the sprint across unscathed. Finally, as Ridgway fed enough units into the battle to gain overwhelming numerical superiority, the defenders melted away into the hedges and the Americans scored a significant, if dreadfully costly, victory.

The men of the other American airborne division, the 101st, soon faced a similar trial by combat as they approached the outskirts of Carentan, the key to linking Utah and Omaha Beaches. The town straddled Route 13, the road that would connect the two American invasion sectors if it could be seized from the elite defenders of the

German 6th Parachute Regiment. The crack Luftwaffe troops had established a series of strongpoints in the formidable stone farmhouses that loomed above the hedgerows and causeways. Lieutenant Colonel Robert Cole, the 29-year-old commander of the 3rd Battalion of the 502nd Parachute Infantry, drew the unenviable task of seizing a causeway over the Douve River on the outskirts of Carentan then capturing a large farmstead that controlled access to the road into town. When the American paratroopers advanced over the road that stood about three feet over the marshes, German defenders concealed in a nearby hedgerow opened fire with automatic weapons and mortars and forced dozens of GIs to hug the ground for cover. As Cole watched his command being annihilated, he ordered his men to fix bayonets and charge. As the young colonel waved his pistol and screamed encouragement, dozen of GIs screamed at the top of their lungs and plunged into trenches that connected to the hedgerows. The German paratroopers dropped dozens of attackers, but not quite enough to stop the growing momentum and the surviving Americans reorganized for a thrust at the farmhouses.

The farm was located in a large orchard and was surrounded by a vast network of hedges that provided excellent cover for the Luftwaffe defenders. Several American attacks were thrown back with heavy losses on both sides as an old cider store between the farm and the outskirts of Carentan filled up with over one thousand wounded American and German paratroopers. Two American medical officers who were captured during the battle joined a team of Luftwaffe physicians in dealing with the overflow numbers that crept steadily higher in the see-saw battle. Finally, Cole organized another massive bayonet attack that captured most of the outbuildings while his counterpart, Colonel Friedrich von der Heydte, cobbled together a last ditch stand at the main farmhouse which he hoped to hold until nightfall. Colonel von der Heydte turned down a polite surrender proposal from 101st Airborne commander General Maxwell Taylor, asking the American general in English, "What would you do in my place?"

The surviving German paratroopers were able to use the cover of darkness to backpedal into Carentan where they began to link up with newly arriving units from the equally elite 17th SS Panzergrenadier Division. The mix of Luftwaffe and SS troops established a strongpoint around Carentan's railroad depot. The Germans even managed to launch a spirited counterattack that pushed the 101st Screaming Eagles back through the cobbled streets of town. Then, at this moment of crisis, Brigadier General Anthony McAuliffe, the artillery com-

German prisoners were made to dig the graves of their fallen comrades while their American captors of the 101st Airborne stood guard.

mander of the 101st, demonstrated the initiative that would make him a hero later in the year in the defense of Bastogne. McAuliffe organized a mixed force of paratroopers and newly arrived Sherman tanks from the 2nd Armored Division in a desperate stand against the onrushing Germans and forced them back toward the railroad station. Finally, General Ostendorff, commander of the 17th SS Panzergrenadiers, decided that his surviving troops were doomed if they remained in Carentan any longer and ordered his men back to the relative safety of the extensive hedgerows beyond the town. Meanwhile, as the German paratroopers and panzergrenadiers were evacuating Carentan, the senior officer in the region, General Erich Marcks, commander of LXXXIV Corps, was killed by Allied fighter-bombers while driving to the front lines. Thus on the morning of June 12 the Utah and Omaha beachheads were finally linked and a full-scale offensive against Cherbourg could begin against an enemy that had just lost one of its most talented leaders.

The linkage of Omaha and Utah set in motion a huge, complex operation in which the VII Corps's thrust toward the Atlantic Ocean and then Cherbourg was incorporated with an advance of the V Corps

The first significant French town captured by the Allies after the D-Day landings was Carentan, finally taken on June 12, 1944.

toward the Vire River city of St. Lô which was seen as the launching pad for an American breakout from Normandy into the heartland of France. Each American offensive soon ran into serious obstacles as the GIs collided with German defenders who made maximum use of their weapons and terrain.

The 29th Division of Leonard Gerow's V Corps quickly captured its first major objective, the small town of Isigny on the Aure River, and in the process mauled several battalions of the German 352nd Division. However, Major General Dietrich Kraiss, the 352nd commanding officer, initiated a skillful series of withdrawals from the Aure River to the Elle River, seven miles north of St. Lô. Kraiss was desperate to buy enough time for the arrival of elements of the 275th and 353rd Infantry Divisions and the 3rd Parachute Division which were all on their way on a nearly two hundred-mile trek from the far reaches of the Brittany Peninsula to the front lines of Normandy. Each division commander elected to use the limited supply of available vehicles to send two or three battalions to aid Kraiss and then rush trucks back to Brittany to transport the next echelon of reinforcements.

Meanwhile, Kraiss's men did everything in their power to hold the Americans at bay until these powerful new units arrived to tip the balance back in the Germans's favor.

The first hint of German resilience occurred during the early morning hours of June 10 about two miles north of the Elle River. The 2nd Battalion of the U.S. 115th Regiment had spent most of the night on a forced march that found the unit in the small hamlet of Le Carrefour at 2:00 A.M. Their commander, Lieutenant Colonel William Warfield, allowed his unit to halt for the night and the utterly exhausted men stumbled into an adjoining field and dropped in exhaustion. Unfortunately, Warfield failed to implement the standard army practice of digging foxholes before bedding down and the GIs simply slumped against hedgerows without even removing their knapsacks. As the weary Americans slept, Germans from the 352nd Division discovered the vulnerability of the battalion and crept stealthily forward, surrounded the fields, and set up mortars and machine guns behind every available hedgerow. Three mobile assault guns maneuvered into firing position and at the firing of a signal flare opened a furious barrage on the startled Americans. In twenty minutes of sheer terror, machine guns picked off GIs before they could reach for their rifles and mortar shells burst among groups of scrambling troops. As the Americans were hit, they tumbled back against the hedgerows in growing heaps while German snipers popped up from a hedge, fired their rifles, disappeared, and reappeared behind another hedge while the defenders fired wildly at phantom targets. A few intrepid bazooka teams managed to knock out the enemy assault guns, but the Germans destroyed the American command structure when they launched a bayonet attack against a farmhouse that Warfield was using for a command post and cut down the colonel and most of his staff as they attempted to retreat from the back door of the building. Fifty Americans were dead, one hundred wounded, scores captured, and the battalion virtually ceased to exist as a fighting unit. Two hours later four survivors staggered into General Cota's headquarters and brought the appalling news of the disaster. While other survivors continued to straggle in after daylight, the drive for St. Lô had suffered a severe check that was about to be followed by an even bloodier setback.

The Germans, flush with the excitement of their one-sided victory at Le Carrefour, leapfrogged back to the next defendable position, the south bank of the Elle River. General Charles Gerhardt, commander of the U.S. 29th Division rushed in dozens of replacements to fill the empty positions in the 115th Regiment and ordered a renewed advance to the town of St. Marguerite, just north of the Elle. However, while the men of the 29th Division spent most of June 11 waiting for the arrival of massive artillery reinforcements that were to be used to support the impending river crossing, Kraiss left a small screening force on the south bank and deployed the remainder of his men in a cleverly constructed new defense line of hedgerows, slit trenches, and dugouts. On the morning of June 12 an American barrage that looked like a re-enactment of World War I bombardments dramatically boosted the assault troops' morale, but did little damage to the main German positions. As the assault companies of the 1st Battalion streamed out of St. Marguerite, unit after unit of German machine guns deployed on the south bank opened a devastating hailstorm of fire which killed or wounded over one hundred GIs before the men even reached their crossing site. The 3rd Battalion, attempting to cross a half mile further east, slammed into the main German mortar positions which produced the same deadly result. Lieutenant Joseph Binkoski of Company M noted that "Captain Fowler and I headed for a sunken road which ran parallel to the river which was to be the line of departure for the attack. When we got down there we found a ghastly sight. Littered over some twenty yards of this road were the badly mangled bodies of our dead and wounded. The medics were on hand immediately doing what they could when the Captain and I came across the body of Captain Hille, the commanding office of Company K, surrounded by a pool of blood."

While most of the American assault units were stopped short of the riverbank, two companies managed to get across the Elle and advanced almost two miles southward while assuming that their counterparts in other battalions were making similar progress. The jubilant GIs pushed into the village of Les Fresnes only to realize they had walked into a trap as German mortars and howitzers pulverized the town and threatened to annihilate the entire force. As the Americans backpedaled toward the river, newly arrived German reinforcements smashed into the flanks and rear of the badly shaken troops. The Germans pursued relentlessly, sensing that they might kill or capture the whole force. The path of retreat was littered with hundreds of discarded knapsacks, weapons, and radios while dozens of badly wounded soldiers were left behind in the rout. Another 130 GIs were added to the mounting casualty toll of the day and the Germans waited eagerly to checkmate the next American attempt to cross the Elle.

The setbacks at Le Carrefour and the Elle River convinced Omar Bradley that the capture of St. Lô was of less immediate importance than the ability of the V Corps to prevent an enemy flank attack on the VII Corps troops advancing across the Cotentin Peninsula. Bradley had issued orders three days earlier for General Collins to use the 82nd and 9th Infantry Divisions to cut off the Cotentin at its neck while the 4th and 90th Infantry Divisions pushed on abreast toward Barneville on the Atlantic coast of the peninsula. Unfortunately, this operation began to unravel when the 90th Division floundered badly in its first operation of the war.

This newly arrived division had come to England under the command of General Jay MacKelvie, a professional artillery officer who had been named to lead the unit only days before the men had embarked from the United States. The new commander found himself saddled with a job for which he had not been trained and a division with far too many officers who could not properly read a map or did not have any idea how to motivate the men under them. When the 90th went into action on June 10 they were ordered to expand the 82nd Airborne's bridgehead over the Merderet River using the 357th and 358th Regiments to make a cautious advance toward Barneville and the Atlantic coast. However, soon after the operation began units of the 90th Division found themselves in a ferocious firefight throughout the orchards and hedgerows of the region. Then it became shockingly

After landing at Utah Beach, soldiers marched inland to secure planned positions. These troops of the 90th Infantry Division marched inland and took part in the battle of Cherbourg a few days after landing.

171

apparent that the "enemy" troops were actually units from the American 325th Glider Regiment as MacKelvie's men had become lost and attacked a friendly force. When the American regiments finally located the *real* enemy, the attack was poorly coordinated and listless and the Texas and Oklahoma draftees watched their leaders attempting to fight a World War I battle that culminated in disastrous charges against the far better deployed men of the German 91st Division. MacKelvie and two of his regimental commanders controlled the battle from command posts filled with color-coded maps in which staff officers distributed an endless supply of crayons while the frontline units were being mauled by a largely unseen enemy that was enormously talented in small-unit tactics.

Finally, on June 13, Bradley fired MacKelvie and two of his regimental commanders and relegated the division to a flank guard while Collins paired the 82nd Airborne with the better-trained 9th Infantry Division for the drive on Barneville and Cherbourg. This maneuver paid quick dividends as an advance unit found a lightly defended approach to the Douve River, the last important barrier to the Atlantic coast of the Cotentin. General Ridgway rushed two regiments forward to secure a bridgehead there while units of General Manton Eddy's 9th Division prevented the Germans from rushing significant reinforcements to the ruptured point in their line. The regiments of Eddy's command soon found themselves in a furious battle with part of the German 77th Division which was fighting desperately to keep the Americans from reaching the Atlantic and cutting the peninsula in two. Finally, German commanders became more interested in saving their units than holding an unraveling line and on the morning of June 18 advance units of the 9th Division entered Barneville and prepared to wheel ninety degrees toward the major prize on the peninsula, the port of Cherbourg.

General Bradley now had six divisions available for the operations on the Cotentin and he realigned his forces to use the two airborne divisions and the 90th Division to face south and deal with any German counterattack while the 4th, 9th, and 79th Divisions were faced northward toward Cherbourg. The First Army commander believed that because the 82nd and 101st Airborne Divisions were now badly understrength because of the intensity of their operations and the 90th Division was disheartened, these units would be better utilized in a largely defensive role in which for once they could use the notorious hedgerows to their advantage. Thus these units were placed under the command of General Troy Middleton's newly operational

VIII Corps while the remaining three divisions would fight under Collins's VII Corps banner.

Collins split the upper half of the Cotentin into three north-south alleys and assigned the 4th Division to advance on the right, the 79th Division in the center, and the 9th Division on the left. At dawn on Monday, June 19, the great offensive against Cherbourg began and the city that had served as the transatlantic gateway to France and the home of spectacular oceanliners now became a grim and bloody battlefield. Adolf Hitler presented the attackers with a major strategic present when he ordered Cherbourg's commander, General Karl von Schlieben, to contest the advance in the countryside, far beyond the formidable defenses of the port. This demand allowed Collins to utilize massive air and armor support in a region that had more open fields and fewer hedgerows than the lower part of the peninsula. Thus the Germans were forced into a grueling, costly battle that gradually whittled down their ability to contest the American advance.

The frustrating nature of the German tactics was typified by the experience of Major Friedrich Kupper, commander of Artillery Group Montebourg which provided fire support for the infantry units defending the left flank of von Schlieben's line. Kupper had deployed five batteries of guns in an area between Quineville and Montebourg and then fronted the positions with several batteries of smaller anti-tank guns. When the first assault units of General Barton's 4th Division advanced through the fields and orchards of the Channel side of the Cotentin, Kupper's masterfully camouflaged guns initially took a heavy toll of the attackers. However, the covering screen of German infantry that was assigned to protect Kupper's guns was too small to cover the whole line. Thus the artillery officer recalled, "I ordered concentrated fire on all enemy penetration points and found that the artillery bombardment at least temporarily slowed the American advance." However, the GIs probed each part of the line relentlessly and eventually found a weak point. Then a stream of Sherman tanks penetrated the defenses and sent the outnumbered German defenders scrambling for the rear. Only the intervention of heavy thunderstorms allowed Kupper to withdraw his men toward Cherbourg while leaving many of the precious guns behind to be captured.

As each successive German defense line was overrun and large numbers of defenders and their weapons were captured, von Schlieben began deploying his four remaining reasonably intact regiments in a wide arc around the city. The 922nd Grenadier Regiment

On the drive to Cherbourg, many French villages and small towns were badly damaged from the fighting, as was this town, Valognes, which lost its church to bombs.

was assigned to hold the Jobourg Peninsula and the strongpoint of Westeck; the 919th Grenadier Regiment covered the left flank of the 922nd; the 739th Grenadier Regiment was assigned to hold the center fronting the city itself; and the 729th Grenadier Regiment was deployed in the area around Cape Levy west of the town. The nerve center of the garrison was an underground tunnel complex in the

174

town of Octeville which included von Schlieben's headquarters and facilities for Admiral Hennecke, German naval commander of Normandy. In a scene reminiscent of the Japanese siege of Bataan and Corregidor just over two years earlier, hundreds of staff workers, nurses, Luftwaffe ground staff, naval personnel, and civilian construction workers inhabited hot, poorly ventilated subterranean galleries, attempting to defend a fortress that seemed doomed to fall because reinforcements could not penetrate the enemy cordon. As lights flickered during American air raids and the air-conditioning system wheezed to a halt, this flotsam and jetsam of a doomed garrison prepared for the inevitable final assault against Fortress Cherbourg.

As Collins brought forward every cannon and tank at his disposal, the Allied navy maintained pressure on the Germans through a massive naval bombardment led by the USS *Texas* and the HMS *Glasgow*. Then once the land batteries were adding their weight of steel against the German defenses, assault companies from the 9th and 79th Divisions converged on Fort de Roule which dominated the southern approaches to Cherbourg and looked down on the city itself. The fort's defenders faced the same impossible situation as the British defenders of Singapore when the Japanese attacked in 1942. The fort's heavy guns were all positioned to repel a seaborne attack and it was virtually impossible to reposition them. Thus huge 150mm guns remained silent as the GIs scrambled toward the walls of the fort and engaged in a wild firefight with the defenders as they climbed over the ramparts.

The only tangible support that von Schlieben received from outside the siege lines was several boxes of Iron Crosses which the Luftwaffe parachuted into the embattled city in lieu of fighter-bomber support. The German commander freely distributed the coveted medals to individuals who were at least slowing, if not entirely halting, the American advance. While the general began issuing rifles to clerks, sailors, and construction workers, Hitler radioed the command bunker and ordered von Schlieben to "fight the battle as Gneisenau once fought in the defense of Colberg," a reference to one of the epic engagements of the Prussians against the might of Napoleon. By Sunday, June 25, von Schlieben's paneled headquarters was covered with maps that showed the Americans completely encircling his last line of strongpoints. He sent a report to Rommel that "enemy superiority in material and enemy domination of the air is overwhelming. Most of our own batteries are out of ammunition or smashed. Troops are badly exhausted, confined to narrowest space, their backs to the sea. Loss of the town unavoidable in nearest future." The Desert Fox's response was terse

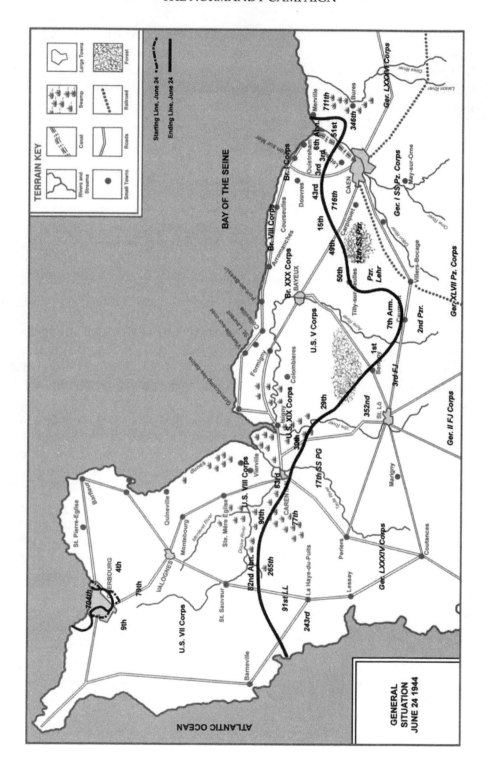

and unsympathetic as he insisted, "you will continue to fight until the last cartridge in accordance with the orders of the Führer."

At this point in the battle American tactics had assumed a deadly regularity. First, fifty or sixty bombers would pulverize a section of the German line. Then an artillery barrage would pound any fortifications that appeared to continue to offer resistance. A small assault force would then move close enough to draw fire, locate the position of the Germans, and call into walkie-talkies to signal the advance of massive reinforcements. Once a strongpoint was overrun, the GIs would organize a powerful defense cordon and wait for an enemy counterattack that almost always proved to be a bloody failure. Then the process would begin again a short time later at another point in the line, forcing the Germans to shuttle ever smaller numbers of troops from one threatened spot to another.

On Sunday morning as Rommel's order to fight to the last cartridge was received, von Schlieben and his naval counterpart Admiral Hennecke picked up carbines and stood behind breastworks at the entrance to their command tunnel, determined to fight side by side with their men when the Americans launched the supreme assault against German headquarters. However, back in the hospital lateral a slightly wounded American captain who had been captured a short time earlier surveyed the deteriorating conditions of the more than two thousand casualties and convinced the senior medical officer to allow him to see von Schlieben. The American officer proposed to cross the lines, point out the location of the hospital to the American gunners, and return with medical supplies. The German general quickly authorized the mission and soon the American captain returned with a supply of painkillers and a letter from General Collins stating, "You and your troops have resisted stubbornly and gallantly," and requesting a parley to discuss terms of surrender. Von Schlieben refused to send an immediate reply for a very important reason. He was busy supervising a massive demolition plan in which thirty-five tons of dynamite were positioned to wreck every maritime facility that might be of use to the Allied invaders. At 7:00 P.M. tremors shook the ground as jetties, piers, dock facilities, and even Cherbourg's famous stone tower blew into thousands of fragments and flames shot up from several parts of the harbor. Then the next morning, just as the Americans were on the verge of advancing on his headquarters, von Schlieben sent out a flag of truce and surrendered to General Manton Eddy.

American news photographs snapped hundreds of photos of von Schlieben and his men capitulating and General Bradley's aides sug-

German resistance in Cherbourg was ferocious as they fought to "the last cartridge." Finally, on June 26, the Germans surrendered the town to the Allies after destroying much of the cities' port.

gested that the German commander should be invited to dinner in light of his stubborn defense of the city. However the crusty general growled, "If Schlieben had surrendered four days earlier, I'd have asked him. But now, that he has cost us a pile of human lives—no!" Bradley's mood was hardly lightened by the discovery that the Americans may have captured a port, but most of the critical facilities in that harbor city were now piles of rubble, useless to the Allied logistics officers. The Americans had won the first significant victory of the Normandy campaign following the invasion, but the momentum for this triumph had carried them away from the heartland of France and the Reich. The next phase of the campaign would initially prove far more frustrating than the drive for the colorful port and its now badly damaged harbor.

Chivalry and Atrocities in the Normandy Campaign

The eighty days of the Normandy campaign featured some of the bloodiest, most vicious fighting of World War II, but the treatment of enemy troops outside the immediate line of battle probably occupied a middle ground between the frequent truces, prisoner exchanges, and individual acts of kindness that dotted the panorama of the American Civil War and the virtually merciless violence that emerged in the fighting between the United States and Japan in the Pacific War. Britain, America, and Germany had all agreed in principle to abide by the series of nineteenth and twentieth century accords, popularly known as the "Geneva Convention," dealing with the treatment of prisoners, medical personnel, and other non-combatants, and in a broad sense these accords were generally either met or exceeded. Medics and stretcher-bearers were generally, although not always, spared from direct fire, although this did not prevent some of these men from being killed or injured by air attacks, artillery fire, or simply by opponents who thought it was silly to have "rules" in deadly combat. There were a number of incidents where an ambulance strayed to the wrong side of the lines and was allowed to return to the other side of the battlefield unharmed. Doctors of both opposing armies routinely teamed up to operate on patients from both armies and even shared surgical techniques with their counterparts. During the last days of the collapse of the Falaise pocket, the Germans put together convoys of ambulances and trucks to carry wounded soldiers to safety and Allied fighter-bombers consistently aborted attacks whenever these convoys were spotted.

At times, the level of chivalry extended even beyond the usually accepted rules of combat. Colonel Hans von Luck noted that at one point in the fighting a column of half-tracks and trucks was caught by surprise along an open stretch of road by a swarm of fighter-bombers flown by Canadian pilots. The German vehicles were virtually helpless, but to von Luck's amazement, the squadron leader made a pass without firing, motioning furiously for the occupants to abandon the trucks before they were destroyed. After the Germans had clambered out of the vehicles, a more serious attack began, but the destruction was against the trucks, not the occupants. On another occasion during the siege of Cherbourg, a slightly wounded American officer was captured by the Germans and was appalled by the crowded mass of enemy casualties stacked up in tunnels that were not safe from American shelling and contained very few medical supplies. The officer asked to see the German commander, General von Schlieben, and offered to cross over to American lines, identify hospital positions to American gunners, and return with medical supplies. A short time later, the shelling of the hospital areas ceased, and the officer returned with a large supply of medicine to distribute to the German surgeon.

Probably the most significant element of the Geneva Accords was the proper treatment of prisoners and men on both sides met with a wide range of experiences if they attempted or were forced to capitulate. While the senior field commanders of both Allied and German armies seem to have encouraged scrupulous adherence to the rules concerning prisoners, it is obvious that at least some men who surrendered never made it safely to the POW cages. In some cases atrocities were made possible when relatively high-ranking officers immediately below the senior command structure tacitly condoned or even encouraged the killing of prisoners. German SS General Kurt "Panzer" Meyer was eventually imprisoned and very nearly executed for condoning the mass shooting of Canadian and British prisoners by his Hitler Youth teenagers on several occasions. However, prosecutors could never fully determine whether Meyer had actually ordered such treatment or simply exercised far too little control over his younger officers who were perpetrating the atrocities. On the other side of the battlefield, there were persistent suggestions in the accounts of American paratroopers landing in the hours before the beach assaults that they had been ordered to "take no prisoners." However, there are few, if any, specific accounts of the paratroopers actually gunning down surrendering enemy soldiers and in the afterglow of a victorious campaign and a victorious war records that might have implicated battalion, regimental, or division commanders were hardly scrutinized by authors chronicling the Allied triumph.

The other way in which a surrendering soldier might never make it to the POW camps often occurred when the passion of a just-completed vicious firefight was carried over to the moments after the battle. If a machine gunner or sniper mowed down several enemy soldiers and then, when either surrounded or out of bullets, threw down his weapon, there was no guarantee that men who had just watched their friends get killed would honor that surrender.

On the other hand, if a soldier in either army survived this initial encounter and made it to a POW camp, the odds of survival were quite good. The survival rate of Allied soldiers in German camps and German soldiers in British and American compounds was in the vicinity of 99 percent, a statistic that compares quite favorably with the 40 percent fatality rate among Americans captured by the Japanese, 70 percent rate among Russians captured by the Germans, and 80 percent death rate among Germans unfortunate enough to be taken prisoners by the Soviets.

CHAPTER XIII

Operation Epsom
The Battle for the Odon

Early on Friday morning, June 17, 1944, as advance elements of the American army closed on the Atlantic coast of the Cotentin Peninsula, a formation of German fighter planes flew through a newly quarantined air corridor escorting a single transport plane. That aircraft was carrying Adolf Hitler from his headquarters in Berchtesgaden, Germany, to an airfield in Metz, France. An honor guard met the Führer at the airport and escorted him to a waiting motorcade which whisked the dictator to a specially built forward headquarters at Marginal, just outside the city of Soissons. The headquarters complex had actually been constructed four years earlier to enable Hitler to direct Operation Sea Lion, the German invasion of Britain. Now circumstances were totally reversed, and Hitler was traveling to France to meet his senior generals to discuss prospects for throwing the Anglo-American attackers back into the sea.

When the two senior generals on the Western Front, Gerd von Rundstedt and Erwin Rommel, were ushered into Hitler's underground conference room, they were given a frosty welcome by their Führer who played nervously with his reading glasses and twirled pencils between his fingers as he listened to their explanations of why the Allies were expanding their foothold in France. Then Hitler began raising his voice and shaking his fists as he insisted that his generals and his soldiers had failed him because of cowardice and obsession with their individual safety. Rommel quickly countered with an insistence that the static divisions had actually fought better than expected and several regiments had been virtually annihilated during the past ten or eleven days. The army group commander then suggested that the only hope to check a continuing Anglo-American advance was to concentrate every available armored division for a massive counterattack that would split the Allied lines before their numerical advantage became overwhelming. Hitler did not categorically reject the field marshal's reasoning but continued to insist that the "real" invasion was still imminent at Pas de Calais and the precious panzers might be far more decisive in that sector. The Führer then designated sixteen French ports as "fortresses" and directed that the 200,000 troops defending these points could not be transferred to field operations and would be expected to fight to the last bullet where they stood.

As tensions between Hitler and his generals rose alarmingly, waiters brought out the typically unappetizing food that passed for a meal in Hitler's presence. In a now familiar ritual, orderlies tasted the dictator's food, two huge SS bodyguards deployed themselves behind his chair, and Hitler began to wolf down an enormous mountain of rice and vegetables topped off by an astonishing array of liquid and tablet medicines prescribed by the quack who masqueraded as the leader's personal physician. Once lunch was concluded Hitler began lecturing his senior officers, admonishing them "don't worry about the future course of the war but rather about your own invasion front." The former corporal from the Great War insisted that he knew far more than his field marshals about long-term strategy and emphasized that his new "vengeance" weapons, the pilotless missiles that were even now beginning to descend on England, would force the British government to sue for peace by the end of summer. The Führer made one concession to his generals; he agreed to visit Seventh Army headquarters with Rommel the next morning. However, in one of the many ironies of World War II, one of the V-1 flying bombs targeted for England ran wild after launching and smashed into the Marginal complex directly above the command bunker. Twenty feet of concrete allowed Hitler to escape injury, but the supposedly fearless dictator promptly cancelled his visit to the forward areas and hurried back to Germany, never to return to France. Adolf Hitler might not have ever appeared near the battlefront again but it was now clear that his will alone would determine the future course of the Normandy campaign, and, for better or worse, his policy of holding out to the last bullet on most parts of the front threatened to turn the expanding battle into a stalemate of Great War proportions.

The three senior Allied commanders who were overseeing the ground battle, Eisenhower, Montgomery, and Bradley, were now confronting a different kind of stress than they encountered in the first phase of Overlord. The five separate beachheads were now essentially linked into one massive battlefront and Allied forces were making some progress in advancing inland, but a whole new set of crises was rapidly emerging. On the evening of June 15 air-raid sirens had begun to scream on the cliff tops of Dover. British antiaircraft batteries opened up as a missile that filled the air with the rumble of an enormously amplified idling engine and then nose-dived out of the clouds, leveled off and detonated with a ton of high explosive. The next day over three hundred of the twenty-foot-long flying bombs headed for London and RAF fighters were scrambled to intercept the strange-looking aircraft that streaked a flame behind them as long as the weapon itself. While some V-1s were shot down or simply veered off target, two hundred of the deadly missiles impacted in and around London and many residents of Britain wondered if Hitler was actually regaining the initiative of the war. The British War Cabinet seemed to be in a panic and Churchill asked Eisenhower to give the secret weapon launching pads one of the highest priorities for bombing or capture, even though they were largely in Belgium or Holland, hundreds of miles from the Normandy battlefields.

Then as Eisenhower and his generals were attempting to placate the politicians over the missile attacks, a new crisis emerged. On the afternoon of June 18, the skies over the Channel lowered and an unusually bad storm lashed the water between France and England. Allied shipping sustained heavy losses in the strong seas as some eight hundred ships were either sunk or beached. An even more spectacular disaster occurred when both artificial harbors were smashed by huge waves which pounded the American Mulberry into rubble and severely damaged its British counterpart. When the storm finally lifted three days later, the Allied troops in Normandy were faced with substantial shortages of almost everything from rations to artillery shells as 140,000 tons of material had been destroyed and the schedule of follow-up landings had almost completely unraveled.

Finally as Eisenhower, Montgomery, and Bradley savored the news of Cherbourg's capture, the reality of the extent of damage to the port began to sink in. General von Schlieben's demolition experts had turned the harbor facilities into a mass of wreckage that would take months to repair and it was increasingly apparent that the city's capitulation was a largely hollow victory that would do little to solve the looming logistics nightmare that was accompanying the expansion of the battlefield. Under Eisenhower's encouragement, Montgomery and Bradley were about to initiate new offensives designed to capture the important towns of Caen and St. Lô and use these newly acquired communities as pivots for the breakout from Normandy into the heartland of France. The engagements that followed during late June and much of the first three weeks of July would become known collectively as the "battle of the hedgerows" and would severely test the courage and endurance of the British, American, and German troops who fought and often died in the "bocage" of Normandy.

The new British offensive, code-named *Epsom*, was developed by General Montgomery as a massive infantry and armored envelopment east and west of Caen. While units in place kept the Germans occupied east of the city, the newly arrived 11th Armoured Division, 43rd (Wessex) Division, and 15th (Scottish) Division would use sixty thousand men, six hundred tanks, and three hundred guns along with massive air and naval support to punch a hole between the Panzer Lehr Division and the 12th SS Panzer Division, swing eastward through the bocage, cross the Odon River and capture the high ground beyond, especially the strategically important Hill 112. At best this operation would force the German evacuation of Caen and at the very least, Operation Epsom would prevent the enemy from launching a massive armored counterattack which the victor of El Alamein sensed was about to begin.

The drive for the Odon was to be spearheaded by the Scots of the 15th Division, a unit that was now concentrated north of Route 13, the main road from Caen to Bayeux. While the Scots could expect massive air, naval, and artillery support, they faced the uninviting prospect of being ordered to walk forward through a succession of cornfields and orchards that featured dozens of German strongpoints all the way back to the banks of the river. On the morning of June 26, just as General von Schlieben was preparing to surrender at Cherbourg, twenty-five platoons of about thirty men each shouldered their weapons and prepared to advance behind an artillery barrage which was gradually rolling its deadly shells forward. This force of slightly over seven hundred men would eventually receive support from dozens of similar platoons, but at this moment they were engaged in an almost isolated advance toward a series of hedgerows, sunken roads, dense orchards, and formidable stone farmhouses that the Germans had spent three weeks turning into a five-mile-wide defense zone.

The soldiers in field gray manned twenty-eight machine-gun nests deployed to cover the approaches to the cornfields and could use a series of covered, sunken roads to scramble back to a new defense line if the forward positions seemed about to be overrun. Two miles further south a ridge that ran along the north bank of the Odon had been laced with barbed wire, strewn with mines, and fitted with an additional twenty-six machine-gun nests manned by the engineer battalion of the 12th SS Division. Finally, situated on the south side of the river was a string of 88mm-gun batteries and mortar pits, centered on the high ground of Hill 112. The defenders had plenty of heavy weapons and were deployed on superb defensive terrain, but they were dangerously short of riflemen who could protect and support the weapons crews. The Germans were attempting to hold a succession of strongpoints with only two battalions, only one of which was primarily a rifle unit. Once the British advance was fully underway, nine battalions of Scots would be employed to storm through the enemy positions. Thus this operation would be a contest between superior numbers and superior positions and no one was quite sure which factor would prove more important.

At 7:30 A.M. on this warm but overcast Monday morning, bagpipes began playing the simultaneously lamenting and inspirational tunes their instruments produced while officers and sergeants walked among their men giving encouragement and artillery shells exploded further down the seemingly endless rows of corn. For a brief moment it appeared as if the enormous fire support had broken the will of the defenders as a stream of men in coal-scuttle helmets appeared in front of the Tommies waving white flags of surrender. However, any sense of quick success was promptly dispelled by the events of the next few minutes. As one member of the assault force recalled, "We arose and saw the wide fields of ripening corn rolling away before us; the mist already lifting to an overcast sky of gray cloud. There were periodic bursts of small arms fire, confused, some way off in various directions." As the Scots advanced, they encountered isolated but dangerous groups of Hitler Youth who were often lying low to let the leading units pass over them in the corn and then would pop up in the rear to spray automatic weapons fire into the ranks of the khaki-clad attackers.

While the attack route of some assault companies led them through a series of fields and orchards, other units had to batter their way through the small hamlets that dotted the region. One combined force of riflemen and tanks entered the town of Cheux, pushed the

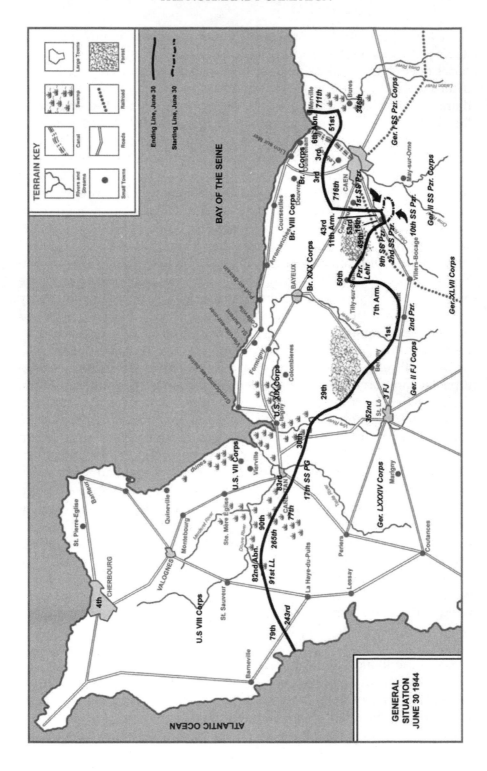

Germans back street by street and then advanced toward the village of Mouen which contained the 12th SS Panzer Division's headquarters on its outskirts. As the Tommies approached town, Kurt "Panzer" Meyer, newly promoted to command the division, formed his available Hitler Youth teenagers into two battlegroups, code-named Granville and Mouen, and mounted his ever-present motorcycle to direct a two-pronged assault to pinch off the British advances. Meyer's command was heavily outnumbered, but the British troops and vehicles were advancing on such a narrow front that their columns were backed up as much as six miles as they clogged the narrow roads of the region. When a small force of Tiger and Panther tanks rumbled into action, the British armored vehicles found it almost impossible to maneuver effectively in the narrow confines of the battlefield. As one member of the Dragoon Guards remembered, "The whole squadron was now in the field with the tanks scattered around the hedges. We soon discovered from the wireless that we were in a trap. There appeared to be Tigers and Panthers all around us. There were about six on the high ground ahead, four in the edge of the wood just across the field to our left. Between them they covered every gap."

Meyer's swift reaction prevented the British offensive from reaching the Odon on the first day of the battle, but the British VIII Corps commander, General Richard O'Connor, was convinced that his troops could certainly cross that waterway the next day. His plan for June 27 was to pull one of the 15th Division's battalions from reserve behind Cheux and order the unit to race southward toward the Odon with no concern for its flanks. At 5:45 on that warm Tuesday morning, the 2nd Argyll and Sutherland Highlanders fell in near an orchard and began marching rapidly toward the riverfront village of Tourmauville, two and a half miles to the south. An accompanying unit of mobile anti-tank guns was used to break through a screen of panzers halfway to the river and then the Highlanders broke into a run, scrambled through cornfields and orchards, and poured across a still-intact bridge to the south bank of the river. Tanks from the 11th Armored Division were quickly deployed to create a small but formidable bridgehead over the Odon. However, the Germans were determined to push the British back across the river and were even now gathering a potent armored force to stage a massive counterattack.

While Hitler had done little to address Rommel's concern over the impact of Allied air and naval support in the Normandy campaign, the Führer had at least agreed to release several powerful armored units to launch a major offensive designed to split the Allied armies in two. The 1st SS Panzer Division was moved from its base in Belgium to the vicinity of Caen, and the formidable II SS Panzer Corps, consisting of the 9th and 10th Panzer Divisions, was pulled back from Poland and sent westward to France. Allied air strikes imposed constant delays on their progress toward the battle zone, but by the evening of June 28 enough units had arrived to permit the Germans to launch a major armored thrust against the British bridgehead.

The panzers were in place, but the utilization of them was quickly wreathed in controversy and contention. Seventh Army commander General Friedrich Dollman had been steadily losing his nerve since the surrender of Cherbourg and when he learned that the British now had a bridgehead over the Odon he became convinced that the whole front was about to disintegrate and ordered the II SS Panzer Corps to launch an immediate counterattack. Then, before issuing more specific orders to corps commander General Paul Hausser, the frantic Dollman took a fatal dose of poison. Since Rommel and von Rundstedt were already on their way to Berchtesgaden to meet Hitler, Hausser was now essentially on his own to stem the British tide in an attack that he had initially opposed.

While Hausser frantically organized the details of the upcoming offensive, General O'Connor's men launched their own attack and early on the morning of June 29 overran the key point in the area, Hill 112. This single hill now became a focal point for an immense slugging match as panzer units that had been carefully hoarded for a much more extensive operation were now thrown into the struggle for the ridge. Two days of vicious battle saw columns of Mark IVs, Panthers, and Tigers trying to push the British defenders off the hill and back toward the river while Shermans and Churchills, backed by some of the most powerful artillery support of the campaign, locked with the panzers in a deadly minuet. Panzergrenadiers and Highlanders blasted away at one another in orchards and fields that changed hands several times during the battle. The infantry battalions of the 15th Division held the south bank of the Odon while their supporting guns mowed down the attacking Germans from their positions on the north side of the river; one enemy thrust at the bridgehead was repulsed so bloodily that the Odon was almost dammed by corpses. Most British rifle companies were reduced to less than half of their original strength with few reinforcements readily available.

By the afternoon of June 30 it was becoming clear to both sides that Hausser's mauled panzer corps simply did not have enough tanks or men remaining to push the British back across the Odon. However,

British Second Army commander General Miles Dempsey made the mistaken assumption that the Germans would renew the attack the next day at some other point in the line and concluded that the units on the south bank of the Odon were far too exposed to meet an even more powerful enemy thrust. Therefore, Hill 112 was abandoned and the largely victorious units were pulled back to a new line north of the river over the protests of incredulous officers and men who had just smashed a powerful German offensive. Dempsey may have underestimated the damage he inflicted. Operation Epsom *had* badly hurt the German army's precious armored forces and more daring British leaders might have thrust their armies directly into Caen. However, even though Dempsey called off the offensive, the operation had still paid handsome dividends. The list of four thousand British casualties was still shorter than the German toll of dead and injured and the Allies could much more easily replace lost tanks and other vehicles than the Germans. Perhaps most important was the fact that Epsom forced the Germans to fritter away a large concentration of armored units intended for a massive counteroffensive on a localized action that did nothing more than maintain the status quo for a few more days. Tanks that might have been put to excellent use in meeting an imminent American drive were now burned out hulks lining the banks of the Odon River. The Germans would dearly miss those panzers as Omar Bradley's GIs trudged toward the crossroads town of St. Lô.

Karl Gerd von Rundstedt

This imposing Prussian general, nick-named "the old gentleman" in the ranks of the Wehrmacht, was a member of an influential family that sent their son to the Main Cadet School at Berlin where he was commissioned a lieutenant in time for his eighteenth birthday. He graduated with distinction from the prestigious Kriegsakademie and was assigned to the German general staff. Von Rundstedt was still a thirty-nine-year-old captain at the beginning of World War I, but that conflict provided the springboard for a series of promo-tions that made him chief of staff of the XV Corps at the time of the armistice.

Von Rundstedt prospered in the small Reichswehr of the 1920s and was already a full general when Hitler took power; the Führer's favor was much less important to this Prussian than most other significant German com-manders of World War II. The general's involvement in the wrangling between the professional officer corps and Hitler's Nazi cronies resulted in his dis-missal in 1938, but the dictator quickly brought him back to duty in time for the invasion of Poland. He commanded Army Group South during the blitz through France and took the same unit into the Soviet Union in 1941 with the rank of field marshal. His forces overran most of the Ukraine and advanced as far as the Don River by December of 1941, but a new round of feuding with Hitler prompted his resignation at the end of the year.

Despite their ongoing differences, the Führer generally admired this old warhorse, and in the spring of 1942 von Rundstedt was assigned commander in chief of all German forces in the West and given responsibility for repelling an eventual Anglo-American invasion. When the wrangling between the two men resumed at full intensity after the Normandy landings, von Rundstedt returned home to snarl about the dicta-tor's incompetence—but he also partici-pated in the Court of Honor proceed-ings against the July 20 plotters.

Hitler did another about-face in the autumn of 1944 and brought von Rundstedt back to command the mas-sive Ardennes offensive, but the col-lapse of that operation prompted still another sacking. At the end of the war, von Rundstedt was captured by Allied forces in the resort town of Bad Tolz. There was considerable argument over what to do with a man who held so much power but seemed to hold the record for the most sackings by Hitler. After three years of varying degrees of captivity in Britain, von Rundstedt was finally allowed to return home and enter the ongoing disputes about who really cost the Germans the war.

Rivalries and Feuds in the German Forces

Adolf Hitler's concept of maintaining absolute power was to tolerate and even encourage a constant state of tension and rivalry among the men who served in his inner circle. The power struggles inside the Third Reich often took on the appearance of the 1920s Chicago gangster scene with its shifting alliances, utilization of groups of armed thugs to eliminate competition and constant vying for the attention of leaders even while plots were hatched to remove that leader.

Much of the German conduct of the Normandy campaign was complicated by the fact that the defenders actually had three distinct ground forces contesting the Allied advance, while their leaders feuded among themselves. The army represented the traditional shield of the German state and considered itself above politics even though a fair percentage of senior leaders were either Nazis or Nazi sympathizers. However, the power of the army was hardly unchallenged as each of the two major reichsführers, Hermann Göring and Heinrich Himmler, essentially controlled his own private army with a significant presence in Normandy. Unlike the United States Army Air Forces, the German Luftwaffe was a totally autonomous service that not only controlled the aircraft of the Reich, but had responsibility for antiaircraft units and paratroopers as well. Luftwaffe control over these essentially ground personnel combined with the creation of more and more Luftwaffe "Field Divisions" out of surplus air personnel meant that Hermann Göring exercised some level of control over a significant proportion of the land forces defending Normandy—a situation which exasperated and infuriated army commanders during the campaign. In turn, Heinrich Himmler's personal army of Waffen SS made up a very large percentage of the armored units that were key to a continued German hold on the shrinking Normandy perimeter. While most of these units fought well, they operated under a very confused command structure. For example, orders from Wehrmacht generals could sometimes be liberally interpreted by lesser SS officers who considered themselves a cut above their army counterparts.

Another frequent catalyst for feuds within the regular army itself was the attempt to fight a war with a command structure that included one set of generals who were descended from the aristocratic Prussian Junker class and upstart generals hailing from far more modest backgrounds. At times, the aristocrats believed that they were in command *despite* Hitler's seizure of power and generally despised the man who had been a lowly corporal in the Great War. On the other hand, the less socially favored generals tended to admit, either tacitly or enthusiastically, that their rapid rise to power and authority was largely attributable to the Führer's creation of the Third Reich. This gap in social background produced a series of feuds that created less than optimal conditions for successful campaigns on more than one occasion. The almost institutionalized feuds of the military leaders of the Third Reich appears to have had dire consequences for the German cause.

CHAPTER XIV

The Battle of the Hedgerows
The Struggle for St. Lô

By the end of June 1944, Omar Bradley's First Army had risen to a strength of fourteen divisions deployed along a forty-mile front. The Americans had captured nearly forty thousand men at Cherbourg and had so extensively mauled six German divisions that those units now fielded only seven understrength regiments among them. Three other German divisions, the 3rd Parachute, 353rd Infantry, and 17th SS Panzergrenadier, were still largely intact but had too few vehicles and tanks to present a major offensive threat. On the other hand, Bradley and his corps and division commanders were obliged to plan offensive operations in a terrain of swampy flooded fields and extensive stretches of hedgerows that gave the defenders an enormous advantage. The Vire River and the powerful German garrison in the key crossroads town of St. Lô discouraged an American advance on the left; the steep wooded hills around La Haye du Puits presented formidable obstacles to an advance on the right; the center featured the flooded ground near the Taute Valley and upper Vire Valley which was broken only by a mile-wide corridor of dry ground that was bristling with German strongpoints. The one initial advantage the Americans did hold was the fact that Hitler's obsession with the possibility of an Allied invasion at Calais and his preoccupation with holding Caen to the last round had starved the opposite end of the German battle line of the tanks and men that could ensure an indefi-

nite stalemate in that region. The Americans would also begin to ben-
efit from the increasingly confused status of the German High
Command that would orchestrate operations in the second month of
the Normandy campaign. General Erich Marcks, the talented, energetic commander of the LXXXIV Corps had been killed by an Allied
air strike during the second week of action and had been replaced by
the somewhat untested General Dietrich von Choltitz. Marcks's death
had been followed by the suicide of General Friedrich Dollman, commander of the Seventh Army. He was replaced by Paul Hausser, the
commander of the II SS Panzer Corps, and one of Heinrich Himmler's
favorite proteges. Then General Geyr, senior officer of Panzer Group
West, criticized the Führer's strategy once too often and found himself
replaced by General Heinrich Eberbach, a competent but colorless
panzer leader. Finally the senior general in the entire west, Gerd von
Rundstedt, irritated Hitler with his constant requests to evacuate
Caen. The German dictator presented his field marshal with oak
leaves for his Iron Cross and then promptly sent him on "extended
leave" with the more malleable Field Marshal Gunther von Kluge
brought in from the Eastern Front to direct the battle in France. Thus
Allied intelligence personnel would be kept working long into each
night attempting to decipher the personalities and intentions of a
largely new roster of enemy commanders in the next phase of
Overlord.

The major change in the American order of battle as the campaign
entered its second month was the addition of the VIII Corps and XIX
Corps to the V Corps and VII Corps that had participated in the D-Day
invasion. Bradley intended to use elements of all four available corps
to capture the cities of Coutances and St. Lô and then use those points
as a springboard for a major breakout into the heartland of Normandy,
and eventually Brittany to the west and the Seine River to the east. The
commander of the First Army intended to use General Troy
Middleton's VIII Corps to advance past two important hills, Mont
Castre and Montgardon Ridge, and capture Le Haye du Puits which
dominated the roads approaching the cathedral city of Coutances.
Possession of this community would force the Germans to withdraw
from the rest of the Cotentin neck for fear of being cut off by a pincer
attack from the west. Meanwhile, General Charles Corlett's XIX Corps
would join elements of the V and VII Corps in advancing on St. Lô in
a multidirectional offensive designed to prevent the Germans from
concentrating their forces on a single threat to that vital community.

Eisenhower, Montgomery, and Bradley were all enormously interested in the progress of an advance toward Coutances and St. Lô as the key to overwhelming the Germans in Normandy before they poured reinforcements into the region from other locations. By the end of June the Allies had landed 875,000 men in Normandy and were in the process of supplying an additional 79,000 men to replace the 37,000 Americans and 25,000 British and Canadian troops killed or wounded during the first month of the battle. The Germans had so far committed 400,000 men to the defense of Normandy, but the 80,000 casualties in the force had been replaced with only 4,000 reinforcements. For the moment, the Allies enjoyed a substantial numerical advantage that was essential for continued offensive operations. However at some point even the obstinate Hitler would realize that there was no imminent Allied landing at Calais and the 250,000 men in the Fifteenth Army would be released for service in Normandy. The Allied leaders fervently hoped that the battle of Normandy would be largely decided before massive German reinforcements arrived on the battlefield. One of the major keys to winning the battle rapidly was the ability of the Americans to launch a breakout offensive in the near future.

The operation that would come to be known as the "battle of the hedgerows," began early on the morning of July 3 when elements of Troy Middleton's VIII Corps moved out from their jump-off point on the west coast of the Cotentin Peninsula toward the high ground of Mont Castre and Montgardon. Middleton's counterpart, General von Choltitz, was initially surprised by the Americans's willingness to begin a full-scale offensive during a driving rainstorm that negated the powerful Allied air support and reduced the effectiveness of artillery units. However, the new LXXXIV Corps commander had deployed a significant presence on the two pieces of high ground and the American drive was initially stopped cold with over one thousand casualties. The Germans had just enough 88s, tanks, and machine guns to counter each of Middleton's assaults while von Choltitz used the time his frontline troops were buying him to establish a formidable new line of defense in front of La Haye du Puit. Five additional days of hedgerow fighting produced another three thousand American casualties so that by the evening of July 8 Middleton had lost nearly 40 percent of his available riflemen for little appreciable gain. By this point Bradley was thinking seriously of writing off the drive to Coutances as a dud and the focus of the battle shifted sixteen miles to the west to the district capital.

St. Lô was a city of just under twenty thousand people located on high ground above the Vire River and a focal point for eight roads and a rail line. The older section of the town stretched along the river bluffs and centered on a fifteenth-century, double-spired church while the newer parts of the city spread across lowland and up the slopes of a series of encircling hills which led to the plateau-like top of Hill 122 to the north and Martinville Ridge and Hill 192 to the east. As the American drive on Coutances unraveled, Bradley saw St. Lô as the key to an eventual breakout offensive and he realized that an advance from only one direction would allow von Choltitz to use the fantastic defensive terrain to his advantage and repulse the attack. Therefore, the St. Lô operation evolved into a series of thrusts designed to keep the German commander off balance while the Americans located a weak spot in the enemy line and punched through to control the town and its vital road system.

One of the prongs of the American advance was led by General "Lightning Joe" Collins and the men of his VII Corps. Collins was attempting to use the single dry road that loomed above a wide stretch of marshes to burst into the outskirts of town with his 4th, 9th, and 83rd Divisions. However, the road was so narrow that he was forced to advance the three units in an enormously long column that provided little firepower at the front. The corps commander decided to lead off with the inexperienced 83rd Division, followed by the 4th and 9th Divisions to stiffen the attack. Their first objective was the small town of Periers which fronted on a somewhat wide stretch of dry ground. The 83rd's commander, General Robert Mason, was expected to begin the operation by squeezing his troops and vehicles through a narrow neck of passable ground that was bristling with German artillery and machine guns. During the first day of the operation Mason's men advanced a mere two hundred yards at a cost of fourteen hundred casualties and captured a grand total of six German prisoners. As a final insult, the local German commander returned to Mason the doctors and medics he had captured during the battle, noting sarcastically that the American general would need them more than he did.

The next day, as the increasingly impatient Collins dropped hints that he was about to fire him, Mason launched a renewed assault that was so futile and costly that the forward attack companies were nearly annihilated and only four hunderd riflemen remained available for combat in one entire regiment. Communication breakdowns, wrong designation of map locations, and less-than-inspired leadership turned what had already been an agonizingly slow advance into a glacial crawl and a furious corps commander abruptly pushed the 83rd aside and rushed the more experienced 4th Division to the front of the assault line. The change accomplished little except to allow a new unit to undergo the horrors of a bloody stalemate and shift the hopes for an American breakthrough to another part of the battlefield.

As prospects for a quick breakthrough by Collins evaporated, the American high command's spirits were raised by the exploits of Charles Corlett's XIX Corps. Major General Leland Hobbs, the big, outspoken commanding officer of the 30th Division was facing the challenge of moving his three regiments toward St. Lô by crossing two major water barriers, the Vire River and the Taute-Vire Canal. The river was a ten-foot-deep stream that featured high steep banks and was sixty feet wide while the canal was five feet deep, twenty feet across, and presented much more gently sloping banks. Hobbs needed to cross both water barriers in order to launch a two-pronged assault on the town of St. Jean de Daye, a crossroads town fronting St. Lô and located about three miles from both the river and the canal.

At 3 A.M. on July 7, thirty-two assault boats were pushed into the Vire River and paddled by engineers to the opposite bank. The assault force met relatively little resistance as most of the available defenders, including about five hundred infantry, were concentrated around the bank of the canal. German riflemen, machine gunners, and mortar crews picked off about three hundred GIs attempting to push across the artificial waterway but the Americans simply kept coming in waves until the defenders were forced to fall back to the relative safety of St. Lô. However, as the men of the 30th captured St. Jean and prepared for another advance, the German High Command was preparing to launch a major counterattack.

General Paul Hausser, new commander of the Seventh Army, had responded to von Choltitz's alarm about the American crossing of the Vire by ordering his corps commander to dispatch units from the St. Lô garrison to block the enemy drive until major reinforcements could be shuttled over from the area around Caen. Soon a reconnaissance battalion riding in half-tracks and trucks and an infantry brigade pedaling forward on bicycles were deploying in blocking positions to keep Hobbs's men at arms length from the city. However, this was a mere stopgap until Hausser could meet with Rommel and von Kluge to secure more tangible help for the threatened left flank of the German line. The Desert Fox's initial preference was to pull the powerful Panzer Lehr Division out of the Caen defenses and swing them westward to cover St. Lô. While von Kluge had no objection to this gambit, he insisted that the flank might crumble before the reinforcements arrived and took the added precaution of ordering the 2nd SS Panzer Division, which was deployed near La Haye du Puits, to send a substantial number of its panzers to the Vire-Taute region in order to smash into Hobbs before he could consolidate his position. Von Kluge believed that the forces around St. Lô were now essentially anchoring the whole left flank of the German line and if the town fell, the whole front might collapse. Therefore the theater commander was now willing to risk two of his precious armored divisions to smash the American advance and send them reeling back up the Cotentin Peninsula.

General Fritz Bayerlein, the energetic commander of the superb Panzer Lehr Division, organized a series of night movements that he hoped would redeploy most of his vehicles without massive interference from Allied air power. By the evening of July 10 Tigers, Panthers, and Mark IVs of the Panzer Lehr and 2nd SS Panzer were preparing for a dawn attack against Hobbs's bridgehead. However, Allied intelligence had begun to sniff out the German offensive and strong elements of the 9th Infantry Division and 3rd Armored Division were rushed into position to meet the enemy onslaught.

The German offensive began at dawn on July 11 when Colonel J. G. Gutmann, commander of the 902nd Panzer Grenadier Regiment, slammed into advance units of the 30th Division with twenty tanks and dozens of armored cars and half-tracks. Meanwhile Colonel Hans Scholze's 901st Panzer Grenadier Regiment struck at the deep flank of the 9th Division, with a dozen Panthers and a mobile company of 88s. As the panzergrenadiers punched holes in the American defenders, Captain J. H. Philipps led a long column of tanks two miles behind the American lines, overran two battalion command posts and encircled and captured several units of GIs assigned to guard the Vire Canal.

The Germans had scored an early advantage in a growing slugging match but the panzer leaders had not expected a seemingly endless line of Shermans to be available to the defenders, and as the battle ebbed and flowed across wheatfields and orchards the German tanks were being steadily whittled down. Now it was the turn of the GIs to savor the defensive advantages provided by the notorious hedges and it was the Germans who were stunned by the deadly crossfire of the bocage. Whenever the panzers broke into the open, they were challenged by the 899th Tank Destroyer Battalion's formidable tank killers supported by expertly deployed field guns. Then, by mid-afternoon, the sun broke from scudding clouds and American fighter-bombers roared over the fields and roads, picking off desperately maneuvering panzers. By nightfall almost two-thirds of the advance tank units had been destroyed, several battalion commanders had been killed or captured, and 25 percent of Panzer Lehr's vehicles were charred or burning wrecks while the 2nd SS Panzer had suffered similar losses. Two of the most elite units of the German armed forces had been badly chewed up and the Americans had proven to be superb defensive fighters. But the Allied forces could not content themselves with defensive victories alone; they had to maintain offensive operations at all costs before the battlefield congealed into a bloody stalemate. The successful stand along the river and canal had siphoned crucial forces from the St. Lô garrison. Now other American divisions would have to use that advantage to burst into the city and capture the base for a massive new offensive.

On the morning of July 11, just as the Panzer Lehr was launching its ferocious attack on the 30th Division, the men of the "Stonewall Brigade," the 116th Regiment of the 29th Division, were advancing behind an artillery barrage toward Martinville Ridge on the eastern outskirts of St. Lô. The German defenders from the 3rd Parachute Division were deployed along a stretch of sunken roadway fronted with barbed wire and hundreds of mines. As the 116th collided with the skillfully deployed defenders, dozens of men fell from explosions and gunfire. Private John Robinson of Company F recalled, "As we were moving out behind a tank, an artillery shell landed short, right among my squad. My squad was really butchered up. Some of us were blown forward, some backward. It was a big mess." One of the battalion officers of the 116th noted, "A pall of smoke was over the fields, holding in the sweet, sickening stench of high explosives which we had come to associate with death." By the time the 116th had even pushed through the first tier of fortifications, "the three rifle companies were down to about sixty men apiece and those were well shaken up. Very, very few of the NCO's and officers from England remained. We were in bad shape."

Large numbers of men from the 29th Division were becoming casualties because their commander, General Charles Gerhardt, was attempting to bludgeon his way through positions that totally favored the defenders. "Uncle Charlie" Gerhardt, as he was called by both supporters and detractors in the 29th Division, responded to the bloodbath on Martinville Ridge much the same way he reacted to the engagements around the Elle River earlier in the campaign. He simply fired or threatened to fire battalion and regimental commanders who were unwilling to keep attacking regardless of casualties. Meanwhile, the officer responsible for defending St. Lô, General Eugene Meindl, was doing his best to ensure that the Americans would pay an exorbitant price for every yard they gained.

While Omar Bradley was exhibiting the same tendency to solve stalemated engagements by firing subordinate officers, he did have enough good sense to realize that the 29th Division was being expected to accomplish more than it could reasonably handle. The army commander assigned the 35th Division to launch a new attack on St. Lô from northwest of the city while the 38th Regiment of the 2nd Division was assigned the capture of Hill 192 which loomed over the approaches to Martinville Ridge. Bradley hoped that these maneuvers would stretch the defenders to the breaking point and allow Gerhardt's men to concentrate on punching through the heart of the city.

On the morning of July 12, Gerhardt ordered his 116th and 175th Regiments to push along the ridge while attempting to bypass the other prominent peak in the area, Hill 122. The operation began on a positive note when an assault force from the 2nd Division clambered to the top of Hill 192 after a bloody shootout with the defenders, but the Germans still controlled the other promintory and they turned the approaches to Martinville Ridge into a shooting gallery with the men of the 29th as the targets. Thus this warm summer day ended with more than one thousand 29th Division casualties and no appreciable progress toward capturing St. Lô.

At this point Gerhardt decided he could not advance without capturing Hill 122, and he ordered clerks, cooks, drivers, and other rear echelon personnel into the front lines with orders to "fix bayonets" and advance toward the city. Some rifle companies were down to their last fifty men and at least one platoon could put only three men into combat. A sarcastic comment began circulating through the division that "Gerhardt has a division in the field, a division in the hospital and a division in the cemetery." The division commander did little to counter this opinion when he told commanders to "expend the whole battalion if necessary" as long as they captured St. Lô.

The renewed assault on the city began on a high note when corps commander Charles Corlett ordered the 35th Division to capture Hill 122 while the 29th would concentrate on a thrust into town. This combined offensive began to pay immediate dividends as Meindl was obliged to cover too many threatened breakthroughs and the GIs of the 35th Division crossed the crest of Hill 122 and chased the scurrying defenders down the other side. Gerhardt's regiments were now able to advance toward the outskirts of the city and their attack culminated in a spectacular battle for control of the St. Lô cemetery. American riflemen and tankers dueled with German machine guns and 88s through a maze of gravestones. The superior numbers of the attackers gradually turned the battle in favor of the Americans, and the Germans were forced back into the narrow alleys and cobblestone streets of St. Lô's residential areas.

The battle for the city became a street battle with each block becoming a battlefield in miniature. By the morning of July 17 Meindl

St. Lô was the scene of major fighting during the Normandy campaign. In this photograph, two French boys watch from a hilltop of rubble as Allied vehicles pass through the badly damaged city.

was convinced that his defenses were crumbling and he requested Hausser's permission to withdraw to a new line south of the city. The Seventh Army commander bumped the request up to von Kluge who was then expected to clear the move with a German High Command that had issued a standing order of no withdrawals. In a move uncharacteristic of his earlier actions, the theater commander insisted that a long debate with Hitler and his subordinates would leave the St. Lô garrison hopelessly trapped and ordered Meindl to withdraw on the field marshal's own authority. The garrison commander left just enough of a covering force to convince the Americans that the Germans were still contesting every foot of the city and during the evening of July 18 pulled most of his garrison out of one of the most hotly contested pieces of real estate in France.

General Omar Bradley had secured the jump-off position he needed to allow the First Army to break out of Normandy into the heartland of France. The "battle of the hedgerows" had cost the Americans over 15,000 men killed or wounded in the struggle for St. Lô alone with additional casualties suffered in the aborted drive to Coutances. On the other hand, some of the most formidable divisions in the German army, including the 2nd SS Panzer, the 17th SS Panzergrenadier, the Panzer Lehr, and the 3rd and 5th Parachute Divisions had been badly mauled. Now both Montgomery and Bradley were planning new operations that were expected to set the whole front aflame.

The Allies were about to initiate massive offensives, but Field Marshal Erwin Rommel would no longer be their main antagonist. At almost the same time the Germans were pulling out of St. Lô, Rommel was returning to his headquarters after a visit to the headquarters of the I SS Panzer Corps. As his highly visible staff car roared along the road three miles outside of Vimoutiers, the field marshal's aide sighted British fighter-bombers sweeping down less than a hundred feet above them. A burst of 20mm cannon shells tore into the car, went through the upholstery and ripped open the left side of the vehicle. Rommel struck his head against the windshield and then was flung out of the car, fracturing his skull when he hit the pavement. In an ironic twist of fate the badly injured Desert Fox was transported to the town of Saint Foy de Montgomery for emergency medical treatment. A charismatic, energetic leader, who even Winston Churchill lauded as a formidable yet chivalrous adversary, was now permanently removed from the chessboard of war just as the Allies were about to dramatically change the complexion of the Normandy campaign.

Erwin J. Rommel

The man who would become the legendary "Desert Fox" was born in Heidenheim, Germany, into the solidly middle-class family of a local schoolmaster. Rommel did not attend any of the prestigious German military academies but was able to secure entry into what was essentially an officer candidate school after he had enlisted as a private. Eighteen months later Rommel was a lieutenant in a field artillery regiment, but at the outbreak of World War I was transferred to the 124th Infantry Regiment. The young officer suffered two fairly substantial wounds on the Western Front and was then assigned to a mountain battalion engaged against Romanian and Italian forces. He won the Pour le Mérite for his heroic role in the battle of Caporetto in the fall of 1917 and was shifted to a staff position for the rest of the war.

Rommel survived the contraction of the German army after the armistice and became an instructor at the Infantry School in Dresden where he wrote a well-regarded book titled *Infantry Attacks* based on his experiences during the Great War. When Hitler assumed power in the early 1930s Rommel's reaction was somewhat ambivalent; while he never became an enthusiastic Nazi official, he did appreciate the promotions and honors that the Führer extended to him. This decidedly middle-class officer who had enjoyed almost no family influence now found himself near the inner circle of German leadership when he was appointed director of the War Academy and later commander of Hitler's personal bodyguard, assigned to the dictator's headquarters staff, and responsible for the Führer's security during the Polish campaign of 1939.

When the war expanded into France, Rommel was given command of the 7th Panzer Division which had one of the best records of success in the ensuing campaign. However, while other successful leaders of the French campaign were assigned to Barbarossa, Rommel was placed in command of the relatively small but tough Afrika Korps sent to the Middle East to retrieve the situation following Mussolini's botched attempts to push the British out of Egypt. Rommel's skillful use of small, highly mobile forces in the seesaw desert war earned him the title of "Desert Fox" and his spectacular capture of the British bastion of Tobruk pushed the German commander to the apex of his career. Only a few months later, however, Bernard Montgomery's massive counteroffensive at El Alamein pushed the Afrika Korps into a long retreat and encouraged Hitler to extricate the field marshal before the front disintegrated.

The assignment in Africa was followed by Rommel's famous role in preparation for the Allied invasion of France, but it was during this time that the Desert Fox began developing serious questions about Hitler's ability to prosecute the war. Rommel finally entered into a tentative relationship with the men who were plotting to overthrow the Führer but he strongly opposed the assassination attempt itself, preferring the arrest of the dictator with a subsequent trial. Gestapo agents implicated Rommel in the July 20 assassination plot and it appears that Hitler had mixed feelings concerning the guilt or innocence of one of his favorite generals. The field marshal was at home recuperating from his near fatal injury in Normandy on October 14, 1944, when his house was surrounded by security agents and Rommel was given the choice of taking a fatal dose of poison and protecting the position of his family or submitting to a public trial with the possible implication of his wife and son. Rommel chose to commit suicide and was given a massive state funeral with the bland official insistence that he had succumbed to his earlier injuries. Rommel remains one of the most enigmatic of German commanders. He was admired by Churchill and Montgomery for his chivalry and fair play yet accused by postwar scholars of being a loyal Nazi who only turned on the Führer when it looked as if he had lost the war.

CHAPTER XV

Operation Goodwood
Climax at Caen

On July 1, 1944, General Dwight Eisenhower flew over the French coastline in a heavily escorted Flying Fortress. It had rained at least part of every day since the great Channel storm of just under two weeks earlier and from the air western Normandy seemed to be little more than a gigantic pond interspersed with island-like clusters of hedgerows. After he landed Eisenhower discussed the details of the latest operation against St. Lô with Omar Bradley, and then the two generals drove eastward to confer with Bernard Montgomery on future Allied strategy. Both of Eisenhower's senior ground commanders agreed that the hedgerow country that their troops were encountering was far more impenetrable than they had been led to believe before the start of Overlord, and they emphasized the need to break out of the bocage into the open country where superior Allied mobility could be far more of a factor than it had been during the first month of the campaign.

The highlight of Eisenhower's visit to the Normandy battlefield was an impromptu fighter sweep organized by General Ellwood "Pete" Quesada, the dynamic commander of American tactical air support. As a routine staff conference was breaking up, the youthful leader announced casually, "I'm flying toward Paris to see if we can't dig up a fight," a challenging escapade that Eisenhower boyishly asked to join. A short time later a 70-gallon fuel tank in the rear of

Quesada's Mustang was lifted out and the commander of over two million Allied servicemen squeezed into the P-51 as it prepared to take off. Ike waved jovially to a somewhat shocked Bradley, "All right Brad, I'm going to fly to Berlin!" A few minutes later Eisnehower, Quesada, and the pilots of the 365th Fighter Squadron were speeding toward Paris over lush countryside dotted with German tanks and antiaircraft guns. When the flight was halfway to Paris, Quesada began to realize the consequences of being responsible for the capture or death of the most powerful Allied leader in Europe and the formation changed direction for the friendly confines of the American beachhead. This excursion may have earned Eisenhower a stern reprimand from George Marshall, but it also provided him with a vivid panorama of the difficulties his generals were facing in the early summer of 1944.

Eisenhower's heightened awareness of the difficulty of fighting and defeating the Germans in some of the finest defensive terrain in Europe made him particularly intrigued by the twin offensives being proposed by his two ground commanders as vehicles for releasing the Allied army from the frustrating confines of the Norman bocage country. While American troops were slogging along the bloody approaches to St. Lô, Omar Bradley installed himself in an oversized mess tent his aide had acquired from the supply corps. For two full days and nights, the commander of the First Army paced the plank floor, clutching a fistful of colored wax pencils and scrutinizing every inch of a detailed map of the Normandy battlefield. The Missourian scribbled boundaries, penciled roads, and colored river lines on a giant eight-foot map of the beachhead while always keeping in mind that the aborted thrust in Coutances significantly reduced the scope and size of any American offensive launched from St. Lô alone. Bradley paid increasing attention to one of the eight roads that ran from that embattled town, a highway that stretched to the small resort community of Periers twenty miles away. This avenue would now replace the St. Lô-Coutances highway as the line of departure for a complex operation named *Cobra*, an offensive designed to allow American forces to thrust simultaneously toward Brittany and the Seine River.

Fifty miles away, as Bradley paced the floor and worked his way through a seemingly inexhaustible supply of wax pencils, General Bernard Montgomery sat at a desk in his spartan headquarters van and pored over every available map and aerial photo of the region around Caen. Just as Bradley was formulating a plan for an American breakout beyond St. Lô, the British general was devising a scheme to push Canadian and British troops beyond the precincts of Caen. Montgomery had two priorities for the British Second Army: an offensive that would allow his forces to push beyond the heights of Bourgebus Ridge and drive southward toward Falaise and an eventual linking with the Americans; while at the same time engaging the bulk of the German armored divisions that would otherwise be unleashed against Bradley's developing offensive to the west.

The main British offensive, code-named *Goodwood*, was to be preceded by a preliminary operation titled *Charwood*, designed to capture the northern sections of Caen and sieze the main crossings over the Orne River while also recapturing Hill 112 and the high ground of the old Epsom battlefield to eliminate enemy interference from that direction. Both of these operations were predicated on massive air support to cripple the Germans's ability to respond to the opening moves of the British drives, and in this case Montgomery had secured the enthusiastic support of Eisenhower when he requested maximum cooperation from RAF Bomber Command and the U.S. AAF bomber barons. A sense of urgency was now developing in the Allied camp as intelligence reports were beginning to identify new enemy infantry divisions streaming toward the battle zone, obviously intended to relieve the panzer divisions for a massive armored offensive against the British and Canadians. Montgomery knew that he must immediately reinvolve this armor against the British and Canadians if Bradley's operation was to have any reasonable expectation for success.

At just before 10 P.M. on the evening of July 7, 460 Lancaster and Halifax bombers droned over the northern section of Caen and dropped 2,300 tons of bombs. Many of the 115,000 ground soldiers designated to participate in Charwood watched in awe as the bombers went about their deadly business as they left behind the rumble of constant explosions and huge pillars of smoke rising upward from the ancient Norman city. However, in their laudable attempts to avoid hitting friendly soldiers, the RAF planes edged further and further away from the front lines and dropped their deadly payloads in the residential and university sections of the town. While several of the most historic buildings of Caen University were turned into heaps of rubble the German defenders on the outskirts of the city were spared the worst of the bombardment.

At dawn on July 8, the massive projectiles of the battleship *Rodney*'s big guns exploded with a terrible frenzy on Point 64 at the convergence of several important roads and British and Canadian soldiers approached gingerly toward the first line of enemy defenses. The

British 3rd Division lurched forward to capture Lebisey and Heroville, the 59th Division struck out for Galmache, and the 3rd Canadian Division's troops thrust toward the town of Carpiquet and its adjacent airfield. All of the units were heavily supported by both conventional tanks and flail and flamethrowing "funnies" that had served so impressively on D-Day. The British and Canadian infantry may have enjoyed an impressive amount of armored support, but keeping the foot soldiers and tanks operating in unison became a recurring headache all along the line of advance. Corporal Dennis Hischier, a crew member of a flamethrowing tank of the 141st (Buffs) Royal Armoured Corps Regiment described the confusion caused by poor tank-infantry coordination:

> We experienced a very heavy German counter-bombard-ment. The South Staffs infantry ran into very heavy fire from the trench system near La Bijude and there were strong anti-tank positions there as we feared. Then we were among the trenches. I gave a long squirt of flame up the left hand one, saw my troop leader close to me just the other side of the right hand trench. The turret gunner was using the Besa to good effect when he had a double feed. I told him to use the 75mm on HE (high explosive) and gave him gun control. He scored a hit some 100 yards ahead in a low bush in which something blew up. German helmets showed in the trench in front and the flame throwers swept along it. Then my face hit the periscope and a sheet of flame flung me into the bottom of the turret. I couldn't breathe as the flames roared out of the driving compartment.

Hischier's tank had been hit by a 75mm shell that killed two crew members instantly while all three survivors were badly burned and forced to crawl on their elbows once they bailed out of the tank. This tragic drama would be repeated with only minor variations for the next two days.

Despite mounting casualties, the Charwood operation was making impressive gains in the northern suburbs of Caen where British troops had inflicted 75 percent casualties on many of the German units they were engaging. However, the Canadian advance on Carpiquet was confronting the ferocious defenders of the 12th SS Panzer Division led with violent gusto by Kurt "Panzer" Meyer. The division commander alternately roared through the cobbled streets on his motorcycle organizing stop-gap battle groups and strode through the masonry strewn alleys carrying a Panzerfaust in a personal duel with Allied tanks. Waves of German panzers clashed over and over again with Canadian 17-pounder antitank batteries in a duel for supremacy of the region around the airport. At the village of Ginchy, the Canadians staged a Wild-West-style charge with sixteen Bren carriers firing their guns in every direction as they engaged in a spectacular shootout with Germans perched in virtually every window and doorway in the community's main street.

Meanwhile, the British 43rd (Wessex) Division and its supporting tanks were slamming into Hill 112 at the old Epsom battlefield challenging the fighting prowess of other units of the 12th SS Panzer Division. Meyer's often fanatical teenagers inflicted two thousand casualties on the attackers, but ended the first day of Charwood reduced to only forty tanks and perhaps a battalion of infantry still in condition to keep fighting. A massive surge among the lifeless trees by the Duke of Cornwall's Light Infantry pushed part way up the deadly slopes, but the defenders promptly staged a spirited nighttime counterattack in which eerie flarelight illuminated panzers crushing British riflemen under their treads as they pushed the Tommies back down the hill. Both sides now poured additional reinforcements into the battle and the fighting surged back and forth over the same blackened, bloodstained ground as men in field gray and khaki grappled in a death grip with one another. While supporting Allied fighter-bombers wheeled and dove in the sky, bombing, rocketing, and machine gunning the Germans on the summit, groups of Tigers rumbled forward like metal predators smashing into clusters of British infantrymen. Panzer Group West decreed that Hill 112 must be held at all costs and elements of the 10th SS Panzer Division, 1st SS Panzer Division, and 102nd Heavy Tank Battalion surged into action to maintain the stalemate on the slopes.

While Hill 112 was still hotly contested, the battle in Caen itself was gradually swinging in favor of the attackers. All day on July 9 British and Canadian attacks on the northern fringes of Caen and the airfield facilities at Carpiquet gradually whittled down the already meager number of surviving German defenders. At the airfield itself a mere fifty Hitler Youth were burrowed in the ruins of stone buildings fighting a one-sided duel with the Canadian attackers. At the town of Ardenne, a single battery of 88s holding back the onrushing surge of Shermans was captured one gun at a time until the battery commander and six surviving gunners fought with spades and rifle butts and finally went down in a final burst of submachine-gun fire. As British

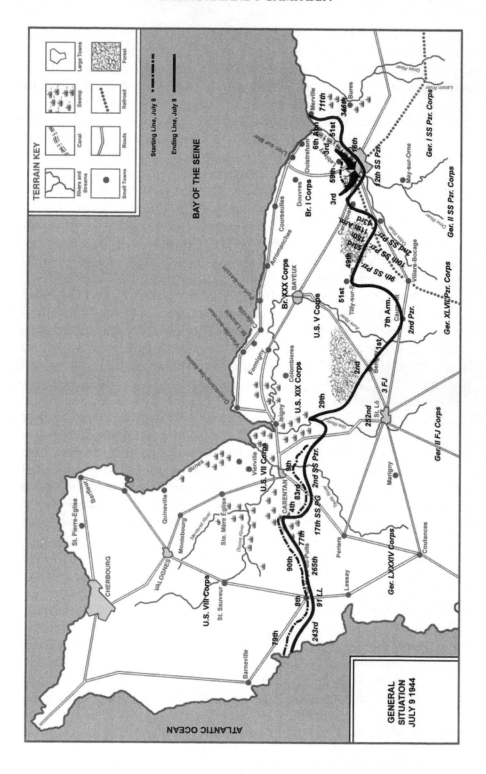

GENERAL
SITUATION
JULY 9 1944

and Canadian troops overwhelmed each of his strongpoints, "Panzer" Meyer finally defied the Führer's orders to hold Caen to the last man and ordered his surviving units to be ferried across the Orne. As the general insisted after the war, "We were meant to die in Caen, but one just couldn't watch those youngsters being sacrificed to a senseless order."

The British and Canadian attackers had accomplished most of the objectives Montgomery had set for Charwood, and now the far larger Goodwood operation was about to be initiated. Much of the concept for this new offensive was based on the fact that the forty thousand British casualties in the first five weeks of Overlord included a far higher proportion of infantrymen than the campaign planners had expected. By early July the pool of available infantry replacements was beginning to dry up. In the summer of 1944 Montgomery and Dempsey were tapping into the manpower of the Royal Artillery, sending field gunners and antiaircraft gunners to a sketchy six-week-long instruction course before being sent to the front lines as riflemen.

However, if Montgomery was short of infantry, he enjoyed a large surplus of available tanks as new vehicles were being landed almost continuously. More than one thousand tanks were already on hand with plenty of replacements available, and the victor of El Alamein decided to use those assets in a huge battle of attrition with the German panzers. While the XXX and XII Corps pinned down the defenders in the old Epsom battlefield area, the II Canadian Corps would capture the huge Columbelles steelworkers complex while the 3rd British Division attacked southeastward to expand the Orne River bridgehead. In the center, Allied firepower would be substituted for infantry as a gap seven thousand yards wide would be blown by more than a thousand heavy and medium bombers, followed by a barrage of 750 guns and a massive fighter-bomber sweep. Then 710 tanks in the three armored divisions of the VIII Corps would cross the Caen Canal and Orne River and advance on a one-regiment front toward the vital high ground of Bourguebus Ridge which was the gateway to the open country beyond Caen.

This massive tank assault would be headed by the 11th Armoured Division under General G. P. "Pip" Roberts, followed by the Guards Armoured Division and 7th Armoured Division on a six-mile advance to the high ground around Caen. Falaise Road, skirting dangerously close to both the heavily fortified Columbelles steelworkers and a series of strongly defended villages, lead to the Caen-Vimont railway line and Bourguebus Ridge beyond.

Montgomery's major objectives for Goodwood were to force the Germans to commit their panzers to battle around Caen rather than swinging westward to interfere with Bradley's offensive; to clear the defenders from Bourguebus Ridge; and finally, to allow reconnaissance units to poke southward toward Falaise to establish the level of enemy strength in the open country beyond Caen. The general insisted that anything short of an actual British retreat would represent some level of accomplishment provided Bradley was given the opportunity to initiate Operation Cobra without encountering massive armored resistance. However, while Montgomery, Bradley, and Dempsey were all in clear agreement that Goodwood was intended mainly to *compliment* Cobra rather than annihilating the German army on the eastern end of the Normandy battlefield, the British commander's communications to Eisenhower regarding the operation were so effusive and full of decisive phrases that Eisenhower expected a massive British breakthrough that would thrust far beyond the environs of Caen.

The British ground forces commander used the tone of his communications to Eisenhower to secure Ike's enthusiastic support for a massive Allied air intervention that would ultimately throw four thousand planes into the offensive. The air attacks were expected to be so extensive that the strongpoint village of Cagny alone would be hit by 650 tons of bombs while the Columbelles complex would be saturated with 2,500 tons of deadly steel. An armada of American bombers would saturate all of the central strongpoints in the path of the armored divisions with thousands of anti-personnel bombs which would kill German soldiers but not crater the approaches the British tanks would require. Also, unlike earlier operations, Goodwood would be initiated immediately after the bombing raids to prevent the defenders from recovering their senses before the attackers were upon them.

Montgomery hoped that the sheer magnitude of surprise and violence would propel the British attack to success, but German agents among the Norman population were beginning to report to German headquarters that a huge British attack was imminent and one of Rommel's last bequests to the German army was to organize a deadly series of impediments to challenge the British offensive.

The Desert Fox established five belts of defenses beyond the Orne. These included a forward crust of infantry and machine gunners; a second line held by the panzergrenadiers of the 21st Panzer Division supported by thirty-six Tiger tanks; a third belt of twelve fortified villages along the Caen-Vimont railway bristling with mobile antitank guns; a fourth line of nearly one hundred 88s along Bourguebus Ridge supported by a final line of 194 field guns and 272 multiple-barreled rocket launchers. Five miles further back German armored units lurked in the woods ready to launch a massive counterattack. When Rommel left the front for the last time on the eve of Goodwood, he was confident that such a formidable defensive array could meet any conceivable British onslaught.

At 4 A.M. on July 18, British and Canadian ground forces looked up in the early morning sky to watch one of the most spectacular aerial displays of the war. One British tanker recalled "a distant thunder in the air which brought all the sleepy eyed tank crews out of their blankets. A thousand Lancasters were flying in from the sea in groups of three or four at 3000 feet. Ahead of them the pathfinders were scattering their flares and before long, the first bombs were dropping. After a few minutes there was a turmoil of dust and smoke while occasionally an aircraft would fall like a swaying leaf flaming to the ground."

While British ground observers could be almost poetical about the massive power that was being unleashed on their behalf, German defenders were much less lyrical about the event. Lieutenant Freiherr von Rosen, commander of a company of Tiger tanks, was shocked at the devastation inflicted by the bombers. "The bombardment early in the morning of July 18 was the worst we have ever experienced in the war. Although we were in foxholes under out tanks, we had a lot of casualties. Some of the 62 ton machines lay upside down in bomb craters 30 feet across; they had been spun through the air like playing cards. Two of my men committed suicide; they weren't up to the psychological effect. Of my 14 Tigers, not one was operational. All had been covered in dust and earth, the guns disadjusted, the cooling systems of the engines out of action."

Then the guns of two Royal Navy cruisers, the monitor HMS *Roberts*, and one hundred batteries of field artillery leveled machine-gun posts, tore antitank positions to shreds, and buried infantry trenches with everything in them, and the first of 877 tanks and 8,000 vehicles committed to the first phase of the operation lurched forward as surviving German tanks and riflemen rallied to challenge their advance. Flail tanks cleared a narrow path through a succession of minefields and tanks of the 3rd Royal Tank Regiment, the Fife and Forfar Yeomanry, and the 23rd Hussars rumbled southward accompanied by supporting infantry regiments including the 3rd Monmouth, 1st Herefords, and 4th King's Shropshire Light Infantry. These territorial units from the Welsh border country were soon heavily engaged in fighting their way through the fortified villages of Cuverville and

Demouville while large elements of the armored regiments rolled toward the first major prize of the operation, the strategically important town of Cagny which provided access to the Caen-Vimont rail line and Bourguebus Ridge beyond. However, as the British tankers drove toward the town from the north, one of the most talented members of the German panzer forces was just entering Cagny from the opposite direction.

Colonel Hans von Luck, commander of the Panzer Grenadier Regiment of the 21st Panzer Division, was just returning from a short leave in Paris where he had been attempting to find a safe haven for his part Jewish fiancée. Von Luck's choice of romantic relationships may have been frowned on by Nazi officials, but he had been nominated by Hitler's old crony Sepp Dietrich for a Knight's Cross for his vigorous defense of Escoville earlier in the campaign and enjoyed the complete confidence of this usually ferocious corps commander. When the young colonel arrived in Cagny he was startled by the impact of the Allied bombardment but climbed aboard a still functioning Panzer IV tank to drive around the area and attempt to cobble together informal battle groups from among the survivors. The panzer commander had been entrusted with authority over Battle Group von Luck which included his own grenadier regiment, a battalion of Tigers, an assault gun battalion, a battalion of Luftwaffe field troops, and a Luftwaffe 88mm battery, with orders to block access to the railway line and the approaches to the ridge beyond. Now much of this powerful force was either destroyed or inoperable and as von Luck would recall, "when I came to the northern edge of the village, I saw to my dismay about 25 or 30 British tanks which had already passed southward over the main road to Caen which ran from east to west. The whole area was dotted with British tanks which were slowly rolling south against no opposition. How could I plug the gap?"

The only reasonably intact unit that was immediately at hand was the battery of Luftwaffe guns which had been supplied by headquarters to provide antiaircraft protection for von Luck's battle group. The colonel quickly perceived another use for these formidable weapons and dashed over to the young battery commander with a request to deploy the skyward pointing guns as horizontal antitank cannon. The Luftwaffe officer had little desire to join the ground battle and insisted that "my concern is enemy planes, fighting tanks is your job. I'm Luftwaffe!" At this point the exasperated panzer officer pulled out his pistol, aimed it at the startled battery commander's head and replied, "Either you're a dead man or you can earn yourself a medal!" This line of reasoning quickly produced the desired effect, and in a few minutes the deadly 88s were deployed in a dense apple orchard adjacent to a cornfield that seemed to be a likely approach route for the British armored column.

A few minutes later a line of Shermans from the Fife and Forfars poked through the cornstalks, ready to sweep into the streets of Cagny. The tankers were startled by the menacing boom of the Luftwaffe guns. As one British soldier remembered, "The strength of the opposition came as a swift and unpleasant surprise. The land laid waste by the bombers seemed like a piece of devastated territory which could scarcely conceal a living thing. Trees were uprooted, fields pitted and littered with dead cattle and theoretically nothing could be left alive on the lunar landscape. Yet suddenly there came evidence that the enemy was there and very aggressive too."

In a barrage that lasted only moments, twelve British tanks were destroyed, almost all seeming to burst into flames simultaneously. When von Luck arrived back on the scene with a hastily organized supporting platoon of panzergrenadiers, he noted "the cannon were firing one salvo after the other and one could see the shots flying through the corn like torpedoes. The men on the guns were proud of their first engagement as an anti-tank unit and in these cornfields north of the village at least 40 British tanks were on fire or shot up. I saw how the tanks that had already crossed the main road were slowly rolling back."

One British thrust had been parried but more lunges were about to follow. A column of Shermans of the 3rd Royal Tank Regiment was rumbling toward the Caen-Vimont railway embankment on it way to Bourguebus Ridge when the unit encountered a mobile assault-gun screen that had been cobbled together by von Luck's trusted subordinate, Major Becker. Becker had personally improvised a force of lethal tank killers by welding German 105mm guns to old French Hotchkiss tanks captured in the blitz of 1940. He now deployed eighteen of these odd looking vehicles straddling the steep embankment of the rail line that the British tanks were attempting to cross. Major William Close, commander of the 3rd Royal Tank Regiment's A Squadron and destined to become a close friend of von Luck's after the war, recalled, "The German gunners frantically swung their guns round towards us, opening fire at almost point blank range. They hit three of my tanks which burst into flames; and I could see that the squadron on my left also had several tanks blazing furiously." Major Close managed to save his surviving tanks by ordering them to drive into a nearby rail tunnel, but the momentum of the attack was broken and the defenders had

The massive tank offensive undertaken by the British, Operation Goodwood, was launched to sidetrack German attention from the American advance. These British soldiers are shown riding to the front on Shermans.

been given time to organize powerful countermeasures to stifle the British charge.

During the morning Panzer Group West commander General Heinrich Eberbach had become aware of the size of the British attack and particularly of the threat along the line of the Caen-Vimont railway. He therefore ordered the powerful panzer regiment of I SS Panzer Division to rush at all possible speed to Bourguebus Ridge to not only support the defense of that high ground but also launch a counterattack designed to push the British tanks back across the Caen-Troarn railway line. Forty-six Panthers and an equal number of Mark IVs were carefully deployed in concealed positions along the ridge and were then bolstered by the Tigers of the 503rd Heavy Tank Battalion creeping forward a short time later. Meanwhile seventy-eight 88mm guns and dozens of smaller cannon were perfectly positioned to meet the British armored charge that was massing on the plain below.

As major elements of all three British armored divisions began to fan out toward Bourguebus, a deadly combination of German tanks

and artillery boomed a startling welcome and Shermans and Cromwells either flared up in brilliant funeral pyres or simply ground to a
halt belching dull clouds of gray smoke from their gutted interiors.
Some surviving tanks rumbled toward the ridge-top villages of Bras
and Huber Folie some three thousand yards ahead across open terrain.
German tank commanders looked down on the almost helpless vehicles on the plain below and maneuvered into optimal firing positions.
Corporal Ron Cox of the 2nd Fife and Forfar Yeomanry barely saw the
enemy tanks firing from their concealment. "At first we seemed to
advance quite rapidly, then suddenly, my tank ground to a halt as did
all the others I could see. The Tigers and anti-tank gunners on our
flanks had apparently let the 3rd Tanks pass through and then opened
up on the Fife and Forfar Yeomanry ... other tanks I could see were all
stationary and several were beginning to brew. There were no targets.
Nothing intelligible was coming over the radio. I watched through the
periscope, fascinated as though it was a film I was seeing." When the
88s and panzers had finished their barrage, four of sixty-one
Yeomanry tanks were still operable and they survived only because
the Germans shifted their fire to the more profitable targets among the
Hussars. A few minutes later their tanks were also flaming in this
awful graveyard of British armor.

Every armored unit that had attempted to climb Bourguebus
Ridge had been shattered in a series of futile charges that was capped
by a vicious German counterattack that pushed the British line back
north of the Caen-Vimont railway line by dusk on July 18. That night,
the Luftwaffe made one of its few effective raids of the Normandy
campaign and caused heavy personnel losses among both headquarters staff and replacement tank crews scheduled to go into action the
next day. The action on July 19 was fierce but largely inconclusive as
the Germans continued to stave off further British attacks on
Bourguebus Ridge while the Canadians were able to clear the
Columbelles factory area and penetrate into the nearby town of
Vaucelles. The onset of another stretch of rainy, miserable weather on
July 20 effectively halted Operation Goodwood and set in motion a
fierce debate over who actually won the battle. The British and
Canadian assault units had lost over four hundred tanks and Allied
reconnaissance units were certainly not poking around the streets of
Falaise as Montgomery had hoped at the onset of the offensive.
However, Allied personnel losses had been remarkable light with only
eighty-one men killed in the four tank regiments of the 11th Armoured
Division and only twenty killed or wounded in that division's four

British and Canadian infantry who fought in Montgomery's Operations Charwood and Goodwood suffered great casualties but laid the way for the success of the American Cobra operation.

infantry battalions. Two German divisions, the 1st SS Panzer and the 21st Panzer Division had lost 109 tanks in the opening phase of Goodwood alone and nearly half of the defenders' antitank guns were put out of commission. Most important, Goodwood had accomplished its primary mission; tanks that could have wreaked havoc with the American advance in Operation Cobra were now locked in a deadly contest with British armored units and would be useless to the German foot soldiers holding the lines beyond St. Lô. The most important offensive of the Normandy campaign was about to be unleashed, and if it succeeded, the days of German control over the Normandy battlefield would be numbered.

Armor in the Normandy Campaign

One of the most high-profile aspects of the fighting in Normandy was the clash between Allied armor and the fearsome panzers. The question of whether armored quality or quantity was more decisive in the campaign has fueled a controversy that continues over five decades later. The most numerous and controversial Allied tanks in Normandy were the M-4 Shermans that became the main medium tank used by both American and British armored divisions in the summer of 1944.

The Sherman was a product of the American army's need for a tank that could be mass produced in staggering numbers, could prove reliable in combat, and yet was small enough to be transported in large numbers across the ocean. The M-4 series of tanks had a .30-caliber bow-mounted machine gun operated by the assistant driver, a .30-caliber machine coaxially mounted with the main gun, and a .50-caliber machine gun placed on the outside of the turret for antiaircraft use. This 32-ton tank was just under twenty feet long with a road speed of twenty-six miles per hour. It was easy to build, easy to maintain, and featured a power turret far superior to its German counterparts. As civilian auto plants geared up for wartime production they were able to produce an impressive 88,000 Shermans, a figure that far exceeded German production figures. However, the Sherman had two major flaws. First, it carried far too little armor. The 76mm of frontal armor and 31mm of side armor meant that under normal circumstances Panzer IVs, Panthers, and Tigers could easily penetrate the hull at relatively long distances, an event that happened so often that Sherman crews mockingly called their vehicles "Ronsons," after the popular lighter that was guaranteed to light

up the first time. Second, the standard gun mounted in the Sherman turret was a low-velocity 75mm gun that was adequate for attacking German infantry units but packed too little punch to consistently penetrate the armor of most German panzers. The British army improved the situation by equipping about one-fourth of their Shermans with the superb 17-pounder antitank gun which gave these upgraded vehicles the punch of a Panzer IV, or possibly even a Panther. The Americans upgraded the M-4 with a 76mm high-velocity gun that was a considerable improvement but few of these models were available during the Normandy campaign.

The Germans approached tank manufacturing in the tradition of their automobile industry—they produced high quality vehicles but in relatively small numbers. The main workhorse of the Normandy campaign was the Panzer Kampfwagen IV, also know as the Mark IV Panzer. This 25-ton vehicle was roughly the equivalent of a Sherman as it carried 80mm of frontal armor and 30mm of side armor and had a road speed of twenty-five miles per hour. The standard Mark IV carried a 75mm gun that had superior muzzle velocity to a Sherman and was roughly equivalent to the punch of the Firefly, the British upgraded model. However, while the Americans built nearly 90,000 Shermans, German factories produced a far more modest 9,000 Mark IVs.

The other main tank that served with panzer divisions was the PZKW V, more familiarly known as the Panther. This was probably the best all-around tank on either side during the Normandy campaign as the 45-ton vehicle featured 100mm of frontal armor, 45mm of side armor, an impressive thirty-four mile per hour road speed and a state-of-the-art 75mm gun. While the British Firefly could engage the Panther on reasonably equal terms, the only proven American weapons that could counter this formidable vehicle were 90mm antiaircraft guns and 105mm howitzers firing a shaped-charge warhead. Unfortunately, the howitzers were usually already engaged in their own fire support missions which allowed the Panthers to sometimes roam the battlefield to the terror of American infantrymen.

The most powerful panzer was the PZKW VI or Tiger tank which was a 54-ton monster that carried 100mm of frontal armor, 80mm of side armor, yet still nearly matched the Sherman's road speed at twenty-three miles an hour. This tank also featured the superb German 88mm gun which could make short work of a Sherman in an individual duel. However, only slightly more than 1,300 Tigers were ever built and most of them ended up on the Eastern Front opposing the Soviets. The Tigers deployed on the Western Front were relegated to special heavy tank battalions under army command and parceled out to smaller units for specific missions before they were returned to headquarters. On any given day the Germans were fortunate to have one hundred operational Tigers available, but they were so fearsome that many Allied soldiers assumed that any enemy armored vehicle they encountered had to be a Tiger, an impression that was a clear advantage for the Wehrmacht.

CHAPTER XVI

Operation Cobra
Breakout at St. Lô

Goodwood and Cobra had been planned as a one-two punch of quick succession and irresistible force against both the eastern and western flanks of the German army in Normandy. However, the same torrential storms that turned the British drive beyond Caen into a soggy stalemate also delayed the start of the American offensive for nearly a week. Dwight Eisenhower spent that time ruminating over the unfulfilled promise of Goodwood, an operation that he had initially found so enticing that he had insisted to Montgomery, "It will make some of the 'old classics' look like a skirmish between patrols." Now the British advance had fizzled out and he shifted attention to Cobra as he declared that "we are pinning our immediate hopes on Bradley's attack." As Eisenhower began to appreciate the mounting public pressure in Britain and the United States to avoid a bloody stalemate in Normandy, Omar Bradley paced his headquarters by day and sheepishly asked his aide for sleeping pills to get him through the incessantly rainy nights of this third week of July. However, as the commander of First Army focused on finalizing each detail of Cobra during this unwelcome hiatus, most of the high command of both the Axis and Allies shifted their attention to the dreary woodlands of East Prussia where a shocking and potentially decisive drama was being played out in Adolf Hitler's headquarters.

On the afternoon of July 20, 1944, just as Goodwood was sputtering to a halt, a deeply religious, somewhat disfigured Wehrmacht colonel was excusing himself from a spartan conference room in a military complex called Wolf's Lair. Colonel Claus Count von Stauffenberg was a staff officer of the training and replacement command of the German army who had been ordered to attend this days' Führer conference to report on the raising of new divisions for the badly mauled Reich forces. The Count had fought bravely in earlier battles, suffering a number of wounds that included the loss of three fingers and one eye, but now he was a part of a conspiracy among a number of German officers to assassinate Hitler and make peace before the Reich itself was overrun. Stauffenberg entered the conference room occupied by Hitler and about twenty generals and staff officers and nonchalantly placed his briefcase under the table. He extracted several folders bulging with official reports but the valise was not quite empty; it contained a powerful bomb designed to kill the Führer and as many of his cronies as the blast could obliterate.

Stauffenberg's plan was not a suicide mission, so he politely excused himself moments before the bomb was set to explode. Then minutes later there was "a blinding sheet of dazzling yellow flame" which filled the room. General Gunter Korten, Luftwaffe chief of staff, was impaled by a large fragment of the exploding conference table while Lieutenant General Rudolf Schmundt, Hitler's personal adjutant, lay dying with both legs blown off. The Führer himself staggered from the building streaming blood from facial cuts and peppered in the thighs and legs with dozens of wooden splinters. However, the Reich dictator had survived the bomb blast because one of his aides had kicked the deadly parcel far down the other side of the table when the briefcase had gotten in his way after Stauffenberg's hasty exit. The Führer's initial euphoria over his miraculous escape quickly shifted into a vengeance mode which would result in the eventual execution of five thousand Germans including the forced suicides of von Kluge and Rommel a few weeks later. Not only were some of the Wehrmacht's more talented generals imprisoned or executed but the ones who were not were convinced that any opposition to Hitler on virtually any point might bring a charge of treason. Thus the rest of the Normandy campaign would be fought entirely on the Führer's terms with the surviving commanders forced to look behind them for the approaching footsteps of the Gestapo as much as in front for the approaching tanks and planes of the Allies.

A new Allied threat was indeed about to crystallize, but in the days immediately preceding Cobra, American officers and enlisted men feared they sniffed the aroma of stalemate in the stormy summer air. As one American tank crew member recalled of the period before the new offensive, "We were stuck; something dreadful seemed to have happened in terms of the overall plan. Things were going awry. The whole theory of mobility that we had been taught, and of our racing across the battlefield, seemed to have gone up in smoke." An armored division officer compared the frustrating campaign to the Persian invasion of Greece twenty-five centuries earlier, as "like an interminable succession of Thermopylaes, in every engagement we are only able to present one tiny unit to the enemy at a time." British soldiers were also bogged down around Bourguebus Ridge but at least they were comforted by Monty's personal attention and he uplifted their spirits with his optimistic rhetoric that their operations were right on schedule for victory. On the other hand, most American troops viewed Bradley as a remote, colorless chief who seemed to be concentrating on firing regimental and division commanders who weren't able to succeed in almost impossible circumstances. The commander of First Army may indeed have been remote and austere, but he was as emotionally charged by the fear of stalemate as any of his men and he fully understood the importance of the upcoming campaign to any hope of victory in France. He freely admitted that ongoing attempts to advance along an extremely broad front were providing an inadequate offensive punch and he envisioned the new operation as a narrow, concentrated thrust along a seven-thousand-yard front supported by one of the most massive aerial bombardments of the war.

Bradley wanted to use nearly 2,500 planes to saturate a rectangle 3½ miles wide and 1½ miles deep south of the vital St. Lô-Periers road that was now seen as the gateway to the open country beyond the bocage. Swarms of fighter-bombers would smash German positions within 250 yards of the road while an armada of heavies would knock out enemy resistance to a depth of 2,500 yards, augmented by the combined fire of one thousand artillery pieces. Then three infantry divisions, the 4th, 9th, and 30th would push forward and hold open the shoulders for an armored advance by capturing the crossroads towns of Marigny, St. Gilles, and La Chapelle. Once these flanks were secured, American tanks would rumble toward the main objective of Avranches, a town which straddled a junction of the Cotentin and Brittany Peninsulas. Once this city was in Allied hands, one part of Bradley's growing army would sweep westward to capture the valuable Brittany ports while the remaining divisions would storm eastward toward Mortain, Argentan, and an eventual linkup with the

British Second Army pushing southward from Caen toward Falaise. It was then expected that a huge ring of steel would be clamped shut somewhere between Argentan and Falaise with much, or perhaps all, of the German army in Normandy trapped within its grip.

The key to this auspicious series of events was the effectiveness of the air bombardment that would provide the opportunity for a massive American breakthrough. To plan the air attack, Bradley flew to Air Marshal Leigh-Mallory's headquarters at Stanmore, a mansion near Harrow, for a final conference on the bombing operation. Air barons such as Tedder, Spaatz, and Leigh-Mallory listened to the First Army commander's proposal for a bombing run on a course parallel to the east-west St. Lô-Periers road so that the attack squadrons would not fly over most of the American ground troops and long or short drops would fall on the German side of the road. Bradley's plan found little favor with the air chiefs who insisted that their planes needed to fly perpendicular to the road in order to minimize time over targets and reduce the impact of enemy antiaircraft fire. The ground commander's insistence that a parallel bomb run at sunrise or sundown would blind German flak crews enough to negate this problem was received very coolly in the conference room and while Bradley left the room under the impression that his plan would be adopted, the air officers later insisted that no such agreement was ever reached; as far as they were concerned there would be a perpendicular bomb run or no bomb run.

Allied weather forecasters gave Bradley the welcome news that there appeared to be a break in the stormy weather beginning on July 24, and on that Monday morning the general's command post was filled with high-ranking onlookers. Lieutenant General Leslie McNair, army ground forces commander, Lieutenant General William Simpson, commander of the newly organized Ninth Army, and Air Marshal Leigh-Mallory, who was taking personal charge of the air bombardment, were all watching for the arrival of the lead squadrons of the great aerial armada. However, a very rapidly developing storm-front caused quickly deteriorating weather conditions and most of the planes were either grounded or called back to England. Yet four hundred planes did not receive the recall order in time and they flew a perpendicular pattern over the St. Lô-Periers road. Large numbers of bombs dropped on the north side of the road among forward units of Americans and when the smoke cleared 25 GIs were dead and 131 more wounded and Bradley was seething at the perceived duplicity of the air commanders while insisting that all prospects for a surprise attack had now been lost. In reality, the bombing attack had little

…d massive carpet bombing to precede the breakout of … 944. The result was an unprecedented rain of steel on … ortunately numerous Allied deaths from friendly fire.

impact on
Montgomei
shal insiste
feint desigr
east.

Tuesday
Eisenhower
Operation (
dred mediu
formation p
opposed bu
numbing b
lucky stars t
were about t
air forces. '
among frier
four thousar
of the road.
mishandled
crept into ou
bombs were
ally forward
picion that t
from us wer
a gentle bre
scribable kir
in muscle ar
pass over us
attack was c
wounded inc
European wa
tion with for
turned away,
his collar.

If this a
Americans, it
of the thousa
sands of Ger
shock and fea
Lehr Division
was wrought

General Omar Bradley order
Operation Cobra on July 25,
the German divisions and ur

forth the bomb carpets were laid, artillery positions were wiped out, tanks overturned and buried, infantry positions flattened and all roads and tracks destroyed. By midday the entire area resembled a moon landscape with the bomb craters touching rim to rim—all signal communications had been cut and no command was possible. The shock effect on the troops was indescribable. Several of my men went mad and rushed round in the open until they were cut down by splinters. Simultaneously with the storm from the air, innumerable guns of the American artillery poured drumfire into our field positions."

When the hurricane of steel finally passed, American officers attempted to rally their alternately shocked and furious men for an advance across this road of death into the enemy-held country beyond. While it appeared that no living thing could have survived the maelstrom of explosives, there *were* German survivors and some of them were even able to rally enough to meet the American advance. Fritz Bayerlein rode around this moonscape on a motorcycle, cobbling together an improvised battle group from his fifteen surviving tanks, a small knot of panzergrenadiers, and a handful of the always invaluable 88mm guns. The initial American advance was gained only grudgingly and over dozens of bodies of men in both olive drab and field gray.

The ground attack of July 25 involved more than 120,000 American soldiers engaged in battle with a little less than 30,000 defenders. Yet the GIs were facing terrain that massively favored the Germans who exploited every advantage they could possible employ. For most of the day the defenders were able to hold the Americans at bay in dozens of incidents in which one or two tanks, an 88mm gun, and a few heavily armed infantrymen used hedges, sunken roads, slit trenches, and stone farmhouses to challenge the olive-drab advancing tide. At the end of the day Eisenhower flew back to England convinced that Cobra was a bust and even optimistic generals admitted that few clean breakthroughs had been accomplished. The infantry had gained some ground, but they had not fully secured the shoulders that seemed to be critical to any armored advance. Thus Bradley and VII Corps commander Joe Collins faced an agonizing decision. Should they commit the main body of American armor without worrying about the safety of their flanks or should they keep bludgeoning the enemy line with successive infantry attacks? Collins convinced Bradley that a massive armored advance was worth the risk and the second day of Cobra would begin with the massive intervention of American armor.

The American leaders from Eisenhower on down were not aware

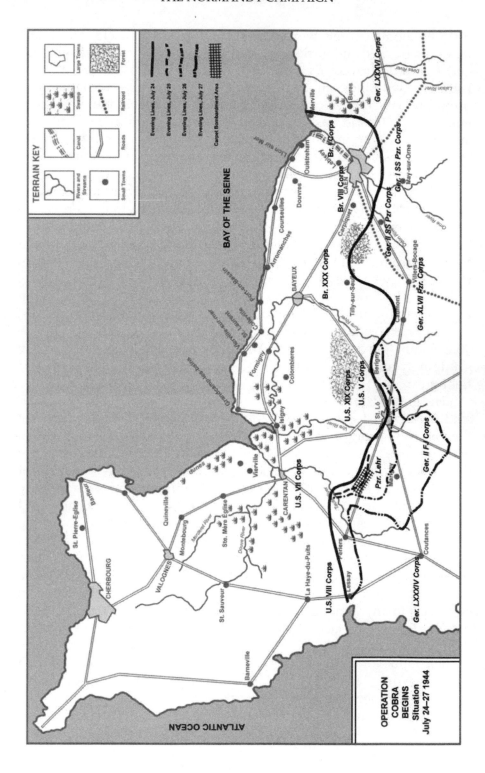

that the massive mobile operation that would begin on July 26 would be aided immeasurably by two potentially decisive developments. First, the Allied generals had not yet appreciated the fact that the formidable German opposition that they had encountered was the main enemy resistance; there were few backup positions or reserve troops available. While the British advance at Goodwood had not encountered the most deadly German resistance until two or three advance lines had been penetrated, the Americans struggling to push past the enemy defenders near the St. Lô-Periers road were actually engaging the only significant force available to stop them. The combination of the massive bombing and the bloody ground engagements on Tuesday had badly mauled the German units assigned to hold back the Americans and by Wednesday morning there was no longer a continuous line, but only isolated strongpoints that could eventually be bypassed.

The U.S. First Army devised these iron "tusks" and affixed them to the front of tanks. The "Rhinos" were used to cut through the hedgerows of Normandy.

Second, American tankers had finally devised a new weapon to counter the effects of the formidable hedgerows. One of the most positive attributes of the American army in World War II was the willingness of unit commanders on all levels to listen to the advice of enlisted men concerning suggestions to improve the army's combat effectiveness. The seemingly endless maze of hedges that confronted the GIs in Normandy became a major topic of discussion among the soldiers and provoked a number of possible countermeasures. The most vital innovation was developed by Sergeant Curtis Culin of the 2nd Armored Division's 102nd Cavalry Reconnaissance Squadron. Culin supervised the construction of an iron "tusk" welded to a Sherman tank which could rip through a hedge in less than a minute. The tanker's device soon gained the attention of the upper echelons of the First Army and on July 14 Omar Bradley attended a demonstration of the new vehicle now nicknamed the "Rhino." The army commander was so impressed with the concept that all available welders and welding equipment were drafted to fashion hundreds of Rhinos using scrap metal from the German beach obstacles that had plagued the GIs on D-Day. By July 26, five hundred of the newly fitted Shermans were available for the great armored offensive that was about to begin.

On the hot, sultry morning of July 26 the three mobile columns of American tanks and vehicles rumbled across the St. Lô-Periers road and thrust into the enemy-held countryside. Lieutenant John Downey of the 18th Infantry Regiment marveled at the new sense of confidence developing among the GIs as they advanced rapidly through a region that clearly showed the impact of Allied air attacks on the German defenders. "Huge craters dotted the fields and the infrequent farmhouses were smashed. Wrecked German tanks and self-propelled guns were encountered at hedgerow corners and near some farmhouses. We emerged into a narrow secondary road and moved up cautiously. We passed wrecked German two-wheeled carts with dead horses lying stiff legged and bloody beside them." When an unseen German gun began shelling a nearby crossroads, "we watched a couple of P-47s swooping down to shoot it up. They were constantly around, looking for something German to shoot at. These two made several passes and then swooped off again." Hour by hour, tanks covered with infantrymen clinging to their hull and trucks crammed with riflemen clad in olive drab raced southwestward passing smoldering German vehicles and somewhat dazed French onlookers who only vaguely realized they were being liberated.

The German High Command had only a vague idea that some-

Once the breakout began, the Americans steadily advanced through Normandy, as these soldiers seen riding in an antitank half-track.

thing was terribly wrong at the front and the generals did not realize how far the Americans had penetrated. General von Choltitz, commander of the LXXXIV Corps, quickly placed a high priority on forming an impenetrable line in front of the vital crossroads town of La Chapelle and he rushed a reserve regiment of the 353rd Division to that community. Meanwhile, Seventh Army commander General Hausser, who was experiencing an almost total communications breakdown with his corps commander, released a reserve regiment of the 275th Division for the same purpose. Both generals assumed that the hard-fighting units of Panzer Lehr would hold back the surging tide of Americans until a new line could be cobbled together in front of La Chapelle. However, the officer most aware of the condition of the Panzer Lehr was far less optimistic about that division's prospects.

General Fritz Bayerlein spent this humid, stifling summer day sitting in his field headquarters near the village of Dangy arguing forcefully with a staff officer sent by Field Marshal von Kluge to emphasize the important role of Panzer Lehr in delaying the American advance.

Bayerlein had hoped that this elegantly dressed visitor was bringing news of large-scale replacement of tanks and men but the colonel merely brought a message from the field marshal that the St. Lô-Periers road was to be held to the last defender. The division commander gripped the edge of the table and spoke in a low, sarcastic voice. "Out in front, everyone is holding out. My grenadiers, engineers and tank crews are all holding their ground. Not a single man is leaving his post. Not one! They're lying in their foxholes mute and silent for they are dead. You may report to the Field Marshal that the Panzer Lehr is annihilated. Only the dead can now hold the line. But I shall stay here if those are my orders."

As German commanders at each echelon marked the progress of the battle on their maps, the American armored columns were making each new stop line obsolete before it could even be communicated to defending units. Major General Edward Brooks, commander of the 2nd Armored Division, had attached a regiment of infantry to the tanks of his "Hell on Wheels" unit and then divided the infantry-tank force into two separate columns that were directed to keep driving until they ran into an impenetrable line of defenders. Brigadier General Maurice Rose, leader of Combat Command A, blasted through a series of German roadblocks, rolled into the town of Gilles, and then rumbled down a wide highway that was supposed to be defended by the Panzer Lehr. The few remaining defenders were routed by incessant fighter-bomber sweeps and by evening the column was on the outskirts of the rail center of Canisy, several miles beyond the original divisional objective for the day. Meanwhile, on the other end of the penetration area, a combined infantry-tank force from the 1st Division and 3rd Armored Division's Combat Command B had smashed its way into the town of Marigny and was preparing to launch a new thrust toward its objective of Coutances, three miles to the southwest.

Omar Bradley's intention for Cobra was to use the infantry divisions to create an open corridor for three separate mobile exploiting forces to thrust westward toward the Cotentin coast, toward Coutances, and ultimately, Avranches. By the morning of July 27 the corridors seemed to be fully developed and each column was now engaged in a wild, often violent ride to the sea. When it became obvious that La Chapelle could not be held, von Kluge authorized Hausser to concentrate every available unit around Coutances to challenge the American advance in that direction. Elements of the 17th SS Panzer Grenadier Division, the 6th Parachute Regiment, and a battalion of the

2nd SS Panzer Division tanks converged on that city and focused their attention on blocking a growing threat from the American 1st Division and its accompanying tank units. However, while the men of the 1st Division were temporarily stymied, Collins ordered General Leroy Watson to lead the remainder of the 3rd Armored Division on a drive to Coutances from south of the city. This thrust was also blocked, but at a cost of using virtually every last reserve unit in the city's garrison. Thus when General Isaac White led the 2nd Armored Division's Combat Command B toward Coutances from yet another avenue of approach there was almost nothing left to prevent a rupture of the tenuous defensive line. The German position began crumbling at so many points that 2nd SS Panzer Division commander General Tychsen was killed by one fast-moving American mobile unit while Seventh Army commander Paul Hausser narrowly escaped death during an enemy armored car assault on his field headquarters.

Von Kluge, Hausser, and von Choltitz spent that night haggling over a decision to either defend Coutances to the last man or evacuate the surviving units to protect Avranches, the last obstacle to an

As the Germans withdrew, they put up stiff resistance in French towns and many were reduced to rubble before they were liberated, as in this town of Coutances.

American invasion of the Brittany Peninsula. Von Kluge finally authorized a compromise fallback to Percy where members of the Coutances garrison were expected to link up with reinforcements arriving from southern France to fashion a new barrier to the Allied capture of Avranches. However, not only did the Americans overrun Coutances on July 28, some armored units began blocking the south-bound roads that the Germans needed to stage their withdrawal. One huge column of five hundred retreating tanks and vehicles was stacked up short of the town of Roncy by a determined American roadblock and then pulverized as squadron after squadron of Allied fighter-bombers peeled out of the summer sky and poured rockets, machine-gun bullets, and cannon shells into the massive traffic jam below. When the smoke cleared 100 tanks and 250 vehicles were burning furiously while surviving foot soldiers fled into the nearby woods. Another German column of one thousand infantry and one hundred armored vehicles smashed into an outmanned American tank battalion sitting astride the road into St. Denis. The Germans initially overran the defenders' outposts, but massive air and armored reinforcements turned the engagement into a rout in which forty-eight vehicles were destroyed and nearly half the infantry force killed or captured. As this scene was repeated up and down the line, the 30th Division commander General Leland Hobbs exulted, "The thing has busted wide open!" As the German lines teetered at the point of collapse, one of the most controversial American generals of World War II was about to regain his place on the stage after an enforced hiatus of several months. Lieutenant General George S. Patton was about to contribute his peculiar, and often brilliant, talents to the next phase of the Normandy campaign at almost the same time that Adolf Hitler was planning the most massive German counterattack of Overlord.

Gunther von Kluge

The second of the three German commanders in Normandy was born in Posen, Prussia, to an old aristocratic family that wielded enormous political influence and secured Gunther an officer's commission while he was still eighteen years old. Von Kluge spent most of World War I as a highly regarded staff officer and was selected to be a member of the 4,000-person officer corps that led the tiny 100,000-man Reichwehr after the Treaty of Versailles was signed. Hitler's rise to power provided an enormous boost to von Kluge's fortunes as he was rapidly promoted to lieutenant-general and appointed to command an entire military district. When von Kluge sided with General Werner Freiherr in a series of disputes with the Führer, he was summarily fired and only reinstated with the outbreak of war.

Von Kluge commanded the Fourth Army in the lightning victories in Poland and France and was rewarded with a field marshal's position in time for Barbarossa. The new field marshal led the spearhead of the German army to the suburbs of Moscow before the onset of winter and then spent the next two years engaging in a bloody series of campaigns at the head of Army Group Center before a serious injury in an automobile accident forced a nine-month hospitalization. Von Kluge spent much of this period of forced inactivity dithering between support and rejection of the men who were planning to assassinate Hitler. While von Kluge eventually withdrew from the plot, Gestapo agents picked up a trail of suspicion and the Führer began to suspect that his field marshal was planning to unilaterally surrender the German army in the west to the Allies. Thus when von Kluge was summoned back to Germany for "consultations," he suspected the worst and took poison near Metz, France, on August 19, 1944.

CHAPTER XVII

Operation Luttich
Counterattack at Mortain

*L*ieutenant General George S. Patton had spent the first several weeks of the Normandy campaign in an agonizing limbo between hope and despair. The general who had gained enormous success in North Africa and Sicily was in England at the time of Overlord's launch but was so far out of Eisenhower's inner circle that he only learned of the actual landings on the radio, remarking in his diary, "I hope I get in before its all over; I have horrible feelings that the fighting will be over before I get in...; admitting it is Hell to be on the sidelines and see all the glory eluding me." This enormously talented, egotistical soldier was on the sidelines to a large extent because of a pair of controversial incidents played out far to the south the previous year. During Operation Husky, the Allied invasion of Sicily, Patton had slapped and threatened two soldiers who were encountered in field hospitals and suffering from battle fatigue. Both men had legitimate health problems but carried no readily recognizable wounds, a sight which infuriated the mercurial general. The incidents very nearly resulted in Patton's dismissal and did generate the strongest words of censure written to a senior American officer in World War II. Eisenhower issued a scathing rebuke questioning his subordinate's judgement and self-discipline and "raising serious doubts in my mind as to your future usefulness." Any prospect of being named senior

American ground commander for Overlord was dashed, but Ike did hold out a lifeline for a person he still considered enormously talented even if far too unpredictable.

Eisenhower's plan for Overlord assured that the enormous infusion of troops into the Normandy beachhead would oblige the Allied command structure to be subdivided into separate American and British army groups under the command of Bradley and Montgomery at the end of July. While Monty would then have immediate responsibility for the Second British Army and First Canadian Army under the umbrella title of 21st Army Group, Bradley's command would expand to become 12th Army Group including the First United States Army and the Third United States Army. General Courtney Hodges, who was serving as Bradley's understudy in the role of First Army commander, would assume responsibility for that force while another officer would step in to command the newly deployed Third Army. Omar Bradley, who had served as Patton's subordinate in the Mediterranean campaign, had become thoroughly disgusted with his antics and apparently had little desire to see the aristocratic, opinionated officer join his command team. However, Eisenhower had the final say in the matter and on July 6, 1944, exactly one month after D-Day, George S. Patton was in Normandy preparing for his role in turning Cobra into a decisive breakthrough. Years later Bradley summarized his mixed feelings about the arrival of his controversial army commander: "He had not been my first choice for Army commander and I was still wary of the grace with which he would accept our reversal in roles. I was apprehensive in having George join my command, for I feared that too much of my time would probably be spend in curbing his impetuous habits." However, the American ground commander admitted that the California-born heir to a wealthy Virginia family offered intriguing assets in the slugging match for Normandy as "I knew that with Patton there would be no need for whipping Third Army to keep it on the move. We had only to keep him pointed in the direction we wanted to go." Patton in turn privately viewed Bradley as an overcautious, colorless pencil pusher whom he called "Omar the tent maker" to members of his inner circle. However, he successfully masked these feelings in public and just as Cobra reached its climax the new commander of the Third Army made his spectacular debut on the stage of the Normandy battlefield.

On July 28, 1944, just as American troops captured Coutances, Omar Bradley assigned operational command of General Troy Middleton's VIII Corps to Patton's as yet unofficial Third Army and directed his former superior officer to capture Avranches which was now the last remaining obstacle to a full-scale breakout into Brittany and the plains of southern Normandy. The provisional Third Army commander quickly displayed the characteristics that would make him both a successful and controversial officer by driving up to the most advanced position of the 6th Armored Division which was attempting to cross a shallow river near Avranches. He quickly noticed a group of officers huddled around a map and demanded to know why they were studying that document instead of advancing across the seemingly shallow water. When their response did not suit him, Patton went to the river and personally tested the depth, ignoring a party of Germans on the other side who, somewhat miraculously, equally ignored him. He then stormed over to division commander Major General Robert Grow and told him that if he valued his job he had better move his men across the river in record time. Germans and Americans alike would now have to get used to the presence of George Patton in the Normandy drama. As his men and vehicles prepared to move out to their potentially decisive breakout, their new commander delivered a speech that would form the introduction to the film biography of his life a quarter century later. Patton gruffy insisted, "I don't want to get any messages saying that 'we are holding our position.' We are not holding anything! Let the Hun do that. We are advancing constantly and we're not interested in holding on to anything except the enemy!"

The initial drive on Avranches proved amazingly successful as botched German demolition activities over bridges on both the Sele and Selune Rivers gave the Americans possession of both Avranches and its twin community of Pontebault with only minor casualties. However, the only road available to move nearly 200,000 men and 40,000 vehicles into either Brittany or southern Normandy was a narrow two-lane strand of rutted asphalt that according to one general offered the daunting challenge of moving a huge army through "what amounted to a straw." Patton blithely intermingled units, encouraged staff officers and even division commanders to double as traffic policemen, and at one point jumped into a police box in the center of Pontebault and directed traffic himself for the next hour and a half to the awed amazement of the hundreds of drivers he extricated from the huge traffic jam.

However, while Patton's units were gaining momentum in an exhilarating if somewhat bizarre advance in two opposite directions toward Brittany and southern Normandy, the operation was being watched carefully in the Wolf's Lair at Rastenburg by a German leader who was equally willing to take risks. Adolf Hitler had an avid interest in American cowboy films and he now saw Patton in the role of the western gambler who ignored long risks, sometimes to his own demise. Hitler told his entourage, "Just look at that cowboy general, driving into the south of Brittany along a single road and over a single bridge with an entire army. He doesn't care about the risks and acts as if he owned the world!"

Hitler was convinced that Patton was overplaying his hand and was engaged in a game so reckless and so contemptuous of a possible turn of his luck that he was providing the Führer with a golden opportunity to make him pay for such arrogance. The German dictator was now about to hatch a plan called Operation Luttich, the German name for the city of Liege that had been a focal point of a brilliant, nearly war-winning offensive in the opening days of World War I. Hitler believed that Patton's lack of caution had given him an opportunity to make this August a month that would go down in the history of his Third Reich.

Operation Luttich was Hitler's plan to concentrate a significant portion of the entire armored striking power of the German army in the west for a large-scale offensive westward from the crossroads town of Mortain toward Avranches and the sea twenty miles away. As the Führer emphasized, "We must strike like lightning toward Avranches; when we reach the sea, the American spearhead will be cut off ... we might even be able to cut off the entire beachhead. We mustn't get bogged down with mopping up the Americans who have broken through. We must wheel north like lightning and turn the entire enemy front to the rear." The offensive would be set in motion when four elite armored divisions, the 2nd Panzer, the 2nd SS Panzer, the 12th SS Panzer, and the 116th Panzer, would be pulled from the eastern flank forces confronting the British and Canadians and shifted westward toward Mortain to smash into the American forces pushing out from Avranches. The German leaders at Wolf's Lair assumed that Patton's units would be helplessly strung out over miles of roads and ripe for a properly concentrated armored counterblow. To this end, Hitler ordered Field Marshal von Kluge to use the four newly deployed armored divisions in a predawn attack on Monday, August 7, which would pulverize any American forces unlucky to be in the way.

As the hour of the offensive approached, Hitler belatedly decided to turn Luttich into an even larger gamble by doubling the size of the strike force through the addition of four more divisions, the 9th and 10th Panzer and the 9th and 10th SS Panzer. It would take several days to fully deploy the additional units and Hitler uncharacteristically advised his field marshal to postpone the attack until the new units arrived. Von Kluge demurred from this offer as he was convinced that the combination of possible loss of surprise and the first stirrings of a new British offensive mandated an immediate thrust toward Avranches with the forces already available. Mortain itself had already fallen to the Americans and the window of opportunity to do any real damage seemed to be closing rapidly.

The Americans who had just liberated Mortain found a small crossroads town of sixteen hundred inhabitants living along cobblestone streets that stretched up toward nearby Hill 317 which was a spur of the wooded highlands that the locals called Norman Switzerland. The top of this hill provided a spectacular view of the region as on a clear day parts of three provinces were visible, Normandy, Brittany, and Maine. One of the most noticeable man-made objects visible from this perch was Route 177 which stretched all the way to the Atlantic Ocean just over twenty miles away. This long belt of asphalt was the initial prize sought by Field Marshal von Kluge in the impending offensive, but in order to fully utilize that highway the Germans would first have to capture Mortain and its nearby hill.

The main obstacle to the first phase of von Kluge's march to the sea was a pair of regiments from the 30th Division. This unit, which had been named "Old Hickory Division" after Andrew Jackson, had regiments with a lineage that stretched back to the dawn of the American nation. The 117th Regiment was a descendant of units that had fought at King's Mountain in the War of Independence and under Old Hickory himself as they annihilated the British attempt to capture New Orleans in 1815. The 120th Regiment traced its roots back to the Confederate States's 1st North Carolina Regiment which had fought its way to the crest of Cemetery Ridge on the third day of Gettysburg and briefly smashed the Union line at a point afterward called the "high watermark of the Confederacy" in the wild melee that was Pickett's Charge. Now this regiment held the high ground against what was about to become a far more technologically advanced, if equally disastrous, version of the storming of the heights attempted by the men in gray and butternut eight decades earlier.

American commanders from Omar Bradley down were quickly aware of the strategic importance of Mortain and Hill 317, but General Leland Hobbs and the men of his 30th Division had only arrived in the area on the afternoon of August 6, hours before the German attack was scheduled to commence. The men of the Old Hickory Division were expected to deploy over a wide area and the force originally allocated to defending Hill 317 was rather slender. The 120th Regiment's 2nd Battalion sent E Company, K Company, two platoons from G Company, and a detachment from its heavy weapons company to secure the hill itself and the whole force numbered a little less than six hundred men. As this compact force of GIs gained its bearings in the fading twilight of Sunday evening, a powerful nemesis was about to strike.

At just past midnight on Monday, August 7, three columns of German tanks lumbered into motion and rumbled down a series of approach roads leading to the main routes to Avranches. As panzer-grenadiers and engineers clung to the top of the mechanical monsters the tanks clanked ahead through a thick, rolling fogbank which turned the night into a soupy blackness. A few minutes later an American forward observer heard the sound of grinding metallic treads and when he realized they were not friendly Shermans, he called in a request for an artillery strike from his battery three miles away. A few minor hits were scored, but a short time later twenty German tanks broke through the first American roadblock and swayed forward toward Mortain.

As supporting Tigers and Panthers poked out of the fog like hungry predators, elements of the Deutchland Regiment of the 2nd SS Panzer Division surged around the base of Hill 317 and poured down Fleur Road and Rochers Road into the center of Mortain. The attackers swept up dozens of prisoners and captured most of the town but the far more important objective, the crest of Hill 317, was still in American hands.

Squad-sized elements of the Der Führer Regiment of the 2nd SS Panzer Division were soon working their way uphill, attempting to infiltrate the American positions. One defender recalled, "They were screaming at the top of their voices 'Heil Hitler' and made enough noise that one could easily believe an entire battalion was attacking." However, the attackers were badly coordinated and the GIs grimly hung on throughout the night and into the early morning hours.

At mid-morning Operation Luttich was at best a mixed success. The Germans had captured Mortain and some panzer units had advanced as much as six miles toward Avranches. However, ominous signs were to appear on the horizon of battle. First, the German offensive was planned on the basis of extensive Luftwaffe involvement as

Hitler had promised one thousand fighters for an aerial umbrella over the armored columns. On the morning of August 7 that number was actually more like three hundred planes and they would prove of little use to the operation. Just as the squadrons of Messerschmitts and Focke-Wolfes were taking off from bases throughout France, seemingly endless flights of Allied fighter-bombers swooped down and mauled the German units so badly that not one plane reached the scene of the battle. As one panzer regiment commander screamed in exasperation, "How can the Luftwaffe be absent from such a vital operation as this? If they're not coming out for this, what *are* they waiting for?" If the Luftwaffe had a low-profile role in Luttich, the same could not be said of the Allied air force. Every one of the six armored columns that took part in the first day of the battle encountered swarms of rocket-firing Hurricanes and Typhoons circling over their vehicles like predatory birds and then sweeping in for the kill with their deadly weapons. At Courdray, American Thunderbolts and British Typhoons engaged in a perfectly choreographed operation of bombing, rocketing, and straffing that significantly whittled down the formidable striking power of a column of Tigers. Wing Commander Desmond Scott left a vivid picture of the scene the Typhoons of his 123rd Wing encountered.

The road was crammed with enemy vehicles - tanks, trucks, half-tracks, even horse-drawn wagons and ambulances, nose to tail, all in a frantic bid to reach cover. As I sped to the head of this mile-long column, hundreds of German troops began spilling out into the road to sprint for the open fields and hedgerows. There was no escape. Typhoons were already attacking in deadly swoops at the other end of the column and within seconds the whole stretch of road was bursting and blazing under streams of rocket and cannon fire. Ammunition wagons exploded like multi-colored volcanoes. A large long-barreled tank standing in a field just off the road was hit by a rocket and overturned into a ditch. The once proud ranks of Hitler's Third Reich were being massacred from the Normandy skies by the relentless and devastating firepower of our rocket-firing Typhoons.

While the high level of Allied air intervention provided one ominous clue that all was not well with Operation Luttich, the events on the ground around Mortain were providing another strong hint that the great German offensive might already be doomed. The simple fact was that as long as American forces occupied the summit of Hill 317, their radios could call in a fearsome level of destruction on the German forces attempting to break through to Avranches. Unfortunately for the men of the American 120th Regiment, the Germans were well aware of this reality and were determined to push the Americans off the vital hill.

The American perimeter gradually contracted as enemy panzergrenadiers overran a succession of the defenders' strongpoints. By the morning of August 8 the men of Old Hickory were desparately short of ammunition, food, medical supplies, and perhaps most importantly, radio batteries. As long as the slim force on the summit could maintain communication with friendly units beyond the besieged area, the defenders could call in enough air strikes and artillery support to keep the gradually advancing Germans at least temporarily at bay. However, the vital radios worked on now overused batteries that were dangerously close to failing totally. The defenders huddled on terrain that was often too rocky to even dig foxholes and awaited the next attack. As Private Leo Temkin of E Company recalled, "We tried to pick out positions where the rocks would give you some protection. I picked out a crack in the wall of soft rock. I can still hear the funny sound the German bullets would make when they hit." Lieutenant Ronald Moody, commanding officer of G Company, used his units two 60mm mortars with deadly effect as the enemy lunged forward. "I had two guys who could lean those mortars on their knees and drop their shells anywhere they wanted; everytime we'd see the Germans forming up for an attack, we'd drop a few shells on top of them."

Commanders at higher echelons attempted to provide supplies and ammunition through airdrops and initiated a number of attempts to push relief forces through the German cordon. However, Hitler was now becoming obsessed over the fighting around Mortain and was raising the table stakes at an increasing rate. The German dictator insisted, "I command the attack be prosecuted daringly and recklessly to the sea, regardless of the risk." He ordered three armored divisions from Panzer Group West, now retitled Fifth Panzer Army, to concentrate near Mortain and "bring about the collapse of the Normandy front by a thrust into the deep flank and rear of the enemy facing Seventh Army." Insisting that "every man must believe in victory," Hitler committed more and more units desperately needed on other parts of the front to the Mortain offensive.

Untimately, Bradley and Montgomery realized that Hitler was doing the Allies an immeasurable service by deploying his most valuable units in open terrain that subjected them to the hurricane of steel that the Allied air forces and artillery units could deliver. In one instance the Allied generals responded to Hitler's challenge by greeting the newly arrived 272nd Grenadier Division and the 89th Infantry Division on their arrival to Normandy with an attack by one thousand Flying Fortresses which utterly pulverized both units. The Germans simply could not maintain an offensive that was bleeding them white at an alarming rate and within five days after Luttich began the Germans were retreating from Mortain and the new heroes of the Old Hickory Division were being lauded for their historic stand. The Germans had now shot their bolt and the gamble had failed. Now it was again the Allies's turn to take the initiative and the momentum would soon be carrying them toward the Seine River and the City of Lights.

George S. Patton

George Smith Patton was born in San Gabriel, California, to parents who both belonged to powerful Virginia families. George attended Virginia Military Institute before enrolling in West Point in 1905. He entered active service as a cavalry officer, competed on the U.S. pentathalon team in the 1912 Stockholm Olympics, and attended the French cavalry school at Saumur. Unlike Eisenhower or Bradley, Patton secured a number of combat assignments during World War I as he accompanied General John J. Pershing to France and became the first American officer to receive tank training. He organized and led the 1st Tank Brigade at Saint Mihiel in September of 1918 and after recovering from a wound incurred in that engagement returned for the climactic Meuse-Argonne Offensive.

After the war, Patton was demoted from temporary colonel to permanent major and placed in command of the 304th Tank Brigade which was actually little more than a battalion-sized training force. He became an honor graduate of Command and General Staff School in 1923, served on the general staff for the next four years, and then attended the Army War College. Despite this rather glittering set of credentials, Patton spent fifteen years in the rank of major and didn't climb back to his World War I rank of colonel until 1937.

When the United States was finally faced with the possibility of war after the German blitz through France, Patton's expertise in tank warfare became a valuable asset and he was assigned to command the 2nd Armored Brigade and then the 2nd Armored Division with a temporary rank of major general. In a series of prewar maneuvers throughout the south, Patton led his woefully undergunned tanks in daring operations that eventually put him on the cover of almost every national news magazine. When America actually entered the war, Patton was given command of the I Armored Corps and then command of the Western Task Force in the invasion of North Africa.

The Kasserine Pass fiasco catapulted the quick-tempered general to command of the II Corps, but a series of quarrels with British commanders prompted the American high command to shunt him over to command of a series of units that would eventually be combined to form the U.S. Seventh Army and take part in the Allied invasion of Sicily. The Husky operation was an emotional rollercoaster for Patton as his highly publicized military successes were counterbalanced by two famous slapping incidents in hospitals. The general was shipped to England with a severe letter of censure from Eisenhower and command of the phantom First U.S. Army Group. Patton's reasonably good behavior in England earned him command of the Third Army for the latter stages of the Normandy campaign.

Patton's post-Normandy career became another rollercoaster as his sensational intervention in the Ardennes campaign and highly publicized charge into Germany were eventually contaminated by his hints that the Anglo-Americans should unite with the just defeated Germans to fight the Soviets. This emotionally charged rhetoric earned Patton a transfer from the real Third Army to the largely paper force of the Fifteenth Army and an effective end of the real military command. Soon after this effective demotion his staff car was involved in a severe traffic accident near Manheim, Germany, and the general suffered extremely painful, and ultimately fatal, injuries. On December 21, 1945, this talented, controversial commander died with his recently arrived wife at his side.

CHAPTER XVIII

From the Corridor of Death
to the City of Lights

Adolf Hitler had presented the Allies with an invaluable strategic opportunity when he insisted on keeping Operation Luttich in progress long after any opportunity for a significant breakthrough had disappeared. Most of the remaining panzer strength in Normandy was being frittered away in a series of unprofitable frontal assaults that were costing the Germans far more tanks than the Americans while in turn setting up exciting possibilities for the Allies in other sectors of the battlefield. Eisenhower, Montgomery, and Bradley were all coming to the realization that Hitler's obsession with Avranches had placed much of the German army in a possible trap from which it would be difficult to extricate themselves. While the Germans flailed away between Mortain and Avranches, the Allies were rapidly taking measures to turn the Normandy battlefield into a pocket and deploying units that, if deployed quickly enough, might trap a huge enemy force on the wrong side of the Seine River. Two of the men heavily responsible for turning an ongoing battle into a virtual siege were a Canadian general fascinated with military innovation and an American general whose original namesake had led an invasion of Canada thirteen decades earlier. General Guy Simonds and General Wade Hampton Haislip were each about to inaugurate climatic phases in the Normandy campaign.

The first counterthrust to Hitler's gamble began only a matter of

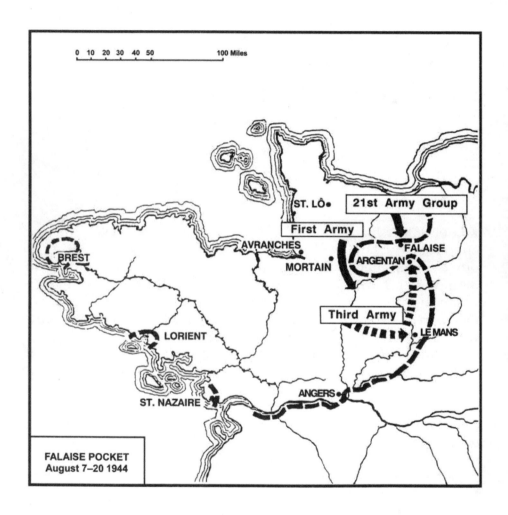

0 10 20 30 40 50   100 Miles

ST. LÔ

21st Army Group

First Army

AVRANCHES

FALAISE

BREST

ARGENTAN

MORTAIN

Third Army

LORIENT

LE MANS

ST. NAZAIRE

ANGERS

FALAISE POCKET
August 7–20 1944

hours after the first Tigers and Panthers rumbled out of the fog toward the Mortain roadblock. General Bernard Montgomery had already authorized Operation Totalize, a massive offensive by the newly designated Canadian First Army to break through the German positions outside the Caen-Falaise road, drive the eighteen miles to Falaise itself, cut off enemy forces facing Dempsey's British Second Army, and unhinge and hasten the German withdrawal from Normandy. The person responsible for the overall implementation of Totalize was General Henry Crerar, a pompous, arrogant windbag who was commander of the Canadian First Army. Montgomery had less than full confidence in this senior Canadian general, but he was far more complimentary of Crerar's immediate subordinate, Lieutenant General Guy Simonds, commander of the II Canadian Corps. The forty-one-year-old corps commander was similar to George Patton in that he was a hot-tempered, often grumpy officer who was invariably intolerant of others' faults yet on the other hand an innovative commander who could command attention wherever he went. Simonds used his innovative nature to prepare Operation Totalize. First he ordered his mechanics to remove the 105mm guns from dozens of "Priest" self-propelled guns and had them converted into open-topped armored personnel carriers code-named *Kangaroos* that could be filled with Canadian riflemen during the drive toward Falaise. Then, in order to rob the German artillery of its accuracy, the attack was scheduled to begin at night.

At 11 P.M. on August 7, twenty-three hours after the start of Operation Luttich, over one thousand heavy bombers dropped thirty-five hundred tons of bombs on the flanks of the German defenses around the Caen-Falaise road while seven hundred fighter-bombers dropped fragmentation bombs toward the center of the enemy positions. A few minutes later 720 cannons began dropping flare shells on the battlefield while dozens of machine guns fired streams of tracer bullets to mark the direction of the Canadian advance. Finally, batteries of searchlights were wheeled into place and began shooting powerful beams of light into the cloudy night sky, deflecting the rays back to the ground in a process called artificial moonlight. The lead assault units of the 2nd Canadian Infantry Division, 2nd Canadian Armoured Brigade, British 51st (Highland) Division, and British 33rd Tank Brigade moved to the start line and prepared to thrust forward.

At 11:30 P.M. the ground shook with the rumble of the flail tanks of the 79th Armoured Division as they lumbered forward and detonated dozens of enemy mines while riflemen jumped from the cover of the

Kangaroos and eliminated German roadblocks along the way. Within a few minutes seven mobile columns, each containing two hundred tanks and other vehicles, advanced four vehicles abreast, less than a yard apart, with each quartet separated from its front or rear counterpart by only a few yards. The procession included Kangaroos, conventional personnel carriers, scout cars, half-tracks, recovery vehicles, bulldozers, and ambulances that together gave the impression of the giant migration of some nomadic yet mechanized tribe. Progress was made but vehicles ran into each other, strayed from the roads, rolled into bomb craters, and crashed into nearby trees. Confused drivers and unit commanders were forced to follow the taillights of the vehicles in front while keeping an eye out for the next barrage from the supporting artillery batteries dropping ahead of them. As one British tanker recalled:

> All went well until the barrage started. The column was then immediately enveloped in a dense cloud of dust in which it was

The Canadian army was part of Operation Totalize launched on August 7 to close in the German army in the area around Falaise. This Canadian tank's crew may have hailed from Vancouver as indicated on the front of their vehicle. The Canadian soldiers who fought in World War II were all brave volunteers.

impossible at more than a few feet to see the taillight of the tank in front. When the barrage started, the needle immediately swung wildly in all direction and the compass became useless; great shapes of tanks loomed up out of the fog and asked who you were. Flails seemed to be everywhere and their enormous ... charging about in the dark seemed to add to the confusion. In fact, some of the Canadians became mixed up with part of our column and one Canadian tank spent the rest of the night with us.

Despite the confusion Simonds's new tactics proved initially successful; by first light advance columns were three miles inside the German lines and had already secured Garcelles, Cramesmil, Caillouet, and Gaumesnil. The two German infantry divisions holding the front line, the 89th Infantry and the 272nd Infantry, had been badly mauled by the Allied air raids and the advance itself and were now scrambling back toward Falaise. But there was still one German unit between the attackers and their objective, the battle-hardened tanks and men of the 12th SS Panzer Division.

As the first rays of summer sunshine sparkled over the French countryside, General Kurt "Panzer" Meyer squinted through his binoculars in his command post near Urville and watched a massive array of six hundred Allied tanks slowly approach on the horizon. Meyer's own tank force was down to thirty-nine Mark IVs of the 2nd SS Panzer Battalion and eight Tigers of the 101st SS Heavy Panzer Battalion under the command of the now legendary Michael Wittmann. The panzer commander was stunned when he watched the vast array of enemy vehicles grind to a halt and deploy in defensive formations rather than smashing their way through the unraveling German defenses. Meyer hopped into his staff car and roared forward to the town of Cintheaux, which lay only one thousand yards beyond the now stationary Allies. He was shocked by the panic sweeping the backpedaling German infantry units. "I am seeing German soldiers running away for the first time during these long, gruesome, murderous years. They are unresponsive. They have been through hell fire and stumble past with fear filled eyes. I look at the leaderless group in frustration. I jump out of the car and stand alone in the middle of the road, talking to my fleeing comrades. They are startled and stop. They look at me incredulously, wondering how I can stand on the road armed only with a carbine. They recognize me, turn round, and wave to their commander to come and organize the defense of the line of Cintheaux."

Meyer cobbled together an improvised defense line from the retreating infantrymen and every 88mm gun he could deploy, and proposed using his small force of tanks in a desperate counterattack. Insisting "you just cannot lead a tank battle behind an office desk," the controversial SS officer shook hands with Wittmann, mounted a motorcycle and led his tanks into a wild melee that erupted between Cintheaux and several adjacent villages. The Germans's most lethal weapon was the small column of Tiger tanks which slashed its way like a phalanx through successive lines of Canadian, Polish, and British vehicles. The Allies responded with a massive artillery barrage and dozens of Typhoons swooping low and firing their lethal rockets. Meyer watched in undisguised admiration as Wittmann launched his desperate attack. "The enemy artillery laid concentrated fire on the attacking Panzers. Michael Wittmann's Panzer thundered into the steel inferno. They had to prevent the enemy from attacking; they had to disrupt his timetable. Waldmuller pursued with his infantry; the brave grenadiers following their officers ... in the face of the terrific Allied power. I watched as an endless chain of large bombers approached." Wittmann's Tiger disappeared into a bank of smoke and haze and never returned as a combination of British and Canadian Shermans and a flight of Typhoons contributed to the annihilation of his tank and much of the column. When the bloody engagement finally petered out, five Tigers, six Mark IVs, and forty Allied tanks were smoldering wrecks and daylight was fast disappearing. The German line had almost, but not quite, unraveled and Simonds reluctantly called a temporary halt to Totalize as German reserves hurried into a hastily prepared new line nine miles north of Falaise.

While Simonds ordered his men to consolidate their gains and prepare for a new thrust toward Falaise, the focus of the battle shifted southward to the activities of his American counterpart, General Wade Hampton Haislip. Haislip had been named after two prominent South Carolina military figures. Wade Hampton Sr. had been one of the senior United States generals during the War of 1812 and had commanded the largest American invasion of Canada, a thrust into Quebec that had been thwarted by a series of monumental snowstorms. Wade Hampton Jr. had been one of the Palmetto State's most successful generals during the Civil War, leading Hampton's Legion, a unique combination of infantry, artillery, and cavalry units. He served in a prominent role at Bull Run, was wounded three times at Gettysburg, and emerged as Robert E. Lee's cavalry chief later in the war. This intelligent, brave, skilled general spent much of the closing phase of the

Civil War fighting a mobile, fast-paced series of battles attempting to keep the Yankees from capturing Petersburg and thus trap the entire Army of Northern Virginia in a great pocket around Richmond. Now Hampton's equally intelligent and skilled namesake was about to fight a mobile, fast battle to accomplish exactly the opposite objective, to burst *into* Argentan and perhaps Falaise and trap the entire German army in Normandy in a huge pocket.

Haislip found himself in this critical situation as he was in command of the American XV Corps, the part of Patton's Third Army that had thrust deepest eastward while much of the German army had been occupied in the attempt to capture Avranches far to the west. Haislip commanded a mixed force of infantry, the 79th, 80th, and 90th Infantry Divisions, and armor, the 4th U.S. Armored Division and the French 2nd Armored Division, and this composite force was in the process of capturing the important city of Le Mans at almost the same time that Michael Wittmann was engaged in his last tank duel about eighty-five miles to the north. Haislip's tankers and riflemen were now poised about sixty miles from Argentan and seventy-five miles from Falaise with only relatively minor German forces between them and these objectives. But Haislip's two principal superiors, Bradley and Patton, now engaged in an emotional debate as to just how to use this powerful striking force to best advantage.

Patton wanted to use XV Corps to thrust seventy-five miles east toward Orleans, cross the Seine River, and then head along the right bank of that waterway to the sea, cutting off all enemy forces to the west in what he called the "long envelopment" plan. This plan would shift the climactic battle for France away from Normandy toward the vicinity of Paris and probably result in an early German evacuation of the French capital. On the other hand Bradley envisioned a more conservative goal of closing the ring on the enemy by an American capture of Argentan or British capture of Falaise while deferring any thought of liberating the City of Lights until the German army had been bagged, supply lines had been improved, and a massive, large-scale offensive could be mounted. Bradley insisted that this "shallower and surer movement" was less risky and better complimented the continuing Anglo-Canadian drive toward Falaise. In fact, Bradley was so sure that his plan would work that he insisted to Secretary of the Treasury Henry Morganthau, who was visiting Normandy, that "the stage is set for an occasion that arises once in a century" as "we're about to destroy an entire hostile army." If this operation was successful, "the Germans will have nothing left with which to oppose us."

General Montgomery's overall vision of how the campaign should unfold was generally closer to Patton's plan than Bradley's but the British commander quickly agreed with Bradley on an inter-army boundary near the towns of Carrouges and Sees eight miles below Argentan. Monty agreed to inaugurate new southward thrusts from Dempsey and Crerar's armies as the upper jaws of a pincer movement while Haislip's forces closed the trap with a series of northbound drives. Patton was bitterly disappointed at the conservatism of this plan as he insisted, "I am the only one to realize how feeble the enemy is. He is finished. We can end the affair, (the war) in ten days." However, the Third Army commander reluctantly put together a detailed plan in which one of Haislip's divisions would cover Le Mans while two armored and two infantry divisions pushed northward toward the outskirts of Argentan "for the purpose of surrounding and destroying the German army west of the Seine." Haislip was instructed to "initially take Sees and Carrouges and prepare for a further advance" and informed that General Walton Walker's XX Corps would be deployed to provide flank protection for the drive northward.

At Wolf's Lair, Adolf Hitler continued to push more units further into the closing noose by fixating almost exclusively on the attempt to push the Americans into the sea at Avranches. However, von Kluge was much more suspicious that the Allies were preparing to spring a trap in the east and he responded to the Führer's calls for a renewed offensive at Mortain by insisting that he could do nothing until at least August 20 and admitting that even then only 120 tanks would be available for the new drive. Even the normally fanatically loyal Nazi Kurt Meyer was beginning to suspect that instead of using the precious time bought by the young soldiers of the Hitler Youth to extricate the German army in Normandy, Hitler was merely throwing more men and more tanks into a noose that was inexorably drawing tighter around the eastern end of the battlefield. As Meyer's 12th SS Panzer and other units withdrew southward in a running battle with the advancing British and Canadians, Wade Hampton Haislip and company were rapidly initiating an American blitzkrieg.

On the morning of August 12, elements of the 4th U.S. Armored Division and 2nd French Armored Division entered the town of Alençon to the welcoming cheers of hundreds of citizens lining the cobbled streets. When Patton received word of Haislip's accomplishments he instructed his corps commander to prepare for an advance at least to Argentan and perhaps as far as Falaise. The Third Army commander then contacted Bradley and, half in jest, said, "We now have elements in Argentan. Shall we continue and drive the British into the sea for another Dunkirk?" Not only was Patton's statement about having troops in Argentan blatantly untrue, his caustic reference to Dunkirk would hardly endear him to a British populace still sensitive about that episode four years later. Bradley was less than amused with Patton's request and responded with a curt "nothing doing." He emphasized the need to avoid an unintended shootout between Americans and Canadians if the armies collided by accident, and he insisted, "Don't go beyond Argentan. Stop where you are and build up on that shoulder. The German is beginning to pull out. You'd better button up and get ready for him." Patton insisted that the Germans were concentrating their forces to counter the Anglo-Canadian southbound drive and that Haislip could probably get to Falaise before Simonds under these conditions. But Bradley insisted that the Americans had far too few troops to hold a defensive line all the way from Alençon to Falaise and would be too thinly stretched to deal with a stampede of German units attempting to push their way out of the closing pocket. He later recalled, "I much preferred a solid shoulder at Argentan to the possibility of a broken neck at Falaise." Not only did

American troops entered the town of Argentan, just a few miles from Faliase, on August 12, 1944. This was part of the offensive to trap the German army in the Falaise pocket.

Although he was not permitted to close the Falaise pocket, Patton's armored divisions continued to drive the Germans back to and across the Seine.

Bradley want a "short hook" that kept the Americans well east of the Seine, he was willing to allow substantial German units to escape rather than risk his own units being overwhelmed in the attempted breakout. An awkward situation was further complicated by the fact that Bradley rather petulantly insisted to Patton that Montgomery's inter-army boundaries were etched in stone and blamed the British commander for the need to halt Haislip's forces. In fact, Monty had clearly established the boundaries as a purely temporary expedient and would have quickly readjusted them if Bradley had only suggested new arrangements. The crisis around Falaise was hardly one of

Bradley's finest moments of the war as he dithered between boldness and caution, made quick decisions that he quickly second guessed, and aborted actions that held promise. Despite their over-publicized "feud," Patton and Montgomery were much more on the same wavelength on how to implement the annihilation of the German army in Normandy. Luckily for Bradley some of his shortcomings were canceled out by the indecision at Wolf's Lair regarding the extent of the growing threat to the German army.

By the evening of August 14, Field Marshal von Kluge was convinced that the Allies were attempting to seal off avenues of retreat to the Seine and he began shifting units toward Argentan to hold open an exit when and if Hitler finally admitted that Operation Luttich had failed. The next day von Kluge set off on a tour of his shrinking perimeter, but a series of encounters with Allied aircraft left the field marshal in a ditch with his radio communications hopelessly shot up. Meanwhile, back at Rastenberg a sense of panic was creeping through the spartan conference rooms. In a day that even Hitler admitted was "the worst day of my life," the Führer received word that the Allies had begun Operation Dragoon, a second landing in southern France which was soon thrusting northward against a German army that had been stripped of many of its best units to reinforce the garrison in Normandy. Meanwhile, word of von Kluge's strange disappearance reached Wolf's Lair just as intelligence officers were informing Hitler that the field marshal seemed to be somehow involved in the July 20 assassination plot. The Führer quickly conjured up a nightmare scenario that had his army commander surrendering the entire German army in France to the gleeful Allies, leaving virtually nothing to stop an enemy drive into the Reich itself. Therefore, on the hope that von Kluge had not yet pulled off this treasonable act, Hitler ordered him back to Germany for "consultations" as soon as he was located and recalled Field Marshal Walther Model from the Eastern Front to replace him. When von Kluge reappeared at headquarters and received the curt orders to travel to Rastenberg, he penned a long letter of explanation to the Führer, was whisked away by a waiting staff car, and took a fatal dose of poison to end his last journey.

When Walther Model took command of the German army in the west, his main concern was the 90,000 men nearly trapped in a thirty-mile by fifteen-mile pocket that was closing rapidly in the east. A renewed Anglo-Canadian offensive named Operation Tractable pushed Canadian forces to the outskirts of St. Lambert and Polish troops to the edge of Chambois while American forces inexorably surged northward from Argentan. Eisenhower exhorted all of the Allies in an emotional Order of the Day in which he stated, "The opportunity may be grasped only through the utmost in zeal, determination and speedy action; if everyone does his job, we can make this week a momentous one in the history of the war; a brilliant and fruitful week for us, a fateful one for the ambitions of the Nazi tryants."

When Model arrived at his headquarters on the evening of August 17, much of his new command was already in shambles. The 1st and 2nd SS Panzer Divisions fielded only twenty tanks between them, a force that was two vehicles short of a full-strength company. Kurt Meyer's 12th SS Panzer Division had only three hundred combat-ready survivors from the twenty thousand men who had gone into action ten weeks earlier. Model spent most of the next day attempting to convince the Führer that if he wished to continue to keep the Allies at bay he must authorize an evacuation of Normandy. Finally a reluctant Hitler assented to a fallback and forty-five Luftwaffe cargo planes were dispatched with gasoline supplies for the units attempting to move eastward. Model assigned the 12th SS Panzer and 21st Panzer to hold the northern flank and the 2nd and 116th Panzer to deploy southward while the rest of the army attempted to squeeze through the narrow exit between St. Lambert and Chambois.

Colonel Hans von Luck watched the retreat from his regiment's position on the heights west of Vimoutiers as his panzergrenadiers fought to keep the escape route open. He adjusted his binoculars and watched the bloody drama unfold in the valley below. "The enemy planes were swooping down uninterruptedly on anything that moved. I could see the mushroom clouds of exploding bombs, burning vehicles and the wounded who were picked up by the retreating transports. The scenes that had to be enacted in the pocket were indescribable and we could do nothing to help." An American artillery observer who was instrumental in calling down this torrent of steel on the Germans watched the retreat from a somewhat different perspective.

The floor of the valley was seen to be alive … men marching, cycling and running, columns of horse drawn transport, motor transport and as the sun got up, so more targets came to light. It was a gunner's paradise and everybody took advantage of it. Away on our left was the famous killing ground and all day the roar of Typhoons went on and fresh columns of smoke obscured the horizon. We could just see one short section of the Argentan-Trun road, some 2,000 yards in all, on which section at one time was crowded the whole miniature picture of an army in rout. First a squad of men running, being overtaken by men in bicycles, followed by a horse drawn wagon at a gallop and the whole being overtaken by a Panther tank crowded with men and doing well up to 30 mph, all with the main idea of getting away as fast as they could.

By the morning of August 19 all eyes were focused on the two-mile-wide corridor between St. Lambert and Chambois and the two bridges that spanned the Dives River along that stretch of ground. Although the Dives was a relatively narrow six-foot-deep waterway, the river had extremely precipitous banks that were eight feet high and impossible for vehicles to navigate. All types of vehicles from horse-drawn wagons to Tiger tanks clogged the narrow roads approaching those two spans and bottlenecks quickly built up providing sitting targets for Allied gunners and pilots. Late in the afternoon a rifle company of the U.S. 90th Division surged into Chambois from the south at almost exactly the same time a Polish company entered town from the opposite direction. Soon British, Canadian, American, and Polish units were stretched across the exit to the Falaise pocket while small knots of Germans searched desperately for a gap in the Allied line. Rank offered few privileges in this bloody retreat. General Paul Hausser, commander of the German Seventh Army, marched along with his men like an ordinary riflemen with a machine pistol slung around his neck. Suddenly a shell exploded in front of the general, who had already lost an eye near Moscow, and the badly wounded commander was propped up in the back of a Panther tank, drifting in and out of consciousness.

At 2 A.M. on the morning of August 20, General Kurt Meyer decided that his teenagers had done all they could to hold open the escape route and he ordered his two hundred surviving men to head for the Dives River. Meyer himself had already been wounded in the head, and bleeding beneath a makeshift bandage he led part of his command to Chateau Quantites, a half mile north of St. Lambert. Two Sherman tanks suddenly appeared in the darkness and the startled division commander attempted to dodge them. "I jumped from cover to cover with pistol in hand; we dashed between the two tanks like a shot from a gun. I cannot go on; the sweat burns my eyes, the head wound reopens. Machine gun fire flew around our ears." Meyer successfully dashed around the tanks and splashed across the river, but when he reached the relative safety of a new rendezvous position his command

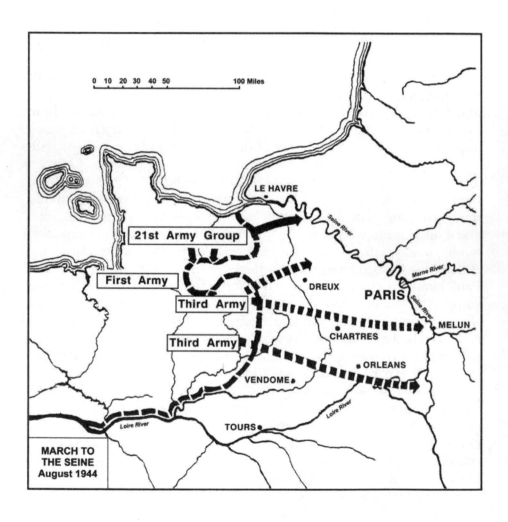

had shrunk to exactly four officers and eight enlisted men. All along this "Corridor of Death" surviving groups of Germans maneuvered their way to safety, abandoning 252 heavy guns, 1,778 trucks, 664 armored cars, 157 half-tracks, and 187 tanks, while Allied planes and guns were turning another 160 panzers and 650 vehicles into smoldering wrecks. Ninety thousand German troops had originally been trapped in the Falaise pocket yet somewhat more than thirty thousand Germans were now being processed as prisoners of war while an additional ten thousand were sprawled as corpses along the length of the now closed pocket. While four corps commanders and twelve division commanders managed to escape in order to reconstitute their units during the next few weeks, the loss in armored assets was little short of total annihilation. Only twenty-five of the fifteen hundred German tanks that opened the Normandy campaign were successfully ferried across the Seine by the end of August. Nine armored divisions now had the combined tank strength of a single company. The Allied commanders now realized, that at the very least, the battle of Normandy was over. However, even before they could fully comprehend the impact of the outcome, a new crisis flared. A lowly French division commander was about to change the focus of the battle of France from the Normandy countryside to the streets of Paris.

General Jacques Le Clerc, whose real name was Phillipe de Hautercloque, had served as a captain in the French army during the debacle of 1940, made his way to England, and was the first regular army officer to swear allegiance to Charles de Gaulle's Free French Forces. Le Clerc's ultimate reward was command of the most elite unit in the Free French Army, the 2nd French Armored Division. This collection of French natives and Arabs and Africans from the colonies stirred their commander's burning desire to erase the humiliation of the 1940 surrender to the Germans and that emotion frequently took precedence over the needs of the Allied army in which the unit served. Le Clerc had followed corps commander Wade Haislip's orders only when they suited his purpose which was essentially to get into position to liberate Paris. Le Clerc's only acknowledged superior, Charles De Gaulle, was incessantly badgering Dwight Eisenhower to initiate an operation to push the Germans out of the City of Lights, but Eisenhower viewed the French capital as little more than a logistic nightmare for his already thinly stretched supply lines. However, just as the battle for Falaise was reaching its climax, the decision began to slip out of Eisenhower's hands.

Lieutenant General Dietrich von Choltitz had been transferred from command of the LXXXIV Corps to command of the German garrison in Paris on August 7. However most of the best combat units in the garrison were pushed into the battle for Normandy so that the new commander now had barely 25,000 troops to hold the city. On August 19 some three thousand Paris gendarmes, most of whom had spent the war collaborating with the occupiers, suddenly rose in revolt and began taking over public buildings. This move emboldened a number of local Gaullist and communist resistance groups to begin attacking the Germans and soon gun shots crackled through the streets and the City Hall, Palace of Justice, and War Ministry were in the hands of the Maquis. Von Choltitz quickly agreed to a four-day truce with the larger resistance groups. The general pointedly ignored Hitler's frantic orders to demolish much of the city and instead used the ceasefire to begin evacuating much of the garrison. A bizarre procession began to move eastward out of the city as German headquarters personnel drove trucks piled high with records, office furniture, four-years worth of loot accompanied by both German and French office workers, assorted girlfriends, camp followers, and small units of pro-Nazi French militia who now began to realize they had picked the wrong side in the war.

Meanwhile, fear of widespread bloodshed in Paris had prompted Eisenhower to order an Allied force to push to the capital and liberate the city. Le Clerc's 2nd Division was paired off with the reliable United States 4th Infantry Division and the two units hurried toward the capital as the truce began to unravel. At just past midnight on August 25 elements of both divisions entered the suburbs of Paris and by morning Le Clerc had established himself at the Hotel de Ville. Huge crowds of Parisians surged onto the streets to greet the liberators. Von Choltitz spent most of the day evacuating as many of his troops as possible and then formally surrendered the city late that afternoon and by evening the French tri-color was waving proudly over every important building in the City of Lights.

Exactly eighty days after the first Allied troops had scrambled ashore on five previously obscure Normandy beaches, the capital of France was in Allied hands and Liberation Day was about to go into the French calendar as one of that nation's most glorious holidays. The great struggle to liberate Europe from Nazi tyranny would rage on for another eight months as the Germans grimly withdrew toward the borders of the Reich. However, even if the Normandy campaign was not the final battle of World War II, it was a decisive step toward the ultimate Allied victory in the defining event of the twentieth century.

Epilogue

Alternatives and Evaluations

On a bright late summer Monday morning, as thousands of Parisians basked in their new freedom, company after company of troops of the American 28th Infantry Division marched in formation around the Arch of Triumph and down the Champs Elysees in a parade that would provide photographic images that evoked many of the same emotions in the United States that would be felt the next year with the raising of Old Glory over the heights of Iwo Jima. By August 28, the day of this victory parade, the war had shifted far beyond Normandy and commanders on both sides could begin to analyze the impact of the eighty-day campaign that had just ended. The sheer scope of the Normandy campaign was monumental. Two million Allied soldiers had served in some capacity in Normandy and 209,672 of them had become casualties. Among the 36,976 men who had been killed in action were just over 14,500 British and Canadian troops, 21,500 Americans, and several hundred Poles, Frenchmen, and other Allied forces. These losses were considerable but still relatively modest compared to the casualties suffered by the roughly one million German troops who had engaged the Allies in Normandy. By the time the Allies entered Paris, the Germans had lost 240,000 men killed or wounded, 210,000 soldiers missing or captured, and an additional 100,000 men besieged in French ports and now useless for future operations. The defenders of Normandy had also lost or abandoned 2,200 tanks and self-propelled guns, 3,500 artillery pieces, and 20,000 other assorted vehicles. The forty-eight infantry divisions that Field Marshal von Rundstedt commanded on June 5, 1944, had been reduced to twenty-one units that could still reasonably be labeled combat effective. The twelve panzer divisions that were available to the German High Command on D-Day could now deploy exactly twenty-four tanks among them. The Allies were about to push eastward from Paris with thirty-nine full-strength divisions and 438,000 vehicles, imbued with the notion that the enemy was reeling toward defeat and eminently beatable.

The Normandy campaign was one of the defining moments of World War II and in many respects one of the most decisive events of the twentieth century. Combined with the massive Soviet summer offensive of 1944, Operation Overlord pushed the Third Reich to the brink of defeat and resulted in Germany's unconditional surrender almost exactly eleven months after Allied troops clambered out of their landing craft on D-Day. However, any concluding chapter on this major episode in the largest conflict in history should probably consider two important questions. First, were other outcomes reasonably possible during the course of this great campaign? Second, how successful or unsuccessful were the commanders who led these mighty forces during "the longest day" and its aftermath?

The range of possibilities for alternative outcomes of the Allied invasion of France is a broad spectrum of scenarios ranging from the virtual annihilation of the German army in Normandy to the elimination of the entire Anglo-American beachhead on, or soon after, D-Day. Any of these alternative scenarios might have become reality if relatively minor changes had occurred in the course of events that marked the actual Normandy campaign. Perhaps the most beneficial outcome of the campaign for the Allied camp would have been the forced capitulation or annihilation of virtually the entire German army west of the Seine River. Such an event would have quite possibly ended the Northwest Europe campaign by Christmas of 1944 and spared millions of civilians in the occupied countries the suffering and death of continued Nazi occupation. This author believes that this tantalizing development would have been far more likely if George Patton had been in command of the 12th United States Army Group instead of Omar Bradley.

Based on the progress of Allied operations in the Mediterranean campaign up to the point of the infamous slapping incident, it is apparent that George Patton was well on his way to one of the highest ground commands of the American army in the European Theater of Operations. However, after the general's emotional outbursts at two army hospitals, Dwight Eisenhower essentially took a compromise position which allowed Patton to retain his eligibility for some command but essentially disqualified him from any prospect of becoming the senior American ground commander in the invasion of France. As Patton was shunted down the pecking order of generals, Omar Bradley filled the void in Eisenhower's eyes and ultimately secured the coveted prize of Army Group Commander. The appointment of Bradley should certainly not be viewed as a military blunder as Bradley emerged as a good, if not great, field commander between D-Day and the German surrender. However this craggy, bespectacled general's prime assets of caution and reliability were not the most valuable characteristics in the final, critical phase of the Normandy campaign. In mid-August of 1944 George Patton was the American general with the clearest vision of the main military objective of the Normandy campaign, the destruction of the German army. On the evening of August 17 Patton envisioned a broad, all-encompassing sweep by three corps down both banks of the Seine to the sea which would have moved across the entire German escape area in Normandy and fashioned a deep encirclement, and the ultimate elimination of the best German units in western Europe, the fighting forces of Army Group B. These forces were the main impediment to an Allied thrust into Germany and the climax of the war.

Somewhat ironically, the role of George Patton as American ground forces commander would have probably produced better, not worse, relations with Bernard Montgomery than was the actual case between Bradley and Montgomery. Despite the emphasis on the rivalry between Patton and Montgomery that is chronicled in numerous book and film accounts, the two generals actually respected one another and exhibited complimentary strengths of risk and balance. There is little reason to believe that Montgomery, as Allied ground forces commander, would have given Patton any less autonomy than he accorded to Bradley and in turn the American general could have very likely implemented the same daring maneuvers to trap the Germans that Bradley refused to authorize. The result just may have been a far more spectacular conclusion to Operation Overlord.

A somewhat more conservative, but still highly acceptable outcome to the Normandy campaign from an Allied perspective revolves around the alternative scenario of a tighter closing of the Falaise pocket that would have bagged thirty to forty thousand German troops who escaped the trap just as the pincers were about to shut tight. During the last few days of the Normandy campaign neither Montgomery nor Bradley seemed to have a clear idea of exactly which German units were inside or outside of the Falaise pocket. The American general then complicated the situation by sticking inflexibly to Montgomery's suggested inter-army boundaries that the British general seems to have had no intention of being etched in stone. Bradley's insistence that he was deeply concerned about Patton's forces pushing too far north and somehow becoming engaged in a pitched battle with the British or Canadian forces seems somewhat ludicrous considering the availability of both reconnaissance forces and radio communication. If Bradley had simply unleashed American forces and told them to keep pushing until they met the first unit wearing British uniforms, there is a strong possibility that the Allied pincers really would have shut tight and a substantially larger haul of Germans would have ended up in prisoner of war camps rather than reappearing later in the year at Arnhem or the Ardennes.

On the other hand, there are other alternative scenarios that might have produced far worse consequences for the Allies and at least one appallingly disasterous outcome might have been played out on D-Day itself. The scenario of the Allies being thrown back into the sea early in the Normandy campaign would probably have started with a shift of emphasis by Hitler on the development of one of Germany's "wonder weapons." By the spring of 1944 the German aircraft industry had produced the first operational jet fighters. These radical planes were far faster than anything the Allies could put into the air. However, Hitler had initially insisted that the revolutionary Me262 be developed as a bomber capable of striking London and precious months had been lost as the Führer dithered between approving a fighter or a bomber. When approval was finally given for development of a fighter it was too late to have substantial numbers in the air in time for the invasion. Even a modest speedup of approval for jet fighter production could have set the stage for a very different response to the Allied landings on D-Day.

Almost any modest acceleration of production of the Me262 A1 fighter would have very likely placed 150 to 200 of these jets in Luftwaffe squadrons by the eve of D-Day. Assuming that these planes were held back as a trump card against the expected invasion and not put into combat until the morning of June 6, 1944, their initial impact would have been stunning. Their speed and armament of four 30-mm automatic cannon made them more than a match for any Allied bomber or fighter and they could be deployed as effective fighter-bombers as well. This force of perhaps ten squadrons of Me262s would not have been enough to clear the skies over Normandy of the twelve thousand Allied planes committed to the D-Day invasion, but they could have both provided a safe attack corridor for conventional medium bombers and dive-bombers over a portion of the beachhead and then served as a potent attack weapon themselves over the same territory. If the jets had been held back as the defenders' trump card against the invasion, the most logical phase to employ them would have been at the point where the Allied invasion nearly unraveled, Omaha Beach.

This alternative scenario would envision the very real crisis of the Americans on Omaha being fantastically worsened by the sudden appearance of jet fighters strafing the invasion beach with their dead-ly cannon and jet fighter-bombers knocking out landing craft and command ships as they came in so fast that the Americans simply had no time to react. Then, using the corridor the jets had established, dozens of medium bombers and Stukas could have pounded the land-ing ships as they lay off the beach and made it virtually impossible to reinforce the decimated GIs climbing their way through the bloody shingle. The addition of massive casualties suffered in air attacks added to the already touch-and-go situation at Omaha in the real bat-tle would almost definitely have either opened V Corps to the proba-bility of a massive counterattack the next day when Rommel returned from Germany or forced Eisenhower to order a withdrawal from "bloody Omaha." In either case the chances of the Allies forming a continuous invasion front would have dropped enormously and the odds would have risen that Ike would have been forced to issue his famous, but unused, message of defeat.

A second, if longer played, Allied disaster might also have sprung from another of Hitler's "wonder weapons." During the spring of 1944, German scientists had been furiously working to complete pro-duction of the V-1 rocket that was essentially a jet-propelled bomb. Exactly one week after D-Day the Germans launched the first of seven thousand of these "buzz bombs" that emitted a low-pitched buzzing sound seconds before impacting with a ferocious explosion. The Germans had plenty of V-1 rockets but Hitler committed a major strategic blunder in their use. He directed their use as a terror weapon against the city of London, insisting that their destructive power would force the British government to sue for peace. However, a far more practical use of this new weapon would have been to shift targets to the invasion beaches and the nearby waters that held the massive Allied fleet. A massive rain of flying bombs may not have annihilated the invasion forces, as the weapons were notoriously inaccurate, but an ongoing barrage of these rockets almost certainly would have complicated an already tenuous Allied supply situation and bought additional time for the Germans to bring up reinforcements to raise the odds of the Normandy campaign turning into a bloody stalemate.

A final, and not particularly far-fetched, alternative scenario could revolve around Hitler going with his own intuition rather than the insistence of his generals that Calais was the Allied invasion site. The Führer had developed a strong hunch that Fortitude was a bluff and began wavering toward deploying much of his powerful Fifteenth Army and formidable panzer reserves very near the Normandy beaches. If Hitler had convinced himself that his intuition was on target, the Allied invasion forces might very well have faced far more powerful German counterattacks than they experienced in the actual battle and in many places the Allied defenses could not have contained the fury of the enemy onslaught. At this point the Allied lines would have been penetrated in at least some areas and it would have been the intervention of the naval gunfire and air support that would have determined whether the beachheads were held. However, even with this formidable support, the panzers probably could have driven right onto the beaches in some places and where they did the casualties would likely have been enormous. It is not unreasonable to picture a newly arrived Rommel driving up and down the battle lines attempting to sniff out the vulnerable points in the Allied positions where a powerful counterattack could possibly be fatal. Here again, even if the Allies were not pushed into the sea, they would have probably faced an extended stalemate with no certainty that a unified front could be cobbled together for weeks to come and it is highly unlikely that Paris would have been liberated a relatively brief eighty days after the invasion.

The second relevant question, how successful or unsuccessful were the key commanders during the Normandy campaign, can quickly generate its own current of controversy and debate. No two people can seem to agree completely on the merits or liabilities of any celebrities whether they are political leaders, sports stars, or major actors in television or films. In this case, high profile commanders are celebrities and their thoughts, pronouncements, and actions are intensively studied by others. This epilogue will conclude with an evaluation of German and Allied commanders based on this author's evaluation of their impact on the Normandy campaign. It must be emphasized here that these evaluations are for this campaign alone; these same commanders might be rated considerably higher or lower in a larger context of the war. Also, commanders were selected due to their overall impact on the campaign not on rank alone. Therefore some relatively high-ranking officers are excluded while lower-ranking commanders are evaluated who seem to have had more influence on the outcome of Overlord.

The person who had direct responsibility for dealing with an Allied invasion anywhere in western Europe was Field Marshal Gerd von Rundstedt. This prickly, opinionated sixty-nine-year-old Prussian demonstrated considerable thoroughness and flexibility combined with tactical and strategic skill in preparing to counter an Allied landing that theoretically could occur almost anywhere along a wide swath of European coastline. This general had one of the clearest conceptions of the immense power of Allied naval and air forces of any German officer and insisted that the best hope of countering the Anglo-American landings was to launch a massive counterattack on favorable terrain relatively far inland from the invasion beaches. While this gambit certainly did not guarantee success, it was probably the best strategy remaining to the Germans by the summer of 1944. One of von Rundstedt's failings was his frequent refusal to make specific requests to Hitler, who he called "the Bohemian corporal," a tactic that tied the field marshal's hands even more than usual with the erratic Führer. Von Rundstedt was relieved of command before he really had an opportunity to fight the campaign he envisioned but he was respected as an honest, loyal commander.

Von Rundstedt's main rival in the preparation for Overlord was clearly the charismatic hero of the Afrika Korps, Erwin Rommel. The Desert Fox, who was fifteen years younger than his superior, was an expert tactician but merely an average strategist who dramatically improved the morale of the German defenders in the countdown to D-Day but designed a flawed strategy to meet the invasion. Rommel placed all of his strategic bets on his ability to stop the invaders on the beaches, and when this concept utterly failed on what he termed "the longest day," the field marshal was forced into a series of mere tactical reactions to Allied initiatives. Rommel was energetic, chivalrous, and both a demanding and fair leader of troops. He was one of the few German commanders genuinely admired by Allied leaders and ultimately became a victim of Hitler's wide net of recrimination after the July 20 assassination attempt. However, while he orchestrated a spirited defense of each square mile of Normandy, he was never able to seriously challenge the inexorable Allied thrust from the beaches to the hedgerows to the French capital. This almost legendary German commander had his share of success in World War II but was an average commander in the Normandy campaign.

The heir to elements of both von Rundstedt and Rommel's strategies was Field Marshal Günther von Kluge. Von Kluge was a generally good improvisational tactician who seems to have been in over his head in the strategic arena of the Normandy campaign. Not only did he personally vacillate in and out of the plot to assassinate Hitler, he demonstrated the same level of dithering during his tenure as senior general in the west. Von Kluge became so obsessed with countering the British offensives around Caen that he produced only weak resistance to the American thrust in the Cobra operation. Then, in a further proof of his strategic shortcomings, he botched an already flamed counterattack at Mortain. When von Kluge ultimately killed himself en route to Germany, he left the Normandy front in shambles and is one of the German leaders who merits blame for the impending disaster.

The final German to hold field command in the west during the Normandy campaign served the briefest time but was probably the most effective leader. Field Marshal Walther Model was essentially placed in charge of a sinking ship as he took the reins of power in the last days of the campaign. However, this talented "fireman," who had accomplished minor miracles in the east, was an aggressive, energetic, and skillful commander who orchestrated the evacuation of 30,000 to 40,000 German troops as the Falaise pocket collapsed and then cobbled together a series of stop lines that temporarily halted the Allied juggernaut driving from Paris toward the Reich. Model provided the German army with significant damage control at a moment of dire crisis and should be given credit for his limited but important actions.

The German commander who played a major role in the final phase of the Normandy campaign, the liberation of Paris, was General of Infantry Dietrich von Choltitz. Von Choltitz not only had both the humaneness and strategic good sense to evacuate most of the Paris garrison rather than follow Hitler's orders to burn the city or, worse, allow most of his men to be trapped by the approaching Allies, he also proved to be one of the most talented corps commanders on either side in the battle of the hedgerows. As commanding officer of the LXXXIV Corps, von Choltitz deployed minimal infantry forces and even less armor to maximum effectiveness in the slow, frustrating

American advance previous to the Cobra operation. He made maximum use of favorable terrain and surprise spoiling attacks to at least partially check a number of American attempts to get beyond the hedgerows into the open country beyond. He made the most of his limited resources in a somewhat abbreviated tenure as corps commander and should be considered one of the more effective German commanders in the campaign.

Von Choltitz's maximum use of minimal forces as a corps commander was reflected on the divisional level by Brigadeführer Kurt "Panzer" Meyer. This young SS general was both a vicious arch-Nazi officer and a fearless, talented tank commander. While Meyer's tactics as commanding general of the notorious Hitler Youth of the 12th SS Panzer Division incurred the justifiable wrath of Allied units and sometimes resulted in appalling casualties among his own indoctrinated teenagers, his constant plunges into the most dangerous areas of a firefight created a bond with his men that a number of American division commanders would have been wise to emulate. Meyer's SS troopers actually met with a number of bloody setbacks when Allied forces had time to organize a proper defense against his aggressive tactics, but his tankers scored enough impressive victories to rate "Panzer" Meyer as a solid and successful commander.

A panzer commander who rivaled Meyer's audacity and courage without the hardline Nazi ideology was Oberst Hans von Luck of the 21st Panzer Division. Von Luck always seemed to be at the critical spot in the battle all during the Normandy campaign and deftly commanded odd assortments of tankers, riflemen, engineers, and Luftwaffe personnel to maximum advantage in crucial points of the fighting. This panzer officer influenced the course of Overlord far beyond his relatively modest rank of colonel as he consistently took charge of improvised battle groups that produced a major impact on the attainment of Allied objectives. Von Luck was clearly one of the most talented officers on either side in the Normandy campaign.

The lowest ranking commander from any of the opposing armies to be included on this list of influential officers is Obersturmführer Michael Wittmann. Although commanding only five tanks at Villers-Bocage and a reinforced company during Operation Totalize, this intrepid tanker significantly affected the outcome of both engagements and encouraged Allied forces to assume they were facing dreaded Tigers anytime they encountered a German armored vehicle even if it was actually an obsolete relic of the 1940 campaign. Wittmann's exploits at Villers-Bocage with a single tank was a remarkable feat of arms and one cannot help but wonder what he might have accomplished with a much larger force under his command.

If Michael Wittmann proved what could be accomplished by a small force that was willing to take enormous risks, Reichsmarschall Hermann Göring demonstrated the ability to turn a feared juggernaut into an almost superfluous weapon of war. This author believes that this bombastic, showy, and self-indulgent commander was one of the two men most responsible for German defeat during the Normandy campaign. The Allied leaders who knew that their ground forces would be outnumbered in the first phase of Overlord, could not even begin to conceive of landing in Normandy unless and until their air forces gained aerial superiority over the Luftwaffe. Göring so badly mismanaged the German air arm during the spring of 1944 that the invaders not only achieved air superiority but enjoyed actual air supremacy during most of the campaign. Göring refused to force a showdown with Hitler over the production of the revolutionary Me262 as a fighter plane, mismanaged the response to the Allied air forces leading up to the landings, and managed to have almost the entire Luftwaffe in the wrong places when the Allies finally stormed ashore on D-Day. The Allies could not win Overlord with air power alone, but without a substantial advantage in the air there was very little prospect of winning the Normandy campaign, and Hermann Göring contributed mightily to giving the Allies that advantage.

The person who was even more directly responsible for the German defeat in Normandy than Hermann Göring was the reichmarschall's only real superior in the Nazi hierarchy, Adolf Hitler. The German Führer is often a difficult person to analyze from a purely military perspective because of the combination of his perpetration of some of the worst crimes in the history of mankind and his own personality which often seemed more suited to a mental hospital than a military conference room. However, he *was* ultimately responsible for the success or failure of the German armed forces on a level far beyond the involvement of either Winston Churchill or Franklin Roosevelt who were more or less his counterparts in a political sense in Britain and America. While the two democratic leaders sometimes dabbled, usually unwelcome, in the development of Allied strategy and tactics, they were certainly not the personification of their nations' armed forces in the same way that Adolf Hitler orchestrated virtually every significant move of the German military machine. Hitler knew that the outcome of the war probably rode on the success or failure of the invasion of western Europe; he took serious steps to counter that invasion;

and then he botched the whole campaign once the invasion actually occurred. The German dictator's obsession with holding every inch of ground in Normandy has often been cited for the eventual disaster that befell the defenders, but the actual case is somewhat more complex. Hitler was intelligent enough to realize that once the Allies were able to penetrate beyond the hedgerow country, there was relatively little to stop their advance into the Reich itself. The Norman bocage was about the best defensive terrain that an army was likely to occupy. However, the Führer became so obsessed with holding ground rather than conserving manpower that he allowed the Allies to bottle up more than 100,000 troops in essentially useless "fortresses" where the men served no more purpose in the war than the Japanese garrisons of islands that had been bypassed in the "island hopping" strategy pursued by the Americans during the Pacific campaign. Even when Hitler authorized withdrawals they tended to be too little, too late and allowed the Allies to scoop up thousands of men and hundreds of vehicles when the defenders were at the vulnerable transition between defense and retreat. This process would then be compounded by ill-advised offensives that were often launched in the wrong place at the wrong time. Thus Hitler frittered away dozens of well-trained, hard-fighting units often enough to give the Allies some margin for error when their own plans were developing short of expectations.

One of the most important characteristics of a brilliant commander is the reluctance to throw away the lives of his men unnecessarily. This was simply not Hitler's style. While his coldblooded tactics worked well in early victories against a hopelessly outgunned Poland, a desperately unprepared Russia, and a hopelessly divided France, when the war became more of an even match the Führer was often clueless on how to stem the tide of defeat. Adolf Hitler was not the only German commander who made serious errors in the conduct of the Normandy campaign but he must bear the ultimate blame for defeat.

While one key component of the outcome of the Normandy campaign was the failure of critical elements of the German command structure to respond properly to the strategic crisis imposed by a number of Allied offensive operations, this reality should not diminish the very real military skill exhibited by a number of Allied commanders. The Allies certainly had their share of marginal or even incompetent officers and in several cases their failings produced disastrous results. However, on the whole, the Allied forces fighting in Normandy were blessed with generally competent and sometimes brilliant leaders who had a clear purpose of what it would require to defeat a highly motivated and often dangerous enemy army.

The person most responsible for actually getting the Anglo-American armies safely onto the Normandy beaches was Admiral Bertram Ramsay, R.N. This energetic, hard-working mariner was the officer who was ultimately charged with orchestrating a gigantic sealift of hundreds of thousands of fighting men across a body of water that could be riddled with mines and serve as the lair for enough German warships to do real damage to the invasion fleet. Ramsay's forces not only got the troops ashore, but once they were on the beaches and the countryside beyond, provided a level of gunfire support that shocked virtually every German commander who encountered it.

If Admiral Ramsay was almost unanimously lauded for his role in Neptune-Overlord, his air-force counterpart, Air Chief Marshal Trafford Leigh-Mallory, receives far more mixed reviews. This often gloomy air commander should be credited with a substantial role in providing a level of air support that Eisenhower insisted he simply had to have if the invasion of France was ever going to become a realistic objective. However, Leigh-Mallory's sour disposition produced often stormy relations with a wide spectrum of British and American air and ground commanders and sometimes impeded the vital cooperation among the services that Eisenhower felt was essential to the success of the campaign. Leigh-Mallory emerged in the campaign as an adequate but certainly not superb commander.

The officer most responsible for the overall day-to-day operation of ground forces during the Normandy campaign was General Bernard Montgomery. This often exasperating officer could be arrogant, petty, and evasive, and his negative character traits produced a host of critics among both contemporary commanders and postwar writers. Sarcastic comments about the general's leadership by Bradley, Patton, and a number of lesser officers produced a virtual cottage industry in Monty-bashing in the United States during most of the remainder of the twentieth century. However this author believes that it is an injustice to utilize Montgomery's admittedly annoying personality to shortchange his very real military talents. Monty, at his best, had a rare ability to engage authentically with common soldiers and convince them that there was virtually no chance that they could lose the next battle. The accounts written by lower-ranking American soldiers, as opposed to the comments of their superiors, are just as effusive as their British counterparts concerning Montgomery's electric impact on their morale. Monty may very well have been able to drive his fellow commanders to distraction, but this general possessed a formidable ability to instill confidence in his men, develop a coherent campaign plan of action, and maintain the self-confidence that even in a temporary crisis the plan would work. His plan to draw in most of the German armor on his (British) left flank while enhancing the ability of the more mobile American units to break loose on the right was clearly the correct way to fight the battle. Montgomery did have an exasperating capacity to oversell and overdramatize what each successive operation was going to accomplish and this led Eisenhower to wonder what his ground forces commander *really* expected to gain from each engagement, but this was an annoying, not a fatal, flaw.

The American officer who would eventually come to rival Montgomery for authority in the ground operations of the Normandy campaign was Lieutenant General Omar Bradley. This taciturn, modest Missourian shared Monty's genuine concern for the welfare of his men and was an intelligent if not particularly brilliant or imaginative commander. Bradley's conduct of the American element of Overlord was generally competent and in the case of Operation Cobra, outstanding. However, this almost legendary general seems to be at least mildly overrated in his overall accomplishments in Normandy. At the outset of the landings he seemed to pay little attention to the lessons learned by army and marine units already fighting their way across the Pacific Ocean. In the period leading up to Cobra he launched a series of poorly focused, poorly coordinated offensives that produced high casualties and minimal results. At the climax of the Falaise operation he petulantly ordered a tactically questionable halt to hard-driving American armored forces rather than merely pick up the phone and rearrange army boundaries with Montgomery. Bradley was not a bad choice for senior American ground commander but he was not the best choice.

The person who this author believes *should* have commanded the American forces in Normandy was Lieutenant General George S. Patton. The mercurial general was at least as exasperating and annoying as Bernard Montgomery but like Monty he was also exceptionally talented. Patton seems to have had a better focus than any other Allied general on what the capabilities, strengths, and weaknesses of the Germans really were and how to destroy their army rather than just grabbing more enemy territory. He had a much better feel for the sort of "knockout punch" that would finish off the reeling German forces than Bradley and his natural audacity would have formed a natural compliment to Montgomery's more cautious approach. This controversial leader merits the highest rating as a field commander.

The senior Allied commander who probably had the most frustrating role in the Normandy campaign was Lieutenant General Miles Dempsey. While Bernard Montgomery accorded Bradley a substantial degree of autonomy, the commander of the British Second Army was subjected to far more control from the ground forces commander. Dempsey performed this difficult balancing act fairly well and provided a steady, competent hand at the head of this large army.

The corps commander among the units that comprised the 21st Army Group who most likely had the largest personal impact on the Normandy campaign was Lieutenant General Guy Simonds. This senior officer of the II Canadian Corps created one of the most effective tank-infantry teams in the Allied forces through a high degree of improvisation during the drive from Caen to Falaise. This general was versatile and imaginative but was not able to generate the momentum that would have more fully closed off the Falaise gap at an earlier date. Despite this drawback, Simonds deserves credit for his effective command.

The closest counterpart to Simonds in the American army was probably Major General Joseph Lawton Collins. As the commander of the VII Corps, "Lightning Joe" successfully melded lessons learned in the Pacific war with a rapid adaptation to the often different battlefields of Normandy. He emerged as an energetic, strong-willed commander who specialized in rapid, audacious movements that caught the Germans by surprise on more than one occasion. He was one of the best.

The relatively junior Allied officer who most likely exerted a decisive impact far beyond his rank was Brigadier General Norman Cota. While the senior American commanders were observing the D-Day landings from naval vessels, this assistant division commander emerged as the most important officer on the bloody shingle of Omaha Beach. Cota's combination of cool leadership and emotional appeals to the beleaguered assault troops was a major factor in turning the landing from a bloody disaster to a dear-bought success. Cota's heroism did not go unrewarded as he was deservedly promoted division commander during the campaign.

If Adolf Hitler personified the German determination to prevent the Allies from landing in western Europe, Dwight D. Eisenhower was the embodiment of the Anglo-American will to launch a successful invasion. This affable Kansan may not have been the most brilliant, imaginative leader in the Allied forces, but he brought to his post a unique combination of cheerfulness, humility, and sincerity that often proved magical to the conduct of Overlord. While Patton and Montgomery exhibited a tendency to become exasperatingly self-assured, Ike's main failing may have been a tendency to tolerate a certain level of incompetence among his varied assortment of Allied officers. On the other hand, that same generosity of spirit toward difficult but talented subordinates helped maintain a sense of unity and common purpose that were vital to eventual victory. Eisenhower also displayed a commendable combination of organizational skills and political awareness that made him an ideal commander for such a multi-faceted alliance. Dwight David Eisenhower had the unique combination of credentials that made this talented officer perhaps the best candidate available to lead the most decisive operation of World War II. This descendant of German pacifists who left their homeland to escape the scourge of war would soon return to that land not as a conqueror but as a liberator at the head of a vast Anglo-American army with a mission to blot out a terrible regime that, as Winston Churchill warned, threatened to produce a new and awful dark age over the shores of the European continent. The Allied landings in France and the subsequent victory in the Normandy campaign ensured that this dreadful nightmare that threatened Europe would not survive another full year. The first step to a return to a better world began in the beaches, hedges, and lush green fields of a place called Normandy.

Eisenhower after the Normandy Campaign, 1945–1969

While Eisenhower directed much of the Normandy campaign from England, SHAEF headquarters was gradually being shifted to France, and on September 1, 1944, Ike assumed direct control of Allied operations in Northwest Europe with Montgomery and Bradley as his army group commanders. Eisenhower approved Operation Market-Garden, the ill fated attempt to secure an early foothold on the Rhine, directed the Allied response to Hitler's surprise counterattack in the Ardennes forest, and then orchestrated the thrust into Germany which was still gaining momentum when the war ended.

After Eisenhower took the surrender of the Germans on May 7–8, 1945, he commanded Allied occupation forces until November, at which time he was recalled to Washington to serve as army chief of staff. In February, 1948, Eisenhower accepted the presidency of Columbia University but it was assumed that this was just a stepping stone to a run for the American presidency in 1952. Ike was in the unique position of being courted by both political parties who saw the hero of World War II as their ticket to holding the White House for most of the 1950s. However, the outbreak of the Korean War temporarily put political aspirations on hold as Eisenhower was put back on active duty as commanding officer of NATO in preparation for a possible Soviet invasion of western Europe. After it became apparent that the Korean conflict was not going to be the opening engagement of World War III, Ike returned to the United States and began dropping hints that he was amenable to a presidential nomination

from the Republican Party. Eisenhower ran a confident campaign against the far more intellectual, and far less popular, Adlai Stevenson, and assured the American public that if elected "I will go to Korea." The former general won a comfortable victory in November 1952, and then flew to Korea to get a first-hand look at the stalemated war. Soon after his inauguration, his none too subtle hints to China that he would introduce nuclear weapons to the conflict combined with the death of Communist titan Josef Stalin convinced Mao Zedong to settle for an armistice in July of 1953.

Eisenhower was now free to pursue a "peace and prosperity" agenda which turned the 1950s into one of the most prosperous decades in American history as Ike seemed to concentrate on unending rounds of golf and his own recovery from a number of serious illnesses. Behind the scenes Eisenhower was deeply involved trying to prevent the Cold War from sliding into a third world war and the president often acted as a brake on more hotheaded advisors who were willing to push toward armed confrontation with the Soviets.

When Eisenhower left the White House in 1961, his replacement, John F. Kennedy, attracted an exuberant response from academics and other writers who contrasted his youthful activism to Ike's apparent nonchalant governance. However, in the closing decade of the twentieth century, the release of hundreds of secret documents and the end of the Cold War encouraged a reevaluation of Eisenhower's presidency and the former general's reputation attracted growing admiration for his role in preventing the Cold War from becoming hot.

Guide for the
Interested Reader

Since D-Day and the Normandy campaign represent the highest profile action of the Western Allies in World War II, the available literature on the event is not just incredibly extensive, it is sometimes overwhelming. Among the available general works on the topic five quite different books are the most valuable for readers. Cornelius Ryan's *The Longest Day*, Max Hastings's *Overlord*, John Keegan's *Six Armies In Normandy*, Carlo D'Este's *Decision in Normandy*, and Stephen Ambrose's *D-Day – June 6, 1944* are each magisterial works in their own way. Ryan's work, which inspired the blockbuster film of the same title, is the oldest of these works, written in 1959. Ryan interviewed a wide cross-section of Allied and German participants at a time when the event was hardly ancient history and the reader can especially sense the conflicting emotions of men who were young warriors in 1944 and were just starting to view the fighting from the perspective of early middle age fifteen years later. This work is extremely well written and easy to follow, but, at just over 200 pages, tends to gloss over key aspects of the landings. Hastings's work is a good, solid narrative of the entire Normandy campaign that frequently suggests that the Germans were far better fighters than the Allies and stresses the resiliency of the defenders after the campaign more than their losses during the campaign. The book's British author is particularly critical of Montgomery's leadership. Keegan's book is somewhat more episodic, attempting to weave a narrative of the whole campaign into extended vignettes of the American, Canadian, Scotland, English, German, and Polish experience during the campaign. The work provides excellent background on the social and political underpinnings of each of the participating armies. D'Este, a retired lieutenant colonel in the U.S. Army, generally places more emphasis on strategy than battle narratives in his work and, ironically for an American writer, views the battle more from a British than an American perspective. This is an excellent picture of the military mind in action but gives less of a feel for the actual experience of combat in Normandy. Finally, Ambrose's book, thanks to the movie *"Saving Private Ryan,"* is probably the best known contemporary work on the Normandy landings and, as a whole, does not disappoint its readers. Ambrose's writing style is excellent and he did a superb job of interviewing an imposing variety of participants in the battle. There is enough background strategy to provide a reasonable picture of why the invasion was so crucial yet the narrative is not so technical as to befuddle intelligent yet rather casual readers.

One profitable way of getting a sense of the competing strategies being considered by both the invaders and the defenders is to peruse the memoirs of those leaders who survived the war long enough to write accounts of their tenure in command. On the Allied side, the three most valuable memoirs are Dwight Eisenhower's *Crusade in Europe* (1948), Bernard Montgomery's *Memoirs* (1958), and Omar Bradley's *A Soldier's Story* (1951). While each one of these works attempts to maximize correct moves and minimize mistakes, they provide a fascinating insight into the thinking of these three giants of Operation Overlord. The memoirs of George Patton, *War as I Knew It*, represent a very different dimension. Patton died before he had an opportunity to develop a formal memoir that could respond to the tomes of his Allied rivals so his wife, Beatrice Ayer Patton, put together a compilation of Patton's diary entries, official and unofficial correspondence, and letters to her—a "provisional narrative." Although this work is more choppy than the previously mentioned trio, it is more frank.

The German leaders during the Normandy campaign supplied much less of a personal perspective of the campaign since most of them were dead long before they could pen a memoir. However, Erwin Rommel's widow enlisted the aid of famed military historian B. H. Liddell-Hart to combine a variety of his surviving papers into *The Rommel Papers* (1953), and Rommel's chief of staff during the Normandy campaign, General Hans Speidel, wrote *Invasion 1944: Rommel and the Normandy Campaign* from the unique perspective of someone who was not only at the field marshal's side during much of this critical period but narrowly escaped execution by the Gestapo for his quite active role in attempting to assassinate Hitler.

Since the Normandy campaign stretched for almost three months beyond D-Day, an understanding of the campaign in its totality requires perusal of works focusing on events after "the longest day." Among the most interesting of these studies are Stephen Ambrose's

Citizen Soldiers, Michael Doubler's *Closing With the Enemy*, Alwyn Featherston's *Battle for Mortain*, J. A. Womack's *Summon Up the Blood*, and Martin Blumenson's *The Battle of the Generals*. The first part of Ambrose's book is a clear sequel to his D-Day work as it picks up almost exactly where the other book leaves off and then continues past the Normandy campaign to VE Day. Doubler's book is a more episodic study of the nuts and bolts of how the Americans fought the Germans and a critique of the tactics that worked and those that failed. The other three works focus heavily on individual battles. Featherston's is essentially a unit study on the 30th Infantry Division's role in repulsing Operation Luttich; Womack's is a first person narrative of Epsom and Goodwood from the perspective of a Royal Engineer; and Blumenson's is a study of Allied command during the contest to close the Falaise pocket.

The German perspective of day-to-day fighting during the Normandy campaign is most vividly portrayed in two personal memoirs and two more general volumes. Kurt Meyer's *Grenadiers* and Hans von Luck's *Panzer Commander* are invaluable sources for gaining a better perspective of the unraveling fortunes of the German defender in their long, bloody battle. Retired British Major General Michael Reynolds's *Steel Inferno* is one of the best operational histories of a German unit, and Paul Carell's *Invasion-They're Coming!* is an English translation of a best-selling German author's chronicle of the campaign written about the same time as *The Longest Day*.

Those readers who wish to place the Normandy campaign in a much broader perspective of World War II have access to a number of excellent general studies. The best general work that focuses on the British Army in World War II seems to be *And We Shall Shock Them* by David Fraser—a measured, readable treatment of that nation's ground forces from the perspective of the 1980s. One of the best American equivalents to this chronicle is Geoffrey Perret's fine *There's A War To Be Won*—a narrative that is a very quick read yet produces fascinating insights into the formation of American strategy in the conflict. Two prominent contemporary American scholars, Williamson Murray and Allan Millett combined forces in 2000 to produce an excellent global narrative of the conflict, *A War to Be Won*.

Index

Afrika Korps, 15, 32
Ajax, the (Britain), 115
Alexander, Harold, 22
All-American Division, 74
Algonquin, the (Canada), 126
Allied Expeditionary Force, 21, 27
American Army Air Force (AAF), 49, 82, 207.
    See also Operation Overlord, air force com-
    ponent of
Argonaut, the (Britain), 115
Arkansas, USS, 96
Army Air Corps (U.S.), 9, 49
Army Group B (German), 32
Arnold, James, 87
Arromanches, 58, 115
Artillery Group Montebourg (Germany), 173
Avranches, France, 233–234, 239, 240, 247

Baldwin, USS, 108
Barton, General, 173
Battle Group von Luck, 214
Bayerlein, Fritz, 148, 149, 198, 225–227, 231
Bayeux, France, 58
Bayfield, USS, 80
Becker, Major, 215
Bedell–Smith, Walter, 24, 29–30
Beer, Robert, 108
Behrendsen, Fritz, 117
Belfast, HMS, 126, 128
Benouville, 69, 70–71, 137
Bieville, 138–139
Big Red One (U.S.), 91, 102. *See also* 1st
    Division (U.S.)
Binkoski, Joseph, 170
Black Prince, HMS, 81, 82
Blue and Gray Division (U.S.), 91, 102. *See also*
    29th Division (U.S.)
bocage (hedgerow) region, battles in, 63–167,
    171–172, 192–198, 205, 230
Bourguebus Ridge, 211, 212, 216–217, 223
Bowen, Dennis, 116
Bowers, H. W., 117
Bradley, Bruce, 81, 85
Bradley, Omar, 69, 92, 94, 95, 106, 184
    assignment to Overlord, 29
    author's evaluation of, 264, 265, 266, 275
    Cherbourg, reaction to capture of, 178

life and personality, 110, 223
meeting with Eisenhower, July 1944, 205–
    206
and Patton, 238, 253, 254–255, 256
strategy for advance on St. Lô, 193–195,
    196, 200, 202
strategy for Operation Cobra, 206, 221,
    223–225, 227, 229–230, 232
strategy for Operation Totalize, 253, 255–
    257
strategy on Cotentin Peninsula, 170–171,
    172–173
British Army
    casualties in June 1944, 195
    casualties in Normandy campaign, 263
    deployment on Gold Beach, 115
    in Operation Charwood, 207–211
    in Operation Epsom, 184–189
    in Operation Goodwood, 211–218
    organization of, 39–40
British Bomber Command, 49
British Expeditionary Force (BEF) 7, 19
Brittany Peninsula, 45, 46, 234
Brooke, Alan, 18, 19, 22, 24
Brooks, Edward, 232
Brotheridge, Dan, 70
Brown, Jack, 116
Bryant, C. J., 108
Bucknall, Brian, 114, 115

Caen, France, 57, 113, 114, 133, 134, 138, 140,
    151, 161, 184, 206–218
Cagny, France, 214–215
Canadian Army, 125–131, 146, 149, 195, 207–
    218, 249–252
Canham, Charles, 107
Cannon, Henry "Chips," 8
Carentan, France, 163, 165–167
Carmick, USS, 108
Carpiquet airport, 130, 131, 146, 208, 209
Carrefour, Le, 169–170
Cherbourg, 19, 58, 161, 163, 172, 173–178, 193
Choltitz, Dietrich von, 194, 195, 196, 197, 231,
    261–262, 270–271
Churchill, Winston, 7, 14–17, 18, 19–20, 21–22,
    24, 52, 55, 61, 65, 183
Clark, L. N., 128

Close, William, 215
Cole, Robert, 88, 166
Collins, Joseph Lawton "Lightning Joe," 80, 161, 171, 172, 173, 175, 196–197, 227, 233, 276
Columbelles steelworks, 211, 212, 217
Combined Chiefs of Staff, 19, 30
Corlett, Charles, 194, 197, 200
Cota, Norman "Dutch," 107–108, 164, 169, 276
Cotentin Peninsula, 58, 74–76, 89, 163, 181
Courseulles, France, 127, 129
Coutances, France, 194, 195, 232–234
Cox, Ron, 217
Cranley, Arthur, 154, 156
Crerar, Henry, 249
Crocker, J. T., 121, 133
Culin, Curtis, 230

Dawson, R. W., 136
D-Day
    air support on, 83, 96
    British advance from Gold Beach, 118–121
    casualties of, 143
    day-after analysis, 143
    German defenses on, 92, 95, 98, 99, 102–103, 117, 127–128, 136, 138
    glider landings on, 69–71
    landing craft problems, 84
    landings on Gold Beach, 115–118
    landings on Juno Beach, 125–129
    landings on Omaha Beach, 91–109
    landings on Sword Beach, 133–138
    landings on Utah Beach, 79–89
    naval support on, 82, 88, 96–97, 108, 115, 116, 126, 135
    paratrooper drops on, 71–78, 88
    pre-invasion bombardment, 81–82
    strategies for, 57–92
Dempsey, Miles, 58, 113–114, 153, 157, 161, 189, 276
Der Fuhrer Regiment, 242
Desert Rats (Britain), 115, 116, 153
Deutchland Regiment, 242
Deyo, M. L., 82
Diadem, HMS, 126, 128
Dietrich, Sepp, 152
Dollman, Friedrich, 92, 188,
Douglas-Pennant, Cyril, 115
Downey, John, 230
Dunkirk, evacuation from, 7–8

Eberbach, Heinrich, 194, 216
Eddy, Manton, 172, 177
18th Hussars (Britain), 134
Eighth Army (Britain), 15, 20
8th Brigade (Canadian 3rd Division), 128

VIII Corps (Britain), 187, 211
VIII Corps (U.S.), 172, 194, 195, 238
8th Infantry Brigade (Britain), 134
899th Tank Destroyer Battalion (U.S.), 198
80th Infantry Division (U.S.), 253
LXXXIV Corps (Germany), 139, 195, 231
89th Infantry Division (Germany), 251
82nd Airborne Division, 58, 68–69, 164–165, 172
83rd Division (U.S.), 196
Eisenhower, Dwight David, 82, 258
    after Normandy, 278
    appointment as supreme commander in Europe, 14–15, 20–22
    arrival in Britain, 27
    author's evaluation of, 276–277
    at briefing in Hammersmith, 55, 57–58
    before Normandy, 23
    choosing of senior commanders for Overlord, 28–30
    conference with Churchill and Montgomery, 14, 15–16
    decision to begin D-Day assault, 63
    and final countdown to D-Day, 63–66
    in France, 205–206
    and Operation Anvil, 60–61
    and Operation Cobra, 221, 225, 227
    and Operation Goodwood, 212, 221
    and Paris, 261
    and Patton, 237–238
    relationship with air force command, 49, 50–53, 68–69
    and rivalries in Allied Forces, 24–25
    strategies of, 45–46, 49, 60–61, 238
11th Armoured Division (Britain), 184, 187, 211, 217
Emerald, the (Britain), 115
Enterprise, the, (Britain), 81, 88
Erebus, the (Britain), 81
Erskine, George, 153

Falaise (Falaise pocket), 212, 249–261, 266
Feuchtinger, Edgar, 139–140
Fife and Forfar Yeomanry, 213, 215
Fifteenth Army (German), 32, 195
XV Corps (U.S.), 253
15th Scottish Division, 184–188
V Corps (U.S.), 92, 161, 167–168, 194
5th Parachute Division (German), 202
Fifth Panzer Army, 244
50th Northumberland Division (Britain), 58, 115
51st Highland Division (Britain), 152–153, 249
59th Division (Britain), 208
1st Airborne Division (Britain), 151, 152
First Army (U.S.), 161, 193, 238
First Canadian Army, 238, 249–252

1st Cavalry Division (U.S.), 9
I Corps (Allies), 121, 133
1st Division (U.S.), 58, 97, 102, 109, 232, 233.
    See also Big Red One (U.S.)
1st Hampshire Regiment (Britain), 117
1st Hereford Infantry Regiment, 213
1st SS Panzer Division, 188, 209, 216, 217, 258
First United States Army Group (FUSAG),
    47–48
505th Parachute Regiment, 76–78
501st Heavy Tank Battalion (German), 154
502nd Parachute Infantry (U.S.), 166
506th Parachute Regiment (U.S.), 76
Flander, Dan, 128
Flores, the (Netherlands), 115
Fort de Roule, 175
43rd (Wessex) Division (Britain), 184, 209
4th Armored Division (U.S.), 253, 254
4th Infantry Division (U.S.), 58, 69, 85, 89,
    165, 172, 173, 196–197, 262
4th King's Shropshire Light Infantry, 213

Gale, Richard, 68
Gavin, James, 165
George VI (Britain), 65–66
Gerhardt, Charles, 169, 199, 200
German Army
    analysis of D-Day, 143–144
    and assassination attempt on Hitler, 222
    casualties in June 1944, 195
    casualties in Normandy campaign, 263–
        264
    command problems in, 194
    counteroffensives of, 149–151, 240–245
    defenses in France, 80, 92, 95, 98–99, 102–
        103, 117, 127–128, 136, 138, 184–185,
        216, 229
    evacuation of Paris, 262
    at Falaise pocket, 257–261
    organization of, 40–41
    rivalries and feuds in, 191
    treatment of prisoners, 179–180
    views of D-Day invasion, 82, 85–86, 95–
        96, 117
    withdrawal at Coutances, 233–234
    withdrawal from Normandy, 258–262
Gerow, Leonard, 92, 94, 95, 106, 161
Geyr von Schweppenburg, Leo, 148–149, 151,
    152, 194
Glasgow, HMS, 175
Glennon, the (U.S.), 88
Gold Beach, 57, 113–118
Göring, Hermann, 272
Gothberg, Wilhelm von, 141–142

Grow, Robert, 239
Guards Armoured Division (Britain), 211
Gutmann, J. G., 198

Haislip, Wade Hampton, 247, 252–253, 254
Harris, Arthur, 49, 52
Hastings, Robin, 119, 121
Hausser, Paul, 188, 194, 197, 202, 231, 232,
    233, 259
Hawkins, the (Britain), 88
hedgerows, battle of the. *See* bocage region,
    battles in
Hennecke, Admiral, 175, 177
Herbert, W. G., 129
Hermanville, France, 137
Herndon, the (U.S.), 88
Heydte, Frederick von der, 82, 166
Hickey, R. M., 130
Hickman, Heinz, 71
Hill 317, 241, 242, 244–245
Himmler, Heinrich, 194
Hinde, Robert, 153, 154
Hischier, Dennis, 208
Hitler, Adolf
    air war against Britain, 17
    assassination attempt on, 221–222
    author's evaluation of military strategy
        of, 272–273
    in France in June 1944, 181–182
    offensive in 1940, 7
    offensive in the Middle East, 19
    offensives in Russia, 17, 19
    and Operation Luttich, 240–241, 244–245
    reaction to Cherbourg attack, 175
    reaction to D-Day, 144
    strategies of, 30–31, 33, 76, 163, 173, 182
        187, 195, 240, 247, 254, 257, 258, 266
Hobart, Percy, 93–94
Hobbs, Leland, 197, 241
Hodges, Courtney, 238
Hof, Major, 138
Holley, I. G., 117
Hollis, Stanley, 120–121
Howard, John, 69, 70, 137

Isigny, France, 168

Jahnke, Arthur, 85–86, 88
Joyce, Albert, 120
Juno Beach, 57, 125–129

Kieffer, Philippe, 136
King, Ernest J., 60, 61
King's Shropshire Light Infantry, 137, 138, 139

Kirk, A. G., 66
Kluge, Günther von, 194, 197–198, 202, 222, 232, 233–234, 235, 240, 254, 257, 270
Korten, Gunter, 222
Kraiss, Dietrich, 168–170
Krakowiok, the (Poland), 115
Krause, Edward, 77–78
Kupper, Friedrich, 173

Le Clerc, Jacques, 261–262
Le Hamel, France, 117
Leigh-Mallory, Trafford, 25, 29, 63, 69, 152, 224, 274
Lightoller, Herbert, 8
Lockwood, Stan, 156
Lofthouse, Robert, 120
London Yeomanry, 153, 154–156, 157
Lovat, Lord, 137
Luck, Hans von, 139–140, 152, 179, 214, 215, 258, 271
Luftwaffe, 49–50, 82, 166, 175, 214, 217, 242–243

MacKelvie, Jay, 171–172
Madill, Laurence, 101
Marcks, Erich, 139, 140–141, 144, 167, 194
Marshall, George, 14, 18, 20–21, 23, 27, 68
Mason, Robert, 196
Maurice, F. J., 137
McAuliffe, Anthony, 166–167
McIntyre, George, 85
McNair, Leslie, 224, 225
Meindl, Eugene, 199, 200, 202
Merville, France, 71–74
Meuvaines Ridge, 119, 121
Meyer, Kurt "Panzer," 145–147, 148, 149, 180, 187, 208–209, 211, 251–252, 254, 259, 271
Middleton, Troy, 172, 194, 195
Minogue, Joseph, 116
Model, Walther, 257–258, 270
Montgomery, Bernard Law, 69, 238
    arrival in Normandy, 147
    assignment as ground forces commander of Overlord, 21–22, 27–28
    author's evaluation of, 274–275
    at briefing in Hammersmith, 55, 57
    conference with Churchill and Eisenhower, 15–16
    and decision to begin offensive, 64
    biography of, 122–123
    and Operation Epsom, 184
    and Operation Goodwood, 206, 211–212
    and Operation Torch, 20
    and Operation Totalize, 249, 254, 256

plan for offensive on Caen, 151–153, 157
    pre-D-Day war service, 15
    strategy for D-Day, 57–58, 113, 115
    tank use by, 114
Moody, Ronald, 244
Moon, Don, 80
Morgan, Frederick, 25
Mortain, France, 241–245
Mulberry project, 58, 161, 183
Murphy, Robert, 74

Neave, Robert, 135, 136
Nevada, USS, 81, 88
919th Grenadier Regiment (Germany), 174
901st Panzer Grenadier Regiment, 198
922nd Grenadier Regiment (Germany), 173
902nd Panzer Grenadier Regiment, 198
XIX Corps (U.S.), 194, 197
90th Infantry Division (U.S.), 171–172, 253
91st Division (Germany), 172
9th Infantry Division (U.S.), 172, 175, 196, 198
9th Panzer Division, 188, 240
9th SS Panzer Division, 241
North Nova Scotia Highlanders (Canada), 130–131, 146
North Shore Regiment (Canada), 130

O'Connor, Richard, 187
Ogden-Smith, Bruce, 13
Old Hickory Division (U.S.). *See* 30th Division (U.S.)
Omaha Beach, 13, 57, 58, 89, 91–109
185th Infantry Brigade Group (Britain), 134, 137, 138, 139
101st Airborne Division (U.S.), 58, 69, 165–167, 172
101st SS Heavy Panzer Battalion, 251
141st (Buffs) Royal Armoured Corps Regiment (Britain), 208
192nd Panzer Grenadier Regiment, 141
102nd Heavy Tank Battalion (Germany), 209
175th Regiment (U.S. 29th Division), 200
117th Regiment (U.S. 30th Division), 241–242
116th Panzer Division, 240, 258
116th Regiment "Stonewall Brigade" (U.S. 29th Division), 97, 98, 101, 109, 199, 200
120th Regiment (U.S. 30th Division), 241–242
Operation Anvil, 61
Operation Bolero, 19
Operation Charwood, 207–211
Operation Cobra, 206, 212, 218
Operation Dragoon, 257
Operation Dynamo, 7–8, 10
Operation Epsom, 184–189

Operation Fortitude, 46–48
Operation Goodwood, 206, 211–218, 221
Operation Luttich (Germany), 240–245
Operation Neptune, 29, 59–60. *See also*
    D-Day, naval support on; Operation
    Overlord, naval support component of
Operation Overlord
    advance to St. Lô, 193, 195–202
    air force component of, 48–53, 66, 67–78,
        83, 88, 96, 151–152, 207, 209, 212, 213,
        224–225, 234, 243, 245
    alternative outcomes, 264–268
    bocage (hedgerow) region, battles in,
        163–167, 171–172, 192–198, 205, 230
    briefing at Hammersmith, 55, 57–58
    capture of Cherbourg, 172–178
    choosing of senior commanders for, 22,
        28–30
    choosing of supreme commander for,
        20–22
    comparison of adversaries' forces in, 35
    comparison of adversaries' weapons in,
        35–37
    D+1, 143–147
    decision on landing sites, 45–46
    different strategies for, 18–19
    effect of storms in mid-June on, 183
    final countdown for, 63–66
    first day of (D-Day), 67–142. *See also* D-
        Day
    formalization of, 20
    genesis of, 16–22
    logistical problems of, 58–59
    naval support component of, 29, 59–60,
        80–81, 82, 88, 96–97, 115, 116, 126, 135,
        152–153, 175, 207
    and Operation Anvil, 61
    and Operation Charwood, 207–211
    and Operation Cobra, 206, 212, 218
    and Operation Fortitude (deception
        component of), 46–48
    and Operation Goodwood, 206, 211–218
    planning of, 10, 11, 45–46, 48–53
    postponement of, 61–62
    reconnaissance for, 13
    risks of, 18
    timing of, 62–63
Operation Pointblank, 49
Operation Round-Up, 19
Operation Torch, 20
Operation Totalize, 249, 252–257
Operation Tractable, 257–258
Oppeln-Bronikowski, Hermann von, 140–141
Orion, the (Britain), 115
Ostendorff, General, 167

Otway, Terrence, 71–73
Ouistreham, France, 57
Oxford and Buckinghamshire Light Infantry,
    69

Panzer Grenadier Regiment (21st Panzer
    Division), 214
Panzer Group West, 31, 148–149, 151–152,
    209, 244. *See also* Fifth Panzer Army
Panzer Lehr Division, 139, 140, 148, 149, 155,
    184, 197, 198–199, 202, 231–232
paratroopers, 69, 72–78, 88
Paris, France, 261–262, 263
Paris, Raymond, 77
Parley, Harry, 107
Parry, Allen, 73
Pas de Calais, 46, 47
Patton, George S., 25, 234
    appointment as commander of the Third
        Army, 238
    author's evaluation of, 264–265, 275–276
    and Bradley, 238, 253, 254–255
    at briefing in Hammersmith, 57
    and Eisenhower, 237–238
    life of, 246
    in Operation Cobra, 238–240
    and Operation Totalize, 253–254
    as part of deception operation, 47–48
    slapping incident, 46–47, 237
Pearce-Smith, K., 137–138
Periers, France, 196
Philipps, J. H., 198
Pluskat, Werner, 95–96
Pluto, 118
Pointe du Hoc, 103–106
Port-en-Bessin, France, 118–119
Powell, Edgar, 108
Priestly, J. B., 8
Pyle, Ernie, 225

Quadrant Conference, 20
Queen's Own Rifle (Canada), 129–130
Quesada, Ellwood "Pete," 205–206
Quincy, the (U.S.), 81

RAF. *See* Royal Air Force
Ramillies, the, 135
Ramsay, Bertram, 29, 63, 64, 274
Regiment de la Chaudiere (Canada), 130–131
Regina Rifle Regiment (Canada), 129, 149
Rennie, T. G., 134
Richter, Wilhelm, 127, 141
Rickers, John, 84
Ridgway, Matthew, 164, 172
Roberts, G. P. "Pip," 211

Roberts, HMS, 213
Robinson, John, 199
Rockwell, D.L., 97
Rodney, HMS, 207
Rommel, Erwin, 133, 139, 222
    author's evaluation of, 269–270
    and defenses around Caen, 212–213
    injury of, 202
    life of, 203–204
    meeting with Hitler, June 1944, 181–182
    reaction to Cherbourg attack, 175, 177
    post-D-Day command, 148, 151
    pre-D-Day war service, 15, 32
    strategies of, 32–33, 95, 182, 197
Roosevelt, Franklin Delano, 14, 16, 19, 20–21,
    27, 60
Roosevelt, Theodore Jr., 86–87
Rose, Maurice, 232
Rosen, Freiherr von, 213
Royal Air Force (RAF), 7, 9, 49, 82, 88, 183,
    207. *See also* Operation Overlord, air force
    component of
Royal Winnipeg Rifles (Canada), 129, 149
Rudder, James, 104–105
Rundstedt, Gerd von, 133
    author's evaluation of, 269
    biography of, 190
    demotion of, 194
    meeting with Hitler, June 1944, 181–182
    strategies of, 31–32
Russell, Ken, 77
Russian Front, 17, 18

Sanders, Harry, 108
Schaaf, Rudolf, 138
Schlieben, Karl von, 173–177
Schmundt, Rudolf, 222
Scholze, Hans, 198
Schonberg-Waldenburg, Prince, 149
Scott-Bowden, Logan, 13
Scott, Desmond, 243
Screaming Eagle Division (U.S.), 74. *See also*
    101st Airborne Division
2nd Armored Division (France), 253, 254, 261
2nd Armored Division (U.S.), 167, 230, 232,
    233
Second Army (Britain), 113, 153, 161, 207, 238,
    249
2nd Canadian Armoured Brigade, 249
2nd Canadian Infantry Division, 249
II Corps (Canada), 211, 249
2nd Division (Canada), 126
2nd Division (U.S.), 200, 262
2nd Fife and Forfar Yeomanry, 217
2nd Panzer Division, 157, 240, 258

2nd Ranger Battalion (U.S.), 104
2nd SS Panzer Battalion, 251
II SS Panzer Corps, 188
2nd SS Panzer Division, 197–199, 202, 233,
    240, 242
Seton-Watson, Christopher, 8
716th Division (Germany), 92, 116, 127, 141
739th Grenadier Regiment (Germany), 174
736th Grenadier Regiment (German 716th
    Division), 116, 127, 138
726th Regiment (German 716th Division), 127
17th SS Panzergrenadier Division, 163,
    166–167, 193, 202, 232–233
Seventh Army (Germany), 32, 188, 197, 231
7th Armoured Division (Britain), 115, 153, 211
7th Brigade (Canadian 3rd Division), 128
VII Corps (U.S.), 79, 161, 167, 194, 196
79th Armoured Division (Britain), 39, 249–252
79th Infantry Division (U.S.), 172, 175, 253
77th Division (Germany), 172
Sherbrooke Fusiliers, 146–147
Shubrick, the (U.S.), 88
Simonds, Guy, 247, 249, 252, 276
Simpson, William, 224
Sioux, the (Canada), 126
16th Regiment (U.S. 1st Division), 97, 98, 102
6th Airborne Division (Britain), 58, 68, 69–74,
    115, 134
6th Armored Division, 239
6th Green Howards (Britain), 119–121
6th Parachute Regiment (Germany), 166,
    232–233
69th Brigade Group (British 50th Division, 115
Slaughter, Robert, 107
Slazak, the (Poland), 136
Smith, Sandy, 70
Soemba, the (Netherlands), 88
South Lancashire Regiment (Britain), 136
Spaatz, Carl, 49, 52, 224
Staffordshire Yeomanry, 137, 138
Stagg, J. M., 63
Stalin, Joseph, 14
St. Aubin-sur-Mer, 130
Stauffenberg, Claus Count von, 222
Steele, John, 77
Stimson, Henry, 27
St. Lô, France, 193, 195–202
St. Mère Église, 69, 74, 76–78
Summers, Harrison, 88
Svenner, the (Norway), 135
Sword Beach, 57, 131, 133–138

tanks, types of, use of, and problems with,
    36–37, 88–89, 93–94, 97, 114, 116, 129, 136,
    137, 138, 140, 141, 147, 154–157, 187,

188–189, 208, 209, 211, 213, 215, 216–217, 219–220, 251–252
Taylor, Maxwell, 166
Tedder, Arthur, 28–29, 50, 52–53, 64, 224
Temkin, Leo, 244
10th Panzer Division, 241
10th SS Panzer Division, 188, 209, 241
Texas, USS, 96, 175
3rd Armored Division (U.S.), 198, 232, 233
Third Army (U.S.), 48, 238–239
3rd Battalion (U.S. 502nd Parachute Infantry), 166
3rd Canadian Division, 57, 208
3rd Division (Britain), 57, 114, 134, 135–136, 208
3rd Division (Canada), 114, 125–131
3rd Monmouth Infantry Regiment (Britain), 213
3rd Parachute Division (Germany), 163, 168, 193, 199, 202
3rd Royal Tank Regiment (Britain), 213, 215
XXX Corps (Britain), 114, 115–121, 211
30th Division (U.S.), 197, 198, 241–245
38th Regiment (U.S. 2nd Division), 200
35th Division (U.S.), 200
33rd Tank Brigade (Britain), 249
Thompson, USS, 108
352nd Infantry Division (Germany), 92, 95, 103, 168–170
353rd Infantry Division (Germany), 168, 193, 231
365th Fighter Squadron (U.S.), 206
325th Glider Regiment (U.S.), 172
Transportation Plan, 51–53
Trevor, Travis, 105
Trident Conference, 20
Tuscaloosa, the (U.S.), 81
12th Army Group (U.S.), 238
XII Corps (Britain), 211
12th SS Panzer (Hitler Youth) Division, 133, 139, 140, 145, 148, 184, 185, 187, 208–209, 240, 251, 258
XX Corps (U.S.), 254
25th SS Panzergrenadier Regiment, 145–147
21st Army Group, 238
21st Panzer Division, 128, 133, 139, 145, 148, 212, 214, 218, 258
29th Division (U.S.), 58, 97, 101, 107, 109,

168–170, 199–200. *See also* Blue and Gray Division
22nd Armoured Brigade, 153
22nd Panzer Regiment, 140
23rd Hussars (Britain), 213
275th Infantry Division (Germany), 168, 231
272nd Infantry Division (Germany), 251
231st Brigade Group (British 50th Division), 115
Tychsen, General, 233

uniforms and equipment, 35–37, 41–43
United States Army
    advance to and capture of St. Lô, 195–202
    advance to and capture of Cherbourg, 164–178
    casualties in June 1944, 195
    casualties in Normandy campaign, 263
    deployment on Omaha Beach, 91–109
    deployment on Utah Beach, 79–89, 91
    at Falaise pocket, 252–261
    in Operation Cobra, 225–233
    organization of, 38
    post-D-Day command in, 238
U.S. Strategic Air Forces in Europe, 49
Utah Beach, 57, 58, 79–89

V-1 missiles, 182, 183, 267
Van Fleet, James, 87
Villers-Bocage, France, 151, 153, 155–157

Waffen SS, 158–159
Walker, Walton, 254
Warfield, William, 169
War in the Pacific, 17, 60
Warspite, the, 135
Watson, Leroy, 233
weapons, 35–37, 111–112. *See also* tanks; uniforms and equipment
Wehrmacht, the, 10, 13, 30, 70
White, Isaac, 233
Williams, Francis, 120
Witte, Fritz, 145
Wittmann, Michael, 145, 154–157, 251, 252, 271–272
Wünsche, Max, 146

Zuckerman, Solly, 50–52